WELLNESS: LIFE, HEALTH AND SPIRITUALITY

WELLNESS: LIFE, HEALTH AND SPIRITUALTY

RICHARD J. WOODS, OP

VERITAS

First published 2008 by
Veritas Publications
7/8 Lower Abbey Street
Dublin 1
Ireland
Email publications@veritas.ie
Website www.veritas.ie

ISBN 978 184730 092 8

Designed by Barbara Croatto
Cover illustration from a piece by Jane LaFazio, entitled 'Tree of Life: Guadalupe'
www.plainjanestudio.com
Printed in the Republic of Ireland by ColourBooks Ltd., Dublin

Veritas books are printed on paper made from the wood pulp of managed forests. For
every tree felled, at least one tree is planted, thereby renewing natural resources.

CONTENTS

FOREWORD

In comments and stories on religion and health, the question often comes up of whether people who identify themselves as religious are more or less healthy than others. Claims and counterclaims are freely bandied about by eminent scientists or well-known journalists, especially in recent years, in regard to the social benefit (or detriment) of religion. Does religion have anything to do with increased (or decreased) longevity? Or with better health and more profound happiness? Can religion be hazardous to health? What factors are involved in measuring the perceived differences in such areas between religious and non-religious people?

Uncovering and, when possible and helpful, illuminating the links between spirituality, health and nutrition have preoccupied and sometimes astonished me over the last forty years. For a time as an undergraduate student, I considered pursuing a medical career, so biology became a major interest and occasionally a passion. As it happened, at the end of my second year of university study I took a road less travelled and entered the Dominicans, a Catholic religious order of preachers and teachers. But I had already pulled back from the pre-medical curriculum to focus on the body politic, aiming toward a career in international relations with a double minor in English and psychology.

What had disenchanted me with the 'pre-med' curriculum was the emphasis on dissection – cutting up increasingly complex animal cadavers to discover the intricacies of structure and function so crucially important to the study of medicine. As an animal lover and, if truth be told, a developing nature addict, I found such an analytic and artificial approach to be sterile and even confusing. I was interested in life and, as it turned out, health, but everything seemed to my still-adolescent mind to be centred on death and dismantlement.

For a time I considered concentrating on botany, and I suppose that if the option were available then, I might well have undertaken a course of study in botanic medicine. But at eighteen years of age, to me the world of plants seemed pretty boring. On the other hand, in the early 1960s political science was anything but dull. However, I never lost my interest in the life sciences. Especially over the last two decades, I have grown increasingly interested in the relationship between botany and medicine. My interest in and love for animals did not abate, at least practically speaking, as I raised and observed generations of hamsters, gerbils and mice, rescued squirrels, raccoons and opossums from the perils of urban foraging, and eventually saw added to our small Dominican community at Loyola University three collies and two cats. The latter five provided endless opportunities to learn and marvel at the richly complex world of animal interaction.

Spirituality had everything to do with it, at least so it appears in retrospect. In the spring of that violent and pivotal year, 1968, I became a vegetarian – technically a lacto-ovarian, as I eat some animal products, mainly eggs, cheese and yogurt. On occasion, I even eat a piece of fish, which is hardly a vegetable, but at least has the distinction of being the only food that Jesus was specifically remembered to have eaten (Luke 24:42). At the time, I was studying eastern religions and had taken up the practice of yoga, both of which had impressed on me the importance of a vegetarian diet for a variety of ethical, spiritual, even economic reasons. My religious order, the early Dominicans in particular, had been largely if not wholly vegetarian. St Dominic himself avoided meat whenever possible. My own decision was cemented when a class of local high school students whom I was tutoring in photography voted to tour the local abattoir. Watching the terrified pigs ascending the long ramp to their doom through a mist of water vapour from the scrubbers and fluorescent lights made an impression that haunted me for years. But that is part of another story.

By stages, an awareness of the connections among spirituality, life, health, diet and nutrition was growing in my experience and study. Eventually, I found myself lecturing on these subjects in a variety of courses at the university level. Today, thirty years later, many of my students, as well as other people in our society, describe themselves as 'spiritual, but not religious'. While I sympathise with their evident discomfort with organised religion, I do not intend to draw hard and fast distinctions between the two areas in these pages. It is very obvious that many people who identify themselves as 'spiritual' do not belong to a church or its equivalent, and equally evident that not everyone who goes to church has a vibrant spiritual life. But to avoid unnecessary repetition and confusion, I will ordinarily use 'religious' and 'spiritual' interchangeably, if not indiscriminately. Exceptions will be noted as they arise. For instance, in Catholic practice, 'the religious life' usually refers to a career choice of women and men who have joined a recognised church organisation such as the Sisters of Mercy, the Jesuits, Carmelites, or Franciscans. That does not imply that every member adheres to the same degree to (for instance) 'Carmelite spirituality' as developed by St Teresa of Avila, St John of the Cross and St Thérèse of Lisieux.

Many scientific surveys of religion and health do not in fact distinguish organisational affiliation too sharply from actual spiritual or religious practice, while others focus on specifics such as prayer, celibacy, or diet, which can vary greatly in a denomination or tradition. Findings have to be interpreted accordingly.

Health, Wealth and Illth: A Meditation on the Meaning of Some Words

By way of an additional preliminary aside, I have been struck by the aptness of the words we commonly use to refer to our situation in the world of nature, other people and God – words that we normally do not think much about. They have something to tell us.

'Wellness' (originally *wealnesse*) came into the language around the middle of the seventeenth century, to refer to a general state of well-being or healthiness, the good fortune expressed by the much older word 'welfare', meaning to 'fare' or go well. The word 'well' itself has multiple origins. As an adverb, it meant 'good', 'satisfactory', or 'right'. It connoted favour or friendliness, as in 'welcome'. As a noun, 'weal' meant 'goodness', 'advantage', or 'profit'. The related word 'wealth' (in Middle English *welth*) originally meant 'happiness' or 'prosperity'. Derived from 'weal', it survives in the word 'commonwealth', meaning the public good. Its opposite was 'woe'. 'Wealth' was not at first a term principally connected with money or possessions.

The similar English word 'health' is ultimately derived from an ancient Sanskrit root which means 'whole', and is related to words such as 'holy' and 'hale'. By contrast, 'ill' comes from a Norse word, *illr*, that fundamentally means 'bad', 'wicked', or 'harmful'. It is indeed an ill wind that blows no good, but as a synonym for 'bad health', it has a long patrimony. 'Illness', however, is relatively recent, like 'wellness'. It means much more than mere sickness, however. In the nineteenth century, John Ruskin coined the term 'illth' on the model of 'health' and 'wealth' to mean their opposite – not just physical disease, but the malaise of mind, emotion, body, spirit and community that results from a fundamental disruption in the order of life as a whole. Whether he knew it or not, Ruskin was articulating a well-nigh universal viewpoint, as we shall have occasion to recall in the following pages.

If the long history of the language of medicine and healing has taught us anything, it is that physical disease, mental and emotional problems, spiritual unwellness and social maladies, from marital unhappiness to nuclear war, all arise out of illth. All are facets of underlying and systemic disharmony. The closer we come to rectifying that, the greater our common health, wealth and prosperity – our wellness. The place of spirituality in achieving and restoring this balance is highly important – *critical* in every sense of that word. The health of the world, both in our own local world and that of 'the great globe itself', hangs in the balance.

The following exploration of health and spiritual will cover a wide range of topics, none in great depth because of the nature of a book such as this. But it should introduce those interested in the relationship between these two great human enterprises (or just curious about it) to some uncharted territory without becoming (I hope!) seriously misleading. The first chapter looks more closely at both spirituality and health care as these evolved over the centuries.

In Chapter Two, I turn to Asian and European traditions that offer a panorama of personalities and procedures standing behind both modern medicine and the developing area of holistic spirituality. I also look into the biblical tradition, which is often overlooked despite its sound approach. The third and fourth chapters take up the knotty question, so much in the forefront of recent media controversy, of whether religion is harmful or beneficial individually and collectively. Despite its general and largely prejudicial condemnations by several famous scientific personalities and journalists, there is a mass of empirical evidence that clearly points in the direction of benefit, not least in the origin and development of nursing care.

The next chapters survey particular areas of research and development as well as traditional approaches to ageing (Chapter Five); sickness, suffering and healthiness (Chapter Six); diet and nutrition, herbal medicine, stress and exercise, and the place of grooming and hygiene (Chapter Seven). Chapter Eight looks into the night world of sleep and dreams as we turn to mental health and healing. Mental and emotional health are the focus of Chapter Nine, and health aspects of dying and death are treated in Chapter Ten. Chapter Eleven explores the realm of friendship, love and sexuality.

The final two chapters take up extraordinary dimensions of healing. Chapter Twelve explores the 'beyond' of health – the sometimes controversial topics of spontaneous healing, the role of prayer, and reported miracles of healing, cures that go beyond the scope of scientific explanation. By way of conclusion, Chapter Thirteen takes up the challenge of trying to heal a wounded and suffering planet.

Both the research and personal reflections in the following pages will inevitably display a North American bias, since I am normally resident in the heartland of the United States where most of my work and research is done. However, many of the findings include information from Europe, Asia and Africa, and I have tried to be inclusive whenever possible. Similarly, as a practicing Roman Catholic, and a Dominican friar to boot, the discerning eye may detect some slant in the direction of Rome, but here too I have tried to be ecumenical and inclusive, not least because so much initial work in the area of spirituality and health was done by Protestant Christians. As a male, I am keenly aware that still another kind of bias may be at work, but I hope to have balanced my observations constructively, since both experience and research indicate that women are generally more attentive than males to issues of spirituality and health. It is hardly by accident that so much pertinent research literature is being published by women, particularly in nursing journals. Personally, I have benefited immensely from listening to and learning from my female colleagues, relatives and friends. I hope it shows through!

Finally, by way of introduction, I should acknowledge my debts – none of which I can hope to repay adequately. First, I wish to thank Mr Tyson Shutz, my research assistant, for his painstaking and valuable sleuthing. I am also indebted to Donna Doherty, Ruth Kennedy and Caitriona Clarke of Veritas Publications for the initial invitation and their unflagging support and patience during the preparation of the book. Finally, over the years, I have been blessed to meet and at least briefly to study under the tutelage of some of the most remarkable healers of recent times in a variety of fields. The blunders that will appear in what follows are in no way their doing – for those I take full credit. But imperfect as it is, to them and to their memory I respectfully dedicate this reflection:

Ursula Fleming
Dr Elizabeth Kübler-Ross
Frank MacNutt
Fr Henri Nouwen
Fr Miceál Ó Regan, OP
Dr Karlis Osis
Dr Domeena Renshaw
Dr Cicely Saunders, DBE
Olga and Ambrose Worrall

Richard Woods, OP, Ph.D.
June 2008

CHAPTER ONE
SPIRIT AND HEALTH[1]

How the earth darts on and on!
and how the sun, moon, stars, dart on and on!
How the water sports and sings! (surely it is alive!)
How the trees rise and stand up, with strong trunks,
with branches and leaves!
(Surely there is something more in each of the trees,
some living soul.)

O amazement of things – even the least particle!
O spirituality of things!
Walt Whitman, 'Song at Sunset', *Leaves of Grass*

During the years following the Second Vatican Council, many tried-and-true definitions, pat phrases and practices of conventional Christian spirituality were openly or tacitly abandoned. For many people today, the meaning of the word 'spirituality' itself has become problematic. The confusion of spirituality with religion, no less than the perception of opposition between them, is reflected in much current literature, especially in the area of health care.[2] It is hardly unusual to hear people (especially, but not only, the young) affirm, 'I'm spiritual but not religious'.[3]

It may be tempting to conclude that such claims simply mean 'I don't go to church anymore, but I still believe that God is real and life has meaning'. Or, as my undergraduate students frequently repeat, 'everything happens for a reason'. But merely discarding past terminological and practical clutter has not ensured anyone a better understanding of spirituality today or an easier pilgrimage toward the future. Spiritual writers and teachers are still groping for clarity regarding fundamental notions. At the same time, people in every area of life are not only manifestly interested in developing a viable spirituality, but searching, sometimes desperately, for assistance and resources for their spiritual journey.[4]

As with *mystic* and also *experience* (which William James called a 'weasel word'), spirituality may resist definition because it is often presumed that everyone already knows what it means, especially in institutions where such matters are investigated by learned scholars. Or, conversely, perhaps because there are too many competing definitions. Some writers simply avoid the problem by refusing to offer an opinion or, at most, by providing 'ostensive' definitions, pointing to someone who possesses whatever it is that *spirituality* is supposed to mean.

Spirituality, *spiritual* and *spirit* are obviously related semantically, but also chronologically, the first appearing last, and the last first, in good biblical fashion. Absent from the Bible and Christian literature before the Reformation, 'spirituality' is in fact a relatively modern word, both in French, where it first appeared, and in English, where it acquired its present range of meanings around the seventeenth century. But it had been used in English a century earlier, and 'spiritual' and 'spirit' about a hundred years before that in each case.

Generally, the word group pointed to aspects of life different from and in some respects opposed to material, worldly, or temporal affairs. In English, *spirituality* originally referred to the properties and influence of the church as distinct from those pertinent to civil society. Gradually, the connotation of non-materiality (if not immateriality) came to predominate, especially in the post-Cartesian period. 'A' spirit was, alternatively, a ghost, the non-bodily aspect or essence of a human being, or a gaseous chemical (we still speak of volatiles such as camphor and ammonia, and even whiskey, gin and their cousins, as 'spirits' because they vaporise).[5]

The Breath of Life
Behind all this lies the story of the word 'spirit', one which makes more sense than might first seem apparent. Proceeding in reverse, translators understandably used the English word 'spirit' and its

cognates (as well as the Germanic 'ghost') for the Latin *spiritus*, particularly in the Bible. *Spiritus*, in turn, was generally chosen to translate the Greek word *pneuma*, which rendered the Hebrew *rüach*. For all three words mean 'air', more specifically 'breath', and sometimes 'wind'. On the other hand, *nephesh* was used in biblical Hebrew to refer to the living soul that animates a human person. The word means something like 'self'. It can also mean '(biological) life' or 'soul.' In Greek, *nephesh* was translated by the word *psyche*, and in Latin by *anima*.

Linguistically the Hebrew *rüach* and the Aramaic *ruha*, the word Jesus would have used, are feminine in form, while *pneuma* is neuter and *spiritus* is masculine. These differences would in time present some serious problems in dealing with genderised references to God in the various languages. In the Syriac liturgy, for instance, references to the Holy Spirit employed feminine forms until about the fifth century, when the Greek-speaking hierarchy of Northern Africa and Asia Minor forced the Syrians to shift to masculine usage.[6] The feminine sense of the divine embodied in the image of the Holy Spirit in the figure of Wisdom (*Sophia*) nevertheless survived, even though conventional pronouns referring to the Holy Spirit in English have for centuries taken the masculine form. The German *Geist* is also a masculine noun. *Spiritus* was nevertheless an inspired as well as obvious choice for *pneuma*, which Greek writers (e.g. Aeschylos and Euripides) had used as a metaphor for the soul. Alexandrian Jews almost always used it to translate *rüach* when preparing the Greek translation of Scripture known as the Septuagint. In the writings of Latin poets such as Horace and Virgil, *spiritus* not only stood in for 'soul' or 'mind', but also meant 'breath' and 'sigh'.

The root of all of this word shifting lies in the poetic ambiguity of the second sentence of Genesis: 'The earth was without form and void, and darkness was upon the face of the deep; and the Spirit of God [*rüach elohim*] was moving over the face of the waters.' Some translations, both ancient and new, actually read 'a wind' of God, and *rüach* can indeed mean 'wind', as in Geneis 8:1 and Exodus 10:13.[7]

But as a metaphor, *breath* is an accurate rendering of the Hebrew in critical passages. Thus in Genesis 2:7, God breathes life into the clay figure of Adam, and the first human being becomes a truly living person, having *soul* or *self* (*nephesh*). Breath remains the chosen metaphor for God's gift of life throughout the Hebrew scriptures (important passages include Ex 15:8-10; Ps 33:6; Isa 11:1-3; and Ezek 36:25-37:10) and for an obvious enough reason. Breathing is the first act of post-uterine life, and its most manifest sign. Human beings, like all animals, can live for weeks without food and days without water but only minutes deprived of air. When we cease breathing altogether, we die, or *expire*.[8]

But above all, the various language groups focus on breathing as the most appropriate image of the life communicated by God, and indeed, God's own life. The associated image of a breeze or even a strong wind (as in Acts 2:2, where the related word *pnoe* is used, from the verb meaning 'to breathe hard' or 'blow') as the sign of God's vital presence probably comes from the properties of moving air – invisibility, power and sovereign freedom, all of which were mysterious to the ancient world. In John's gospel, the ambiguity is used to great effect: 'The wind [*pneuma*] blows [*pnoe*] where it wills, and you hear the sound of it, but you do not know whence it comes or whither it goes; so it is with every one who is born of the Spirit [*pneuma*]' (Jn 3:8). The ambiguity is not merely biblical, however. When out of breath, speakers of English sometimes still say they are 'winded'. Runners also talk of getting their 'second wind'.

In general, images of breath and wind (like the more concrete symbols of the dove and tongues of fire with regard to the Holy Spirit) point to the intangible, simple essence of life – both divine and human. But like *experience*, the term 'life', even 'the breath of life', seems to mean most when it is devoid of concrete references. It is hard enough to define biological life. *Eternal life* beggars the imagination.

So, in a word, with *spirit* indicating breath, moving air, the Holy Spirit, and the inner life of human beings, we discover the fundamental biblical and poetic acknowledgment of spirituality as a living relationship between God and the human person. Breathing is more intimate than anything else in life, physical or mental. Spirituality is as close to us as breathing, and more importantly, as vital to us. Similar notions can be found, importantly, in other traditions, as we shall see, the most important being Indian and Chinese medicine, with their doctrine of *prana* and *qi* (*chi*), both of which refer to the vital energy contained within or at least associated with breath.

However conceived, spirit gives unity to the human person, establishing and maintaining the essential and unique psychosomatic character of the individual, even beyond death. Spirit permeates our humanness – it is not opposed to the body, nor to the mind. Thus, as St Paul would insist (see Rom 8:4-13; 1 Cor 2:13ff, 3:1, 15:44), only the 'pneumatic' person is truly individual, that is, balanced within and undivided with respect to the presence and plan of God, because open to and able to transmit the fullness of life.[9]

The pneumatic or 'spiritual' person is thus also at home in the world, both the natural and social orders. It is in this respect we can understand the remark of St Irenaeus: 'The glory of God is the fully living human person.'[10] Significantly, the Hebrew word used even today in Jewish spirituality for such a whole person, a true 'individual', is *shalem*, which has the same root as the familiar word for peace, health and prosperity, *shalom*.

Interior Life, Common Life

Over the past two millennia, the word 'spirit' has become less specific, coming to mean not merely the vital principle, especially of human life, but the immortal, invisible dimension of persons, whether divine, human, or angelic (including 'fallen' angels). Not surprisingly, as it entered French literature and then English in the early modern era, *spirituality* was commonly used to refer to the character of human life as informed by a sense of other-worldliness, focused on the eternal and immaterial. In theological and pastoral circles, this etherialisation of spirit was especially pronounced.[11]

In a seminal article of 1980, noting the shift from the concrete to the abstract in efforts to define spirituality, Jon Alexander proposed three working definitions which encompassed the range of meanings given to the word 'spirituality':

> For some recent writers, spirituality refers to how people live their faith. Although this definition makes spirituality virtually the equivalent of religion, writers seem to use spirituality in order to indicate that they are referring to an affective and personally integrated religion rather than a superficial assent which has few observable effects on life ...
>
> A second definition at a higher level of abstraction has the word spirituality point to the integration of ultimate concerns and unrestricted values in concrete life ... In this sense, spirituality can be used to speak of the affective side of religion in general ...
>
> The broadest way to think of spirituality as the word is used by some recent writers is to think of it as a heuristic, or analytical, concept. In this sense, spirituality is a word used by contemporary writers when they are discussing those aspects of human life which are seen by their subjects, or interpreted by their observers, as intentionally related to that which holds unrestricted value. Spirituality in this sense may be used to discuss phenomenon [sic] not generally considered 'religious'.[12]

Conversely, a more concrete understanding of 'spirituality' views it biographically as the form or shape of one's life as a whole, particularly as integrated around a core set of beliefs, values and practices that are usually to some degree consciously religious. Thus, one could speak specifically of the spirituality of Francis of Assisi or Mother Teresa, while recognising them as instances of a more general tendency. This tendency could be understood, helpfully, as the actualisation of that original receptivity to divine life that constitutes the core reality of a human being.

Similarly, *spirit* and *spirituality* have also been associated with social, ethnic, linguistic and national groups, so it has become common to speak of Jewish spirituality or Jesuit spirituality or even 'Western' spirituality, referring not to the lives of individuals so much as to the general sense of belief, value and practice that animates communities, ethnic groups and possibly whole civilizations. Needless to say, communities are composed of individuals, and also shape them, so that the various contemporary concepts of spirituality are in the end dialectically related. That is, individuals actualise their capacity for self-transcendence, their 'openness' to the world, God, and each other only in the midst of a social group which is itself the on-going product of individual activity.

Thus *spirit* and *spirituality* encompass a wide range of meaning from the most abstract and general to the most concrete and particular, all of which fall to some extent under the purview of a field of study that also calls itself 'spirituality'. In the following pages, I will be using the term generically as a human faith-response, individually and collectively, to the felt sense of personal, life-giving mystery at the heart of experience, and also as a more narrowly prescribed tradition within specific communities, whether identified as religious or not.

A Whole in One

What is *holistic* spirituality, then, and how does it differ from other spiritualities?

The qualification arose from developments in the health field during the last quarter of the twentieth century. Of course, 'holistic' adds no more significance to 'health' than 'hospital' does to 'care'. Literally, the words mean the same thing. The fact that we create such expressions mainly testifies to a felt lack somewhere, something missing from conventional spirituality or health care systems. Similarly, since we speak almost as casually today of spiritual health as we do of physical or mental health, the advent of 'holistic spirituality' should not have been any more surprising than that of 'holistic health'. But again, what 'holistic' adds to 'spirituality' is less specific content than a corrective. The expression bears witness to what was often felt to be lacking in previous spiritualities.

What health care systems and spiritualities were both felt to lack was in fact *wholeness*. (Significantly, as noted earlier, the English words 'heal', 'holy', 'whole' and their cognates all stem from the same Anglo-Saxon root, *hál*, which means 'entire' or, simply, 'whole'. Its closest surviving equivalent is 'hale'.) Over the past several centuries, conventional medicine had become increasingly oriented toward the alleviation of specific symptoms by treatment of suspected causes rather than the art of healing the person as a whole. Over the years, increased specialisation further fragmented research and theory as well as practice. Holistic medicine attempts to remedy that imbalance.

Similarly, conventional spiritualities (much like modern medicine) tended to concentrate upon certain isolated areas of life rather than lived experience as a whole. Whatever failed to fit into the narrow categories and behavioural restraints of attendant spiritual 'disciplines' was either ignored or condemned. As a result, what came to pass for spirituality by the time of the Second Vatican Council was in large measure incomplete, negative, clerical, and most often verbose if not trivial – in short, out of phase with the real world and therefore with the authentic thrust of the Church's pastoral mission. In effect, holistic spirituality attempts to regain a sense of life-embracing Christian wholeness.

Spirituality and Health: A Holistic Perspective
It should be evident by now that I see a close connection between spirituality and health across a wide range of interest areas, and the key to the connection is *wholeness*. Both spirituality and health refer to the harmony or integration of the whole person – body, mind and spirit as William Stringfellow insisted, 'throughout the era of time'. Like health, spirituality is not only embodied experience, it is embodied in history.[13]

Even contemporary spiritual writers sometimes refer to the mind, body and spirit – the accepted holistic trinity – as if they were distinct parts of human life or the person. Biblically (and holistically), such a view is as fundamentally untenable as it is pervasive. A truly holistic approach simply embraces the person as a whole – that is, the unity of every activity, attitude, feeling and thought, every relationship, hope and goal that make up the concrete life events of the historically existing, real individual. In his remarkable study of St Paul's theology of the body, J.A.T. Robinson notes that '*soma* [body], like *sarx* [flesh], is used to indicate the external presence of the whole man [*sic*] …'[14]

From a biblical viewpoint, the human person is never merely a juxtaposition or sum of parts, but in every respect a whole which, metaphorically, any aspect or part can represent. Further, body, mind and spirit are not something we have or possess; rather, we *are* them.[15] What's more, we are *all* body, *all* soul or mind, and *all* spirit. But it is spirit that defines our special relationship with God. According to Robinson, when *pneuma*, spirit, is used of a human being, it means 'that in virtue of which [one] is open to and transmits the life of God …'[16]

Health, Wholeness and Holiness

Like spirituality, health is not a state, but a dynamic transactional alliance with the physical environment, the social system and the divine milieu in which we live, move and have our being. No one is either holy or healthy in isolation. A healthy and social, physical and spiritual 'ecology' permits and fosters health in each of us as an individual. Healthy people also create healthy living situations for others and for the planet as a whole.

Also like spiritual traditions, health has its history – it is a temporal dialogue with both our ancestors and our progeny. It is not simply a present characteristic of a person, place, or group. Like height, weight, skin and eye colour, a robust or feeble constitution, immunities and susceptibilities to certain diseases from heart disease, cancer and sickle cell anaemia to asthma and allergies are passed from generation to generation, often but not exclusively by genetic inheritance. Immediate inheritable effects can result from diet and behaviour, as I have seen in Latin America and the Middle East with their problems of chronic hunger and malnutrition.

Whether in developed or developing countries, smoking and drug abuse on the part of parents can adversely impact the health of their children even before they are conceived. Behaviour is also formative – healthy and unhealthy lifestyles are passed from generation to generation by modelling and imitation.

Simply speaking, health, both good health and poor health, is a habit – actually, a whole system of habits. Because they are a form of learning, good health habits can be developed and bad ones corrected. Those are not easy tasks, however, especially in a world dominated by commercial interests whose profitability largely depends on consumer trust – and ignorance. (Reading labels on food and drink purchases sometimes seems pointless unless the reader holds a degree in biochemistry.) It is here that a vital spirituality can make a real difference.

The Holistic Health Revolution
Strictly speaking, 'revolution' means 'turning around', as in 'going back to the beginning'. In many respects, the holistic health movement is a revolution, because it hearkens back to the integrative approach of early Chinese, Tibetan, Egyptian and Greek medicinal theory and practice, which understood illth as a disequilibrium of the whole person – being 'out of whack' with the universe. Sickness was simultaneously a disruption of the body, spirit, mind, emotions, social relations and the heavens. Hebrew thought tended in the same direction. Treating a single symptom was not a cure. Finding the source of illness might be.

Traditional or 'allopathic' medicine is founded on the assumption, one borne out by over two centuries of scientific investigation, experimentation and analysis, that all ill health – disease, and in some instances, injury – is caused by both physical factors: bacteria, viruses, parasites, toxins and injuries that invade the body from 'outside', and also by internal factors, mainly genetic inheritance, mutation, birth defects, or malfunction that arise from 'within'. Alternative or 'homeopathic' medicine (now often referred to as Complementary and Alternative Medicine, or CAM) is based on the belief that 'illness results when emotional, psychological or spiritual stresses become overwhelming and thus cause a weakening of the body'.[17]

From a holistic or integrative perspective, both approaches are partially correct, but incomplete. They are complementary rather than antagonistic, however. Especially as promoted by physicians such as Norman Shealy, Bernie Siegel, Andrew Weil and Mehmet Oz (to name a few well-known proponents), integrative medicine and health care approach illness by taking the patient's entire situation into account – social, emotional, mental and spiritual factors as well as physical ones.

It would thus be well to recall in considering the psychological and spiritual genesis of illth that the bubonic plagues of the sixth and fourteenth centuries were spread by fleas, not by emotional stress. Like AIDS, the great 'Spanish' influenza epidemic of 1918 was transmitted by a virus. MRSA infection is caused by exposure to bacteria. Cholera is contagious. Malaria is transmitted by a mosquito bite. But resistance to such contagion and infections is undeniably lessened by emotional, spiritual and social stress. And as Sigmund Freud showed over a century ago, even physical injury may occur because of emotional and, I would add, spiritual conflict. Consequently, preventing and coping with illness and injury, including infectious illness and the deliberate injury of invasive surgery, require emotional, psychological and spiritual resources as well as physical assistance in the forms of medicines, antiseptic practice and bed rest. Spiritual and emotional factors may well contribute decisively to recovery and no doubt play an important role in maintaining the immune system: 'Hope deferred makes the heart sick, but a desire fulfilled is a tree of life' (Prov 13:12).

It is now a mainstay even of scientific medicine that true healing arises primarily from 'within'. Medical arts remove obstacles and create optimal conditions for recuperation. In themselves, they do not heal. Nature heals. Thomas Aquinas was fond of insisting that 'Grace completes nature, it does not destroy it' (*Summa Theologiae*, I, Q.1, A.8, ad 2). The same may be said of medicine.

Just as allopathic and homeopathic strategies complement each other to produce optimal health, several troublesome consequences arise from divorcing these two aspects of medicine. First, externalising health by placing too much emphasis on physical factors, seeing the sick as passive targets ('patients') of disease needing only external assistance – often in the form of prolonged and expensive institutionalisation – further victimises those already suffering from illness. Second, by over-internalising illness, the 'patient' is often portrayed as a perpetrator, as if the external environment had little or no role in creating or fostering disease. Guilt feelings can result, especially in the case of frightening diseases such as cancer – the gnawing suspicion that 'I must have brought this on myself. I am to blame'.

We *do* sometimes bring ill health on ourselves by carelessness and vice, but writhing in remorse and shame is hardly likely to make matters better (although changing vicious behaviour will). Blaming ourselves (or others for that matter) may in fact make matters far worse.

A third consequence of the schism between standard medical practice and holistic health care is that physicians, nurses and other medical professionals come to regard intractable illness or injury as a personal failure, a defeat, as if recovery were completely up to them. Not surprisingly, some of the 'heroic' measures prescribed to assure 'successful' healing may be undertaken not so much to benefit the patient as to forestall the guilt of failure. Extraordinary measures may also deprive the patient of the tranquility and dignity of their last moments that would allow them to encounter death not as a technological *gotterdämmerung*, but, as Shakespeare had it, 'as a bride'.[18] Who would want to meet their Maker drugged, slapped, pounded, shocked and surrounded by bleating machinery into which veins, arteries and airways have been 'plugged', rather than quietly, in the mist of their family and friends?

A more integrated, humane and therefore spiritual approach to health care can and will avoid such extremes. Over the centuries, in those ancient cultures where health care and spirituality flourished, a variety of such approaches did in fact arise and still have medical and spiritual relevance. In the following chapter I propose to conduct an altogether too-brief tour of some of the most relevant of them. For every story, there is a back story.

NOTES

1. Parts of this chapter were adapted from my article 'Spirit and Word', *Presence: The Journal of Spiritual Directors International* 3 (May 1997) 2:62–7. Unless otherwise indicated, scriptural citations are from *New Revised Standard Version* of the Holy Bible.

2. Among recent examples of both the fusion of spirituality with religion and their radical separation are M.J. Brady, A.H. Peterman, G. Fitchett, M. Mo and D. Cella, 'A case for including spirituality in quality of life measurement in oncology', *Psycho-oncology* 8 (1999) 5:417–28; T.P. Daaleman and B. Frey, 'The Spirituality Index of Well-Being: A New Instrument for Health-Related Quality-of-Life Research', *Annals of Family Medicine* 2 (2004) 5:499–503; W.L. Larimore, M. Parker and M. Crowther, 'Should clinicians incorporate positive spirituality into their practices? What does the evidence say?' *Annals of Behavioural Medicine* 24 (2002) 1:69–73; and W.R. Miller and C.E. Thoresen, 'Spirituality, religion, and health: An emerging research field', *American Psychologist* 58 (2003) 1:24–35.

3. Marsha Sinetar's early study, *Ordinary People as Monks and Mystics* (New York: Paulist Press, 1986), is still an excellent and relevant source for understanding the apparent divorce between spirituality and religion coincident with the quest for social and self-transcendence. For a recent critique of the dichotomisation of spirituality and religion, see Reid Locklin, *Spiritual but Not Religious? An Oar Stroke Closer To The Farther Shore* (Collegeville, MN: Liturgical Press, 2005).

4. For an excellent example, see Kathleen Norris, *Dakota: A Spiritual Geography* (New York: Tichnor and Fields, 1993).

5. For an older but still useful survey of the origin and range of the term, see Jon Alexander, OP, 'What Do Recent Writers Mean by Spirituality?' *Spirituality Today* 32 (Sept 1980) 3:247–56.

6. See Sebastian Brock, 'The Holy Spirit as Feminine in Early Syriac Literature', *After Eve*, ed. by Janet M. Soskice (London: Collins / Marshall Pickering, 1990), pp. 73–88.

7. The word *rüach* appears some 400 times in the Hebrew scriptures, and generally means 'wind'. The Greek *pneuma* and Latin *spiritus* can also mean 'wind', which is, however, more normally rendered by *anemos* and *venter* respectively, words that do not convey the idea of breath and were not used to refer to God. Hebrew, too, had other words for naming the wind.

8. The English word 'breath' comes from the Anglo-Saxon *braeth*, which referred to odours and smells, especially the aroma of something cooking. It arose from an earlier word which simply meant to burn or to heat something. Eventually, it came to convey the sense of an exhalation of anything being heated, but particularly the warm air expelled from the lungs. In English, many Latinate words associated with physical and religious life are also based on breathing,

among them *aspiration, respiration, inspiration, perspiration* and, as noted, *expiration.*

9.   Exploring the full significance of Paul's teaching about the relations of mind, body and spirit is the burden of J.A.T. Robinson's remarkable little book, *The Body: A Study in Pauline Theology* (London: SCM Press / Philadelphia: Westminster Press, 1952).

10. *Against Heresies,* 4.20.7. Irenaeus is also credited with the view that 'Spirits without bodies will never be spiritual men and women. It is our entire being, that is to say, the soul and flesh combined, which by receiving the Spirit of God constitutes the spiritual human being'.

11. Karl Rahner and the Transcendental Thomists tended to see spirit as 'openness to being'. By the middle of the twentieth century, the term 'openness' became almost synonymous with spirituality, as in 'openness to experience', 'openness to relationship', 'openness to the world', 'openness to God', etc. But while elegant, precise, profound and useful, all such concepts are also abstract and general and to that extent relatively empty.

12. Alexander, art. cit., 253–4.

13. Stringfellow's comment is worth citing more fully: 'spiritual maturity or spiritual fulfillment necessarily involves the whole person – body, mind, soul, place, relationships – in connection with the whole of creation throughout the era of time. Biblical spirituality encompasses the whole person in the totality of existence in the world, not some fragment or scrap or incident of a person.' William Stringfellow, *The Politics of Spirituality* (Philadelphia: Westminster Press, 1984), p. 22.

14. Robinson, op. cit. p. 27.

15. Cf. Robinson, p. 28.

16. Robinson, p. 19.

17. Carolyn Myss, 'Shifting Our Thinking about the Cause of Illness,' in Norman Shealy and Carolyn Myss, *The Creation of Health* (New York: Three Rivers Press, 1993), p. 16. Homeopathic medicine or homeopathy is now largely associated with the theory and practice initiated by the German physician Samuel Hahnemann (1755–1843).

18. 'If I must die, / I will encounter darkness as a bride / And hug it in mine arms.' *Measure for Measure,* III, i, 82.

CHAPTER TWO
EAST MEETS WEST

Is there no balm in Gilead? Is there no physician there? Why then has
the health of my poor people not been restored?
Jeremiah 8:22

It is generally conceded that in both Asia and Europe, religion figured
prominently in the origin and development of medicine and health
care. In ancient Egypt, China, India, Israel and Greece, medical care
was the secondary occupation of the priestly caste, next only to
worship and directly related to it. The ill, infirm and injured resorted
to temples for skilled treatment and recuperation. It was there that the
arts and sciences of pharmacology, surgery and therapeutic practice,
even forms of psychiatry, were studied, practiced and slowly
perfected. The biblical tradition is no less indicative of the close
connection between religion and health. It was not accidental that
Jesus told the ten lepers he had healed 'to go and show yourselves to
the priests', for only the priests could properly examine and
pronounce on such skin diseases (Lk 17:14; Lev 13:2-59).

Writing around the same period, Philo of Alexandria commends
the Therapeutae, members of a Jewish monastic community located
near the Egyptian capital who were renowned for their healing
abilities. St Luke himself was reputed to be a physician and came to be
regarded as a patron saint of the healing profession. Later, not only
spiritual healing but physical health care provided by early Christians
figured importantly in the growth of the new faith.[1]

But long before the healing arts were discovered and developed in
Judaism and Christianity, or even Greece, medicine had flourished in
East Asia – especially in India, China and Tibet. They would do so
with amazing success in the progressive era of Muslim expansion,
especially in Spain. As scientific approaches slowly displaced the

older western traditions in Europe, however, the Asian arts of healing continued their own developmental process, one that has survived to the present despite the inroads made by western medicine over the last century.

Ayurvedic Medicine

In the last decade, the ancient Indian art of Ayurvedic medicine has found a listening and often practicing audience in Europe and North America. The leading proponent of Ayurvedic medicine as an alternative form of health care is the prolific author and speaker, Dr Deepak Chopra, whose first appearance in the West was as a member of the Transcendental Mediation movement of the Maharishi Mahesh Yogi, who seems to have been largely responsible for the recovery and rebirth of interest in the ancient medical lore of India.[2]

Some form of traditional *Ayurveda* ('knowledge of healthy life') is followed by millions of Asian peoples of the subcontinent. In western countries, Ayurvedic practice is mainly limited to herbalism, exercise and diet. In India, where schools of Ayurvedic medicine are recognised, both theory and practice are much more extensive, encompassing internal medicine, surgical practice, paediatrics and psychotherapy, among other areas.

For centuries, probably well over a millennium, Ayurvedic theory and practice were passed on by oral tradition before being committed to palm-leaf books and later to metallic plates sometime around the beginning of the Common Era. By then Ayurveda had spread widely throughout south-east Asia from Ceylon (Sri Lanka) to Tibet. As with most of the major healing systems of the ancient world, the objective of Ayurveda is to preserve or restore the appropriate balance of body, mind and spirit. The intersection of Ayurveda and yoga, with its emphasis on enhancing *prana*, the life force (sometimes identified with breath), produced both occasional friction and frequent advances in the understanding and practice of health care.

Somewhat like the later Greek and Roman medicinal theory of 'humours', Ayurveda maintains that health consists in a balance of factors called *doshas* that correspond basically with the physical elements of the world. These are not physical substances, but manifestations of energies or forces within the body. *Vata* represents a combination of air and space, *Pitta* represents fire, and *Kapha* represents a combination of water and earth. One or other of the *doshas*, or a combination or two or even all three, will predominate in a person's constitution, giving rise to different personality and physical types.

Like other traditional systems of medicine, some western physicians consider Ayurvedic procedures to be hazardous, particularly applications involving the use of heavy metals – lead, arsenic and mercury. At the same time, research is underway to evaluate many of the traditional ingredients used in Ayurveda such as the common spice turmeric, which has been shown to produce remarkable effects in the prevention and treatment of cancer, among other uses. (We will consider later the burgeoning interest in culinary herbs and spices that are slowly revealing their curative secrets.)

Traditional Chinese and Tibetan Medicine

Toward the end of a university study trip to China in the spring of 2007, after a brisk walk through the congested streets of old Shanghai, so different from the post-1992 ultra-modern city, our little caravan finally arrived at the Temple of the Jade Buddha, which was built in 1882 and houses two priceless effigies of the Buddha, as well as a collection of superb bonsai trees which I have to confess interested me even more. But the main purpose of my visit was to find the medicinal tearoom.

For centuries, the monks have blended herbs, blossoms and other ingredients into a collection of ten very remarkable teas which are specific for a variety of ills and ailments, including one that had bothered me for several months. I discovered that here it was called 'shoulderitis'. I thought my malady was arthritis or bursitis, or as several friends had suggested ominously, a torn rotator cuff. I was sure that wasn't the case, but my right shoulder had bothered me sufficiently to be curious about 'Number 7' tea, which, I was assured by the charming attendant, Ling Ling (her real name, which, like that of the lovable panda in Washington National Zoo, means 'clever'), would probably cure or at least considerably reduce the persistent pain and occasional weakness. I was happy to learn that Number 7 was also good for arthritis and lower back pain. The teas are surprisingly inexpensive, but they cannot be ordered by mail or on line. One must go to the Temple to obtain them.

Herbalism and the use of a variety of animal-based medicines have been major features of Traditional Chinese Medicine (TCM) from very ancient times. Invasive surgery was not well developed, but physical manipulation was practiced in the form of acupuncture and acupressure, which rely on the stimulation of certain points located on the skin over 'meridians' of vital energy or *qi* (or *chi*) that courses through the body.

Acupuncture originally employed thorns but now uses fine needles to contact the desired points, while acupressure relies on precise physical pressure to activate them. A third system, moxibustion, was widely practiced in ancient China and is still widespread. *Moxa*, the mugwort plant (*Artemisia vulgaris*), is prepared and warmed or burned at certain acupuncture points, with or without the use of needles, to stimulate the flow of *qi*, which is the equivalent of *prana* in traditional Indian medicine. (Mugwort, a relative of the herb tarragon and wormwood, all of which belong to the sunflower family, was also prized for centuries in Europe and the Americas for its curative powers and reputed capacity to enhance psychic prowess.)

Like the *doshas* of Ayurvedic medicine, TCM postulates a physiological basis of health as a balance of material and energy factors in the body – what the western tradition knows as humours. These *Wu Xing* or Five Elements – metal, wood, water, fire and earth – constitute the material and dynamic constitution of all phenomena, including the human body. Disruption or imbalance of these factors produces ill health. The task of the healer is to diagnose and prescribe remedies that will restore the appropriate balance.

Tibetan healing resembles that of other ancient Asian traditions in many respects, but also has many distinctive features.[3] Based on a theory of interacting biophysical elements, as are Chinese, Mongolian, Korean and early Greek medical traditions, the objective in Tibetan healing is to maintain or restore the appropriate balance of the three main humours – bile, air and phlegm. A wide range of remedies and therapies, many involving esoteric forms of yoga, were incorporated into Tibetan medicine after the arrival of Buddhism in the seventh and eighth centuries of the Common Era. The possibility of influence of 'demonic influences' is also a major factor in diagnosis and treatment.

As in the cases of traditional Chinese and Indian medicine, the art of Tibetan healing is attracting increased attention today in the scientifically oriented West, but remains more resistant to materialistic, secularised comprehension, particularly as the spiritual element is an inextricable component.

Into the West: Greece and Rome
Medical arts developed at a very early date in Mesopotamia and Egypt, but it is to Greece and Rome that we look for the real antecedents of the western medical tradition.

Many volumes can – and have – been written on the origin and development of Greek medical theory and practice, which are more familiar to Europeans than the arts of East Asia, for our systems have their roots in the soil of Greece and later Roman medicine. The religious aspect of medical practice is as characteristic of the Greeks as of any other ancient people. When medical schools began to be established, they were first attached to temples dedicated to Asklepios, the god of healing.

Asklepios was most likely a real physician who lived in the second millennium BCE, roughly contemporary with Moses. He is mentioned in the *Iliad*. Over the centuries, his memory was enshrined and embellished until he achieved the stature of a deified being. As such he found mention in Plato's *Republic*, and a number of statues depicting him have been recovered. The Greek guild of physicians was named the Asklepiades in his honour. Healing temples dedicated to Asklepios were erected throughout the Greek world, the most famous of them all being the shrine at Epidaurus. The emblem by which he is remembered is a representation of his staff around which a serpent, the symbol of healing, is entwined.

The most famous figure in Greek and early European medicine is, of course, Hippocrates, who practiced healing at the Asklepion of Kos, an island near Rhodes. An entire corpus of medical treatises was eventually ascribed to him, materials undoubtedly collected by his followers over the centuries which came to constitute the historical foundation of western medicine.

Never divinized, Hippocrates lived sometime in the late fifth century BCE. He is mentioned favourably by both Plato and Aristotle. Although a practitioner at the Asklepion, Hippocrates seems not to have been a priest and his approach to illness and healing was decidedly naturalistic. He did not neglect the psychological and spiritual dimensions of either, however. His insistence on treating patients holistically, especially taking into account their social situation, clearly makes him a harbinger of contemporary holistic practice. His most famous and perhaps lasting contribution to medical ethics is found in the lines of the Hippocratic Oath which, among other pledges, assures that 'I will apply dietetic measures for the benefit of the sick according to my ability and judgement. I will keep them from harm and injustice. I will neither give a deadly drug to anybody who asked for it, nor will I make a suggestion to this effect. Similarly, I will not give to a woman an abortive remedy. In purity and holiness I will guard my life and my art.'[4]

Much like ancient Indian and Chinese healers, Hippocrates and his followers believed that optimal health was achieved by a balance of bodily elements, the classical humours: blood, phlegm, yellow bile and black bile, which were, in turn, related to the four natural elements: air, water, fire and earth. A preponderance of one or the others produced the four temperaments: sanguine, phlegmatic, choleric and melancholic. But when the relative balance was disrupted, illness resulted. Medical practice aimed at restoring this critical balance. The general theory was accepted by Aristotle and through his writings influenced European medicine for well over a thousand years.

Divergent schools of theory and practice that followed Hippocratic teaching to a greater or lesser extent developed in Greece in later periods. Already influential in Greek-speaking parts of southern Italy, after the conquest of Greece by Rome in the Second Macedonian War (200–197 BCE) and especially after Octavian's defeat of Marc Anthony's forces in 31 BCE, Greek medicine spread to Rome and eventually throughout the Roman Empire. It was surely under Greek influence that in the late second century of the Common Era the Roman poet Juvenal described optimal health as *mens sana in corpore sano*:

> It is to be prayed that the mind be sound in a sound body.
> Ask for a brave soul that lacks the fear of death,
> which places the length of life last among nature's blessings,
> which is able to bear whatever kind of sufferings,
> does not know anger, lusts for nothing and believes
> the hardships and savage labours of Hercules better than
> the satisfactions, feasts, and feather bed of an Eastern king.
> (*Satire* X,10, lines 56–64)

Among the great physicians of the later Roman period, Claudius Galenus, or Galen as he is known (131–c. 216 CE), stands out as a precursor of modern medicine in several regards. A native of Pergamum in what is now eastern Turkey, he too was trained at the local Asklepion. Although limited by Roman civil law to animal dissection, Galen was able to advance knowledge of anatomy and physiology to some extent, despite some serious blunders. He performed delicate eye and even brain surgery requiring skill far ahead of his time. Attracted to Rome, the brilliant physician, now a middle-aged man, eventually was invited to attend the Emperor Marcus Aurelius.

Under Roman auspices and eventually under the Byzantine Empire that succeeded it, the Greek medical tradition flourished and eventually inspired the far greater flowering of theory and practice from the tenth to the thirteenth century in the Muslim world of Baghdad, Egypt and especially Moorish Spain. By that time, Jewish and Christian traditions of healing had long since encountered and benefited from Greek approaches, but medicine was about to make a quantum leap forward.

The Biblical Faiths: Judaism, Christianity and Islam
Stories of the origins of medicine involving the accomplishments of the Greeks, Egyptians and Romans might be at least vaguely familiar to many of us. The great advances of Chinese and Indian healers, herbalists and physicians are understandably less so, although the situation is changing with the publicity given to Ayurvedic medicine in recent years. Similarly, the popularity of Chinese techniques such as acupuncture and acupressure, and the use of Chinese herbal supplements, have introduced many westerners to aspects of Traditional Chinese Medicine. But the ancient legacy of Hebrew, Christian and Muslim medicine seems to be largely unknown to many students today.

Judaism
The biblical tradition is far sketchier than those of India and China, but it provided a foundation on which great medical schools would one day be raised by practitioners among the Children of Abraham, members of the three great faiths that share that tradition. Medieval Islamic medical schools in Seville and Cordoba, where Muslims, Christians and Jews mingled amicably, were arguably the greatest in the world until destroyed by political rivalries and religious reaction in the late Middle Ages and Renaissance.

Like early Greek and Asian traditions, the Hebrew healing tradition emphasised the bond between spirit and body with regard to the origin and treatment of disease. Health was prized as a blessing and gift from God. Human responsibility for preserving and restoring health was not overlooked. But among both the ancient Hebrews and later Jews (literally, the people of Judea), theory was relatively undeveloped and practice was limited to much simpler procedures than those developed elsewhere in the ancient world. By the eleventh century of the Common Era, however, Jewish medicine would be the equal of any in the world.

Possibly the most central thesis of the early Hebrew understanding of the human person in relation to health and healing concerns the unity of body and spirit, an emphasis at odds with the Greek, especially Platonic, view. J.A.T. Robinson observes in this regard.

> ... perhaps [the] most far-reaching of all the Greek antitheses, that between body and soul, is also foreign to the Hebrew. The Hellenic conception of man has been described as that of an angel in a slot machine, a soul (the invisible, spiritual, essential ego) incarcerated in a frame of maker, from which it trusts eventually to be liberated. The body is non-essential to the personality: it is something which a man possesses, or, rather, is possessed by. 'The Hebrew idea of the personality', on the other hand, wrote the late Dr Wheeler Robinson in a sentence which has become famous, 'is an animated body, and not an incarnated soul' ... Man does not have a body, he is a body. He is flesh-animated-by-soul, the whole conceived as a psycho-physical unity: 'The body is the soul in its outward form' ... There is no suggestion that the soul is the essential personality, or that the soul (*nephesh*) is immortal, while the flesh (*basar*) is mortal. The soul does not survive a man – it simply goes out, draining away with the blood.[5]

The care and treatment of the body was therefore focal in healing. Despite advances in psychosomatic therapy, healing the body would remain paramount, even in the Hellenistic period. Greek medicine was certainly known to the Jews of Jesus' time, but there is reason to believe that specifically Jewish approaches also and characteristically developed in Palestine but especially in the Diaspora, where exposure to Greek and Roman culture was inevitable and less fractious. This was especially true in Egypt, where the largest number of Jewish émigrés outside of Palestine had congregated in the capital, Alexandria.

The Therapeutae

Around the beginning the Common Era, the greatest Jewish scholar of his time, Philo of Alexandria, described in one of his most influential works the ministry of an association of Jewish healers who lived in the seaside desert near the great city. If Philo's description of the *Therapeutae*, as he called them, refers to historical fact, their presence and activity was as unusual as it was beneficial to both Jews and pagans.[6]

The title comes from the Greek noun *therapeia*, which meant 'service', particularly temple service, and eventually 'healing service'. The verb *theapeuo*, a classical Greek term found in Hesiod, Aristotle and other writers, means 'to serve, or be a servant', particularly of a divinity. It also came to mean 'to care for, wait upon, or to treat medically', and eventually 'to heal', mainly because the ancient practitioners of health care in both Egypt and Greece were priests in attendance at temples known to be healing sites. In biblical literature, the derivative noun *therap?n*, 'servant', used by the Greeks for attendants at the temples of Dionysios and Asklepios, was used exclusively to describe Moses, as in Exodus 4:10, Numbers 12:7, Wisdom 10:16 and Hebrews 3:5.

The religious and indeed spiritual dimension of healing contained in the term 'therapy' was emphasised by Philo in his description of the monastic healers that lived near Alexandria and apparently elsewhere. It is interesting to note that on reading Philo's account the Christian historian Eusebius, writing early in the fourth century, mistook the Therapeutae for Christian monks, so closely did their style of living and even physical appearance resemble the coenobitic communities of Christian Egypt in his time.

Philo tells us that these early 'monks' were called both *Therapeutae* and *Therapeutrides*, either 'because they professed an art of healing better than that current in the cities which cures only the bodies, while theirs treats also souls oppressed with grievous and well-nigh incurable diseases, inflicted by the pleasures and desires and griefs and fears, by acts of covetousness, folly and injustice and the countless host of other passions and vices', or else in the sense of worship, 'because nature and the sacred laws have schooled them to worship the Self-Existence who is better than the good, purer than the One, and more primordial than the Monad'.

According to Eusebius, 'Whether [Philo] invented this designation and applied it to them, fitting a suitable name to their mode of life, or whether they were actually called this from the very start, because the title Christian was not yet in general use, need not be discussed now'.[7] Clearly, however, Eusebius thinks they were Christian monks. It was not a unnatural mistake; the Therapeutae lived celibately, apparently professing life-long vows, studied scripture, prayed, fasted, and lived a life of poverty and simplicity, being vegetarian and abstinent from alcohol. Their habit was a plain white robe. Like medieval Carthusians, they spent most of the time in solitary contemplation, but gathered for worship, vigils and reflection, following by a common meal which Philo compares favourably to the licentious symposia described by Plato and Eusebius mistakes for the Christian Eucharist.

Philo claims that these Jewish philosopher-priests, both male and female,

> exists in many places in the inhabited world, for perfect goodness must needs be shared both by Greeks and the world outside Greece, but it abounds in Egypt ... and especially around Alexandria. But the best of these votaries journey from every side to settle in a certain very suitable place which they regard as their fatherland. This place is situated above the Mareotic Lake on a somewhat low-lying hill very happily placed both because of its security and the pleasantly tempered air ... [owing to the] continuous breezes which arise both from the lake ... and from the open sea hard by. For the sea breezes are light, the lake breezes close, and the two combining together produce a most healthy condition of climate.[8]

Their houses, Philo says, were simple and not too close together. In each, 'there is a consecrated room which is called a *monasterion* and closeted in this they are initiated into the mysteries of the sanctified life'. One of the most interesting aspects of their life was the absence of a servant class. 'They do not have slaves to wait upon them as they consider that the ownership of servants is entirely against nature. For nature has borne all men to be free, but the wrongful and covetous acts of some who pursued that source of evil, inequality, have imposed their yoke and invested the stronger with power over the weaker.'[9]

After noting that the Therapeutae 'practice contemplation but also compose songs and hymns to God', Eusebius cites their emphasis on temperance in food and the study of scripture, which he mistakenly assumes were 'the gospels, the apostolic writings, and in all probability passages interpreting the old prophets, such as are contained in the Epistle to the Hebrews and several others of Paul's epistles'.[10]

Beyond their contributions to medicine, if we accept the testimony of Philo and Eusebius as reliable, the Therapeutae can be credited with the invention of Christian monasticism! However that may be, the monastic devotion to healing and hospitality was established at a very early period and would remain a cardinal characteristic for centuries to come.

Jesus the Healer, his Disciples and Health

Like the Greek versions of Hebrew texts and works from the Intertestamental Period, the Christian scriptures reveal a variety of terms for health and healing, a vocabulary much richer than our English translations suggest. One thing stands out above all the rest, however. From the beginning, Jesus saw his ministry and it was seen by others as one focused on healing. He was remembered for a praxis that ranged from simple folk remedies such as mixing spittle with dust and applying it over the eyes to clear clouded vision (see Jn 9:6) to astounding feats of compassion such as the cleansing of lepers and even restoring the dead to life (Mt 9:23-26; Mk 5:38-42; Lk 5:17, 7:1-10,11-16, 8:49-56, 17:12-19; Jn 11:38-45). Often, the evangelists simply record that Jesus went about healing the sick and, in regard to spiritual and possibly psychiatric illness, casting out evil spirits (Lk 6:18, 9:42; Jn 4:46-53; Acts 10:38).

When Jesus sent word to John in prison to reassure him that he was the one John had hoped for, he told the messengers to say 'the blind receive their sight, the lame walk, lepers are cleansed, the deaf hear, the dead are raised, and the poor have good news brought to them (Mt 11:5; Lk 7:22). For one so well versed in the prophetic literature, the condensed allusions to Isaiah 29:18, 35:5-6, 61:1, and possibly 26:19[11] would have been sufficient. Whether or not these are the actual words Jesus sent to John, they testify to the faith of the early Christian community that Jesus not only fulfilled the prophetic promise, but exceeded it.

Jesus also clearly meant for his disciples to follow his example. He was remembered to have instructed them, 'Cure the sick, raise the dead, cleanse lepers, cast out demons. You received without payment; give without payment' (Mt 10:8, Lk 9:1-2). That they did so is borne out by the Acts of the Apostles in a host of examples (see Acts 3:2-9, 16, 9:32-35, 36-42, 14:8-11, 20:9-12).

One of the most charming asides in Scripture is found in 1 Timothy 5:23, in which the author, writing in the person of Paul, advises the young bishop Timothy, 'No longer drink only water, but take a little wine for the sake of your stomach and your frequent ailments'.

But if the health benefits of wine were part of early Christian wisdom, the perils of over-consumption were hardly ignored, especially in the case of senior members of the churches, as we also discover in the pastoral epistles: 'Deacons likewise must be serious, not double-tongued, not indulging in much wine, not greedy for money' (1 Tim 3:8). Similarly, 'a bishop, as God's steward, must be blameless; he must not be arrogant or quick-tempered or addicted to wine or violent or greedy for gain' (Titus 1:7). The formulaic tone of the warnings may be cautionary, but it might also testify to a perennial problem, not least among the clergy.

Armed with the exegetical tools of several generations of skeptical scholars, one might quibble over the accuracy of reports of healings by Jesus and his disciples, but whether or not one accepts the accounts as being literally true, the importance given to health and healing in the early Christian communities is beyond doubt. In addition to the frequent allusions to ministries and gifts of healing in Scripture (1 Cor 12:9, 28, 30; Jm 5:14-16), the history of the post-Apostolic churches testify to the continued role it played in the life and expansion of Christianity. Rodney Stark, the sociologist of religion, has in his book, *The Rise of Christianity,* provided corroborative detail in regard to this feature of early Christian life.[12]

The treatment of disease, especially during the plagues of 165 and 251, had a great impact on the rise of Christianity, largely because of the response of Christians pastorally and theologically. Christians not only nursed their own members, but extended their compassion and skills to pagans, behaviour that in a world in which callousness was common occasioned significant attention and became a factor in additional conversions.

Within Christian lore itself, several physicians achieved prominence among early saints – among them Saint Luke, Saints Cosmas and Damian, and the martyr Pantaleon, who became the earliest patron saint of physicians.

Beloved Physician

According to tradition, St Luke the Evangelist was a physician, although textual evidence depends on a single statement of St Paul in Colossians 4:14 ('Luke, the beloved physician, and Demas greet you'). Traditional sources from centuries later agree, however. Having been impressed over the years by the persistence and accuracy of oral tradition, I am inclined to grant the argument to be very probable. However that may be, we know nothing about his medical theory or practice. He was originally the patron saint of portrait painters, by the way, rather than physicians, with that honour going to St Pantaleon as well as Ss Cosmas and Damian (although it must also be admitted that in popular thought Luke is undoubtedly one of a host of patron saints of physicians and doctors). Physicians are mentioned only once in the gospel that goes by his name (Lk 8:43), and while the reference is not particularly positive, it is not as unflattering as the parallel verse in Mark: '[The woman] had endured much under many physicians, and had spent all that she had; and she was no better, but rather grew worse' (Mk 5:26).

Scholarly conjecture based on early Church histories by Eusebius and others suggests that Luke most likely studied medicine in Tarsus, where a famous medical school existed. It is possible that he met St Paul there. Given his later travels with Paul and his other companions, it seems probable that Luke served as the ship doctor. His subsequent story is as obscure as that of any of the early disciples. But his memory as a doctor would be honored forever.[13]

Cosmas and Damian, twin-brother Arab physicians, were born to a Christian mother and pagan father. With their three brothers, they were raised in the faith after their father's death. Apparently the twins studied medicine in Syria and practiced in the Celician region of what is now eastern Turkey. Like Hippocrates, they refused to charge fees for their services, a feature of their practice that became the subject of several amusing tales of fraternal discord. The accounts of their martyrdom during the Great Persecution, probably in the year 287, are adorned with typical hagiographical exaggeration added by later generations. Among other feats, they are credited with performing the first leg-transplant operation in history! But the fact that they and their brothers were martyred at the end of the third century is part of the solid tradition that identifies the twins as renowned physicians.

Like Cosmas and Damian, Pantaleon (whose name means 'All-Compassionate') was martyred during the Great Persecution, probably around the year 305. Also the son of a Christian mother and pagan father, Pantaleon abandoned the Faith as a young man. Later he became court physician to the Emperor Maximianus. Brought back to the Faith by the priest Hermolaus, he was denounced by jealous rivals. Refusing to repudiate Christianity and despite supposed entreaties by Diocletian himself, Pantaleon remained steadfast and was decapitated.

Like those of Cosmas and Damian, most of Pantaleon's exploits later recounted by Christian writers are legendary and untrustworthy. But his stature was sufficient to earn him a place in the Middle Ages among the Fourteen 'Auxiliary' or 'Helping' Saints as the patron of physicians and midwives.

In looking back over historical and legendary accounts, I have found no justification for the notion that early Christians (or for that matter Jews and Muslims) either feared or opposed the theory and practice of medicine. Health was a primary value in the biblical tradition, and the healing arts were believed to have been a sacred gift, a blessing from God. Jewish, Christian and Muslim physicians continued and developed both theory and practice often, it would seem, at considerable personal cost and even risk. Restrictions on human dissection that so hindered the understanding and treatment of disease and injury were not unique to the biblical faiths – Roman civil law prevented Galen's study and similar restrictions held back medical experimentation in India and China longer than in the West.

Despite inevitable exceptions, in all these instances it also should be remembered that it was respect for the sanctity of the human person even in death that held back scientific study of cadavers, not antagonism towards medicine or science themselves.

The Medical Traditions of Islam

As had Judaism and Christianity before it, Islam also developed healing arts. As the Muslim conquest swept over North Africa and Mesopotamia in the seventh century of the Common Era, Arab healers came into contact with traditions from both the Eastern Roman Empire and pagan influences, particular that of the Greeks. By the end of the ninth century CE, the works of Galen had been translated into Arabic under the influence of Hunayn ibn Ishaq, although astute Muslim physicians such as the brilliant Muhammad ibn Zakariya Razi (864–930 CE, known to the West as Rhazes), who first used alcohol – an Arabic invention – in medicine and introduced opium as an anaesthetic, and Ibn al-Nafis (1210–1288), recognised and corrected a number of his errors. One of the greatest of the Muslim physicians, Ibn Sina (980–1037), who became known to the West as Avicenna, was particularly favoured by St Thomas Aquinas, not so much as a doctor, however, but as a philosopher. Yet it was Ibn

Sina who first recognised the contagious character of tuberculosis and prescribed surgical excision of tumourous tissues to treat cancer, among other outstanding contributions.

Other notable Muslim physicians were Abu al-Hasan Ali ibn Sahl Rabban al-Tabari (c. 838–c. 870 CE), Razi's teacher; Abul Qasim al-Zahrawi (963–1013), who became known as 'the father of surgery' and was known as Albucasis in the West; and Ibn Zuhr (1091–1161), known as Avenzoar in the West.[14]

Like Jews, Christians and Romans, Islamic surgeons were not permitted to dissect human cadavers, and their knowledge of anatomy and physiology was proportionately limited if still far better than that of their European contemporaries. Nevertheless, capitals such as Baghdad and Cairo became centres of the healing arts. By the early Middle Ages, the greatest medical schools in western Europe flourished under the aegis of the Moors in Spain at Cordova, Seville and Toledo, while western Europe was just entering the golden period of its Middle Ages.

The contention that the origins of modern medicine lie in the integrated cultures of the ancient world, in which religion played a dominant role, seems to be safely beyond cavil. Despite other admittedly baneful effects of the confluence of religion, power and money (including human sacrifice, 'holy' wars and the development of privileged priestly castes who sometimes preyed upon devotees as much or more than they prayed for them), the elaboration and cultivation of the healing arts remains a preeminently lasting contribution to human civilization – not just one among many, but one of the most important of all. The question continues to arise, however, especially today in a world in which secularisation, materialism and consumerism have become dominant social forces: is religion still all that healthy? Is religion good for you? Is it good for the world?

NOTES

1. See the remarkable account in Rodney Stark, *The Rise of Christianity: How the Obscure, Marginal, Jesus Movement Became the Dominant Religious Force* (HarperSanFrancisco, 1997), especially Chapter 4, 'Epidemics, Networks, and Conversion', pp. 73–94.

2. Dr Chopra's most famous book is still most likely *Ageless Body, Timeless Mind: The Quantum Alterative to Growing Old* (New York: Harmony Books, 1993).

3. For a still-excellent overview of traditional Tibetan medicine, see Theodore Burang, *The Art of Tibetan Healing*, trans. by Susan MacIntosh (London: Watkins, 1974).

4. Ludwig Edelstein, trans., *The Hippocratic Oath: Text, Translation, and Interpretation* (Baltimore: John Hopkins Press, 1943).

5. Robinson, op. cit., p. 14, citing H. Wheeler Robinson, *The People and the Book*, p. 362 and J. Pedersen, *Israel*, I-II, 177.

6. Philo [of Alexandria], 'On the Contemplative Life' (*De Vita Contemplativa*)', trans. by F.H. Colson, Vol. IX, Loeb Classical Library (London: William Heinemann / Cambridge, MA: Harvard University Press, 1967), pp. 104–69.

7. Eusebius, *History of the Church*, II, 17.3, trans. by G.A. Williamson (Minneapolis, MN: Augsburg Publishing House, 1975), pp. 89–90.

8. Philo, op. cit., iii, p. 125–7.

9. Ibid., p. 157.

10. Eusebius, op. cit., p. 92. By way of indirect commentary on the contemplative ideals of the fourth century, Eusebius adds that 'These statements of Philo seem to me to refer plainly and unquestionably to members of our Church. But, if after this someone insists on denying it, he will surely abandon his skepticism and be convinced by still clearer evidences which cannot be found anywhere but in the religious practices of Christians who follow the gospel'.

11. See Isaiah 26:19: 'Your dead shall live, their corpses shall rise. O dwellers in the dust, awake and sing for joy! For your dew is a radiant dew, and the earth will give birth to those long dead.'

12. See Stark, op. cit., Chapter 4, 'Epidemics, Networks, and Conversion', pp. 73–94, and Chapter 5, 'The Role of Women in Christian Growth', pp. 95–128. Morton Kelsey's earlier work, *Healing and Christianity in Ancient Thought and Times* (New York: Harper and Row, 1973) may also still be read with profit.

13. For relevant details, see among other works Adolf Harnack, *Luke the Physician*, trans. by J.R. Wilkinson (London: Williams and Norgate, 1908 / New York: G.P. Putnam, 1909); R.J. Knowling, 'The Medical Language of St Luke', *The Biblical World* 20 (Oct 1902) 4:260–71; Alfred Plummer, *The Gospel according to St Luke, International Critical Commentary*, ed. by Alfred Plummer, Charles A. Briggs and Samuel R. Driver (Edinburgh: T & T Clark, 1901); and John Wenham, 'The Identification of Luke', *Evangelical Quarterly* 63 (1991), 3–44.

14. For an overview and brief history of the rise and development of medicine in Islamic society, see Seyyed Hossein Nasr, *Science and Civilization in Islam* (Cambridge: Islamic Texts Society, 1987).

CHAPTER THREE
IS RELIGION GOOD FOR YOU?

The fear of the Lord is the crown of wisdom,
making peace and perfect health to flourish.
Sirach 1:18

Books dismissing religion as a hazard to civilization and even personal
health and happiness have gained considerable attention in the
popular media over the past several years. Biologist Richard Dawkins'
The God Delusion[1] reached best-seller status on both sides of the
English-speaking Atlantic, while Christopher Hitchens' ill-tempered
God is Not Great: How Religion Poisons Everything[2] was nominated in
October 2007 for a National Book Award in the United States.
Dawkins took his campaign to a wider audience with a television
series which disparaged a wide variety of beliefs and practices, some
of which were only vaguely religious if at all, as superstitious
distractions and foolhardy pursuits.[3] Now that publishers have
scented the lure, one can expect a shelf more of such books in the
coming years as well as efforts to refute them.[4]

Attacks on religion by philosophers, journalists, scientists,
politicians, or aggressive atheists such as the notorious American
controversialist, the late Madalyn Murray O'Hair and her son, are
hardly novel. The eighteenth and nineteenth century produced a
library of assaults, some of which achieved 'classical' status – the
essays and plays of Voltaire, the diatribes of Marx, Schopenhauer and
Nietzsche being paramount among them.

Sigmund Freud later added his considerable weight to the
campaign.[5] But despite outbreaks of sometimes violent anti-
clericalism, anti-religious legislation, and outright persecution in
Germany, France, Mexico, the Soviet Union and China (among other
countries), religion has not only survived but, especially in the United

States, Latin America, Africa and parts of Asia, has flourished – if not apparently in western Europe.

The survival and growth of religion in the world today might well suggest that it is not only relatively harmless, but positively beneficial. Despite the considerable furore in the news media, the vast majority of people on this planet not only ignores the diatribes of Dawkins, Hitchens, Dennett, Harris and their sympathisers, but refutes them with their feet and their faith. But that in itself does not prove that 'religion is good for you' or for the world. That is a claim that warrants further investigation. After all, the inhalation of tobacco smoke and other truly poisonous substances continues to flourish in many parts of the world, while diseases such as malaria and tuberculosis have survived the introduction, a century ago now, of antibiotic drugs and are actually increasing their sway along with other drug-resistant diseases. Persistence is not necessarily evidence of benefit. But, as Dawkins asserts, is religion itself a kind of virus that survives and spreads despite the advances of science? Or could he be wrong? Might religion be a cure rather than the cause of the discontents of civilization?

So the issue at hand is not merely whether religion somehow manages to endure and even grow, but whether it exercises a positive influence on individual physical, spiritual and moral health and in regard to the state of the world as a whole. Perhaps surprisingly, the answer seems to be coming from science rather than religion itself. Two areas thus invite exploration: the actual benefit that religion (including and especially spirituality) confers on people with regard to health, but also the social benefit that religion has conferred on the world in the larger sense, pursuit of which will necessarily take us back in time to investigate the origins of modern health care in the religious practices of the past.

Assessing the Evidence

Both life-long ('diachronous') and current ('synchronous') studies have produced volumes of material on the relationship between religion, spirituality and health. A large number of professional journals now exist which report on findings in this area,[6] but a whole library of books and articles in related medical, psychological and sociological areas of research has added greatly to our understanding of the often-complex connections between religion and health.[7] While widespread agreement exists that religion is remarkably beneficial with regard to longevity, decrease of morbidity, recuperation from illness and an extensive range of improved physical and mental health measures, opposition has also found its voice within the medical and scientific community. Most of the objections focus on propriety and methodology: is linking religion with health care disrespectful of religion, as Richard Sloan claims? And are findings related to non-allopathic healing biased by prejudice and founded on faulty analysis of data?[8]

To begin with, I find it difficult to comprehend how appealing to faith in God for healing can be construed as disrespectful of religion, especially given the many accounts of such cries for help that appear in the Bible, and particularly given Jesus' affirmation of the faith of the sufferers when he healed them. True, many investigations can undoubtedly be faulted for concluding too much from too little evidence. Even so, the cumulative support for a positive relation of religion and health is not only overwhelming but at its best scientifically unimpeachable as demonstrated by decades of highly critical analysis and assessment. Ultimately, however, the choice whether to accept or reject such findings rests with each of us.

The catalogue of the beneficial effects of religious involvement in general (from affiliation and attendance at services to active participation in a variety of activities) tends to manifest a similar pattern: religious participation reduces mortality rates, extends life expectancy, predicts better physical function and reduced disability over an eight to twelve year period, lowers rates of cardiovascular disease, hypertension, obesity, depression, anxiety and gastrointestinal distress, and similarly lowers psychological distress, depression, suicide, illicit drug use, alcohol abuse, violence, delinquency and divorce.[9] This seems to be the case across the whole spectrum of age from adolescence to advanced seniority.[10]

To grasp how the influence of spirituality or religion on health came to be recognised as a major factor in the preventive medicine and the treatment of disease, it is first necessary to go back a generation to review the major paradigm shift that occurred with regard to social factors and health in general. The specifically religious factor would emerge later.

The Framingham Study

In the 1970s, the medical community of North America and much of Europe had retreated to a largely physicalist interpretation of heart disease despite growing suspicions among some physicians that something other than physical factors such as smoking, obesity, lack of exercise and genetic defects could be contributing to the perceived increase in heart-related disease and mortality. Then in the mid-1970s evidence that social factors, including isolation and loneliness as well as stress from a variety of sources, could impact heart health adversely began to gain attention, first in the popular media, then in professional circles as the evidence became more and more convincing. The religious connection gradually emerged as a highly significant factor.

Among long-term projects that pointed to a positive link between religion and health was the 'Framingham Study', so named for the town in Massachusetts selected for the study. Begun under the auspices of the National Heart Institute in 1948 and continued over the decades, this landmark study has achieved classic status in the field of cardiovascular medicine. Since 1971, the study has been continued with assistance from Boston University. The objective was to disclose the factors that lead to heart disease by examining the lives of thousands of women and men with no previous history of such disease.[11]

Over the last sixty years, the results of the Framingham study have contributed very significantly to understanding the causes of heart disease and stroke by identifying major risk factors with scientific precision including high blood pressure, high density blood cholesterol, smoking, obesity, diabetes and lack of physical exercise. Among these factors, by 1978 psychosocial pressures were shown to affect heart health adversely, much as James Lynch had just proposed from his practice as a heart surgeon (see below). Confirmation came from a number of other directions, and by 1988 the impact on cardio-vascular health of stress-driven 'Type A Behaviour', first identified by Drs Meyer Friedman and Ray H. Rosenman in 1974, had been clearly demonstrated.[12]

Although the Framingham study did not undertake to investigate the specific contribution of religion to lower risk of cardiovascular disease, the manifest role of social factors quickly led to studies that did in fact establish that link statistically, beginning on the opposite coast of the United States.

The Alameda County Study
In 1965, investigators in California began a survey of more than 6,000 adult men and women regarding their health, medical history and other behaviour including family life, social activities, hobbies, as well as emotional attitudes. Follow-up studies have continued to monitor the health of the original participants.[13]

Over the years, it became unmistakably evident that religious affiliation and especially frequent attendance at religious services resulted in a statistically significant decrease in mortality in comparison to the general population.[14] Increased longevity was still evident more than thirty years later. Moreover, despite the effect of unhealthy practices such as smoking, obesity, lack of exercise and inattention to routine medical care among many participants, and regardless of gender or age, people who regularly attended religious services tended to manifest significantly lower rates of death from circulatory, digestive and respiratory diseases.[15]

Regrettably, recent follow-ups on the health of Alameda County residents reveal a significant decline in health based on increasing disparities in economic status which limit access for growing numbers of the urban poor to clean air, a healthy diet, recreational areas, as well as educational opportunities, equitable salaries and decent housing. How religious faith might help people cope with or overcome such problems has yet to be determined.[16]

Irish Connections: James Lynch and the Broken Heart

Dr James Lynch was one of the most important contributors to the scientific change of heart with regard to the social sources of cardiac arrest. A cardiologist, Lynch stunned the members of his profession with the publication of his 1977 book, *The Broken Heart*, which detailed cases in which stress, social isolation, loneliness, the death of a spouse and grieving took a heavy toll on the hearts of women and men.

Among other evidence, Lynch had come across comparative studies of Irish men who emigrated to America and a matched group of blood relatives who remained in Ireland, usually brothers and, in one of the most interesting studies, twins, which indicated that disproportionate coronary death rates (four times higher in America) were traceable to factors other than diet and exercise. The largely unexamined but common surmise that the relatively sedentary lifestyle of the American Irish as opposed to the more vigorous lifestyle of the siblings in Ireland was the likely factor in the disproportion did not sit well with Lynch, who suspected for other reasons (including studies done in Japan and elsewhere) that social factors, particularly loneliness, played a much greater role than the researchers were prepared to admit. As Lynch complained, 'Little recognition was given to the social stability of Ireland versus Boston, and scant attention was paid to the stresses involved in leaving one's family and homeland to come to a new country. No data at all were given on the marital status of the relative populations'.[17]

Yet, as the Framingham Study would show, social stresses were beginning to appear in research studies as factors contributing to cardiovascular disease. By targeting the specifically religious dimension of social relationships, the Alameda County Study provided a clear link that led to hundreds of further studies.

Once the connection between social stress and illth, particularly heart disease and then cancer, was recognised, the important contributions of religion and spirituality to the preservation and promotion of health became more and more evident. An area that had been considered strictly off-limits to investigators soon became a promising field for research. And for some fifty years now, a number of these studies have looked directly at the lives of professedly religious women and men to see how they fared over time compared to the population as a whole. Were they more or less healthy? Did they live longer or die younger?

The Lifetime Study of Religious Men and Women

This very long-term study, in some respects a small replica of the Framingham Study, was begun over sixty years ago in order to examine the lives of about 200 men and women from the religious mainstream, mostly Protestant and Catholic churchgoers born in the Depression era. The subjects were interviewed at twenty-year intervals, providing researchers with a vast store of data with which to assess the effects of religion in the actual lives of ordinary people.

Among other variables the researchers examined were how religious involvement fluctuated over the course of a lifetime, the transformative effects of religion, spirituality and the quest for meaning, and the effects of religion on persons in late adulthood. Recently, the findings of the study were further analysed by a sociologist and psychologist.[18]

Among other conclusions, the researchers found that, contrary to expectations, the elderly did not become more overtly religious as they neared the end of life, but tended to return to the religious observance of early adulthood. However, Catholics who tended to soften their attitude toward church discipline and doctrine in the wake of the Second Vatican Council did not as a whole revert to earlier attitudes in their later years. Measures of altruism and civic involvement did not vary greatly between churchgoers and the unchurched, nor did the very elderly use religion as a 'buffer' when their health declined. On the other hand, participants who were more religious tended to fare better psychologically. Overall, religion offered a framework for interpreting life events in a positive way. Significantly, those who most feared death were people who identified themselves as religious but did not in fact practice their faith.

Related Benefits: Drug Use and Mental Illness

More recent studies of the impact of religion on mental illness, such as clinical depression and anxiety disorders, and forms of chemical dependency and drug abuse supports the thesis that religion plays a positive role in supporting mental health and alleviating drug-related problems. One of the more impressive projects examined a population sample to determine the character of religious participation and its relation to lifetime psychiatric illness and substance abuse.[19]

The research team identified seven factors: general religiosity, social religiosity, the sense of an 'involved' God, God as judge, 'unvengefulness', forgiveness and thankfulness. The researchers concluded that these dimensions of religiosity are variously related to reduced risk for mental illness and drug-related problems. Social religiosity and thankfulness were associated with reduced risk for both kinds of disorder, unvengefulness with reduced risk of mental disorders only, while reduced risk for both mental illness and drug problems was associated with general religiosity, a caring God, obtaining forgiveness and God as judge.

Measuring the physical benefits of religious involvement has continued to occupy researchers over the years. The evidence clearly points to positive differences, but the dimensions of 'religiousness' and spirituality are notoriously difficult to determine. Not surprisingly, a number of researchers turned to men and women whose lives are focused on religion in a far more intense manner than ordinary citizens – nuns, monks, priests. How do they fare physically, mentally and socially compared to lay members of society?

The Nun Study

This major long-term research project was initiated as a pilot study by Dr David Snowdon in 1968 to investigate the relationship between ageing, educational level and Alzheimer's disease.[20] Snowdon recruited nearly 700 School Sisters of Notre Dame, a teaching order, to participate by submitting to a periodic battery of tests and, after death, to having their brains autopsied. Religious sisters, after all, live longer than the population in general and their educational level is higher as a rule. In 1990, funding obtained from the National Institute on Ageing permitted a major expansion of the scientific and medical aspects of the project.

The School Sisters were particularly recruited because of their strong educational background, a factor already highly correlated with better health, including a lower risk of developing Alzheimer's disease. The common features of the sisters' lifestyle eliminated a host of potentially complicating variables such as income, social class, marital status etc.

Eventually, much like the Framingham Study, the Nun Study enabled medical researchers to make a number of highly significant findings about ageing and health. Among other results, Snowdon and his team were able to show that sisters with a college education had a much higher probability of surviving into old age enjoying both good health and independence than sisters with a lower level of education. Long-term study also revealed that lycopine, a carotenoid obtainable from external sources – food and supplements – performs a vital role in maintaining physical ability in old age as well as providing protection against heart disease and a variety of cancers. Similarly, brain autopsies revealed that the level of folic acid (a B vitamin) in the blood was inversely related to brain atrophy. Research also clarified how homocysteine, an amino acid homologue, affects heart disease and stroke.

Other less directly physical findings indicated to Snowdon that profound faith, prayer and contemplation can provide a buffering effect against the inevitable mental and physiological deterioration associated with ageing. Similarly, emotional openness and expressivity were positively correlated with longevity.

Overall, the demonstrably better health, increased longevity and persistent mental acuity of these remarkable and generous women made them almost ideal subjects with regard to furthering our understanding of a host of medical, psychological and spiritual factors associated with the ageing process. The study also demonstrated the advantages to physical and mental health that derive from a healthy spiritual life.

Do Monks Live Longer?

Several generations of research have by now indicated that social isolation, often experienced as loneliness, has a pronounced effect on life span, reducing longevity by a factor of years. Statistically, married couples can be shown to have a longer life expectancy than singles. The exception to this general rule seems to be those embracing the monastic life. Monks seem to live longer than other people.

Recent studies indicate that despite their single state, monks seem to live longer than men in general in a given social group, including married men. A study reported in 2007 in the Benedictine review *Missionblatter* cited a study by Marc Luy of Rostock, Germany, who examined the age of monks in a number of monasteries and discovered that monks live about four years longer than other men.[21] Luy suggests that the healthier lifestyle of the monks contributes to their longevity. They smoke less, enjoy a steady and relatively stress-free work schedule, and do not face retirement at sixty-five. But their spirituality also plays a positive role in coping with stress. The length of the monks' average lifespan does not differ, however, from that of nuns. This is itself interesting, given the general tendency of women to live longer than men in western society.

A previous report on mortality rates published in 2002 in the *Journal of Religion and Health* based on a comprehensive study of clergy and religious in the UK, Europe and America had already revealed that the rates were consistently lower than those of the average population.[22] Protestant clergy were found to have more than a 25 per cent mortality advantage, while Catholic nuns had a mortality advantage of roughly 20–25 per cent. (The mortality advantage of diocesan priests was just over 10 per cent, however.) The religious professionals also tended to have a lower rate of disease, including heart disease and cancer, than the population at large. One significant finding showed that in a monastery of Italian nuns who had taken a vow of silence, the nuns' blood pressure remained virtually unchanged for the thirty-year study in contrast to women in nearby towns who showed the typical increase in blood pressure associated with advancing age.

Religion and Health: Calibrating the Connection

Over the past twenty years, reports of similar studies demonstrating the positive role played by religious involvement in regard to health maintenance, the prevention of disease and longevity have proliferated in professional journals.[23] Epidemiological research has convincingly shown that in regard to virtually every significant parameter of health – physical, emotional-mental and social – religious affiliation and especially regular participation exercise a strikingly positive influence on people apart from age, gender, class, race, geographical location, or even denomination. Perhaps even more telling, however, is the fact that statistical study conducted for over fifty years has never discovered that religion or spirituality are negatively correlated with health or injurious in any significant way to human welfare.

From just a cursory examination of the literature, even admitting the methodological problems inevitably involved in any area of social research, much less one as complex as this, it is difficult to resist the conclusion that religion and spirituality exercise a distinct, positive and lasting influence on personal health and well-being. But what about the larger picture? Is religion all that good for the world as a whole? Hundreds of studies of many thousands of individual subjects interviewed and studied with regard to religion and health may well have indicated that the contribution of religion and spirituality is in fact highly constructive. But what does social history show? Has civilization generally benefited from religious involvement (one might say preoccupation) with health and health care? Or, as the 'cultured despisers of religion' maintain, does religion 'poison everything'?[24]

NOTES

1. New York: Houghton Mifflin, 2006 and London: Black Swan, 2007.
2. New York: Twelve Books (Hachette), 2007 and London: Atlantic Books, 2007.
3. Other recent anti-religion books include Sam Harris' *The End of Faith: Religion, Terror, and the Future of Reason* (New York: Free Press, 2006), Daniel Dennett's *Breaking the Spell: Religion as a Natural Phenomenon* (London and New York: Penguin, 2007) and John Allen Paulos' *Irreligion: A Mathematician Explains Why the Arguments for God Just Don't Add Up* (New York: Hill and Wang, 2007).

4.   Among recent works that undertake a rebuttal to Dawkins, Hitchens, Harris et al. are Tina Beattie, *The New Atheists* (New York: Orbis Books, 2008) and John E. Haught, *God and the New Atheism* (Louisville: Westminster John Knox Press, 2008).

5.   Freud's tirades against religion permeate his works, but his magnum opus in this respect is surely *The Future of an Illusion* (London and New York: W.W. Norton, 1989 ed.).

6.   Among them are *The International Journal for the Psychology of Religion, The Journal of Health Care Chaplaincy, The Journal of Pastoral Care & Counseling, The Journal of Psychology and Christianity, The Journal of Psychology and Theology, Journal for Religion and Health, The Journal for the Scientific Study of Religion* and *The Review of Religious Research.*

7.   When Professor Jeff Levin's book *God, Faith, and Health: Exploring the Spirituality-Healing Connection* (New York and Chichester: John Wiley and Sons, 2001) came to my attention, the present work was nearing completion. An epidemiologist, Levin's approach is based on hundreds of studies of the positive impact of religion on health throughout the world. His evaluation of the health benefits of religion and spirituality was not only uncommon in the 1980s, when he began his evaluation, but contributed powerfully to the attention paid to this neglected area in medical research in the following two decades.

8.   Richard Sloan, a professor of medicine but not himself a physician, has emerged as a consistent and strenuous opponent of claims that religion and health are positively correlated. See especially his recent book, *Blind Faith: The Unholy Alliance of Religion and Medicine* (New York: St Martin's Press, 2006). R. Barker Bausell, the former director of the Complementary and Alternative Medicine sector of the National Institutes of Health in Washington, D.C., has expressed a similar and comprehensive rejection of research claims supportive of faith healing and other forms of religious influence on health based on his professional expertise as a statistician. See especially *Snake Oil Science: The Truth about Complementary and Alternative Medicine* (Oxford and New York: Oxford University Press, 2007).

9.   In addition to the resources listed in H.G. Koenig, M.E. McCullough and D.B. Larson, *Handbook of Religion and Health* (Oxford: Oxford University Press, 2001), see Robert Roy Britt, 'Churchgoers Live Longer', *Livescience.com*, www.livescience.com/health/060403_church_good.html, posted 3 April 2006; Stuart M. Butler, Harold Koenig et al., 'Is Prayer Good for Your Health? A Critique of the Scientific Research', *Heritage Letters* 816, Washington, DC: The Heritage Foundation, 2003:1–24; Gillian Friedman, MD, 'Religion & Health', *Ability* Magazine, on-line edition: www.abilitymagazine.com/Health_Religion.html; Daniel E. Hall, MD, MDiv, 'Religious Attendance: More Cost-Effective Than Lipitor?', *The Journal of the American Board of Family Medicine* 19 (2006) 2:103–9; Loren Marks, 'Religion and Bio-Psycho-Social Health: A Review and

Conceptual Model', *Journal of Religion and Health* 44 (Summer 2005) 2:173–86; and Kenneth Pargament, 'The Bitter and the Sweet: An Evaluation of the Costs and Benefits of Religiousness', *Psychological Inquiry* 13 (2002) 3:168–81.

10. John Wallace notes in his comprehensive review of the literature on religion and adolescent health that 'religious youth are less likely to engage in behaviours that compromise their health (e.g. carrying weapons, getting into fights, drinking and driving) and are more likely to behave in ways that enhance their health (e.g. proper nutrition, exercise and rest)': John M. Wallace Jr., Ph.D., *'Is Religion Good for Adolescent Health? A National Study of American high School Seniors'* (Waco, Texas: Centre for Religious Inquiry across the Disciples, Baylor University, 2006), p. 3.

11. The original cohort of over 5,000 subjects was interviewed and examined every two years. Twenty years later, a second cohort was added – a similar number of adult children of the original cohort and their spouses. In recent years, a third generation consisting of 3,500 grandchildren of the original subject group has joined the previous cohorts.

12. Meyer Friedman and Ray. H. Rosenman, *Type A Behaviour and Your Heart* (New York: Fawcett Columbine, 1981 [1974]). Later research showed that so-called 'Type A Behaviour' was not uniformly correlated with heart disease, and some persons seem positively to thrive on competitive, driven activity. But the association of social stress and heart disease has remained constant.

13. See George A. Kaplan, 'Alameda County [California] Health and Ways of Living Study', 1974 Panel [Computer file ICPSR06838-v2] (Berkeley, CA: Human Population Laboratory, California Dept. of Health Services, 1974); and Lisa F. Berkman and Lester Breslow, *Health and Ways of Living: The Alameda County Study* (New York: Oxford University Press, 1983).

14. See Lisa F. Berkman and S. Leonard Syme, 'Social Networks, Host Resistance, and Mortality: A Nine-Year Follow-Up Study of Alameda County Residents', *American Journal of Epidemiology* 109 (1979) 2:186–204; and William J. Strawbridge, Richard D. Cohen et al., 'Frequent Attendance at Religious Services and Mortality Over 28 Years', *American Journal of Public Health* 87 (June 1997) 6:957–61. For further discussion, see Levin, op. cit., 38–9.

15. See Doug Oman, John H. Kurata, William J. Strawbridge and Richard D. Cohen, 'Religious Attendance and Cause of Death Over 31 Years', *International Journal of Psychiatry in Medicine* 32 (2002) 1:69–89.

16. See 'Life and Death from Unnatural Causes: Health and Social Inequity in Alameda County', an executive summary published by the Alameda County Public Health Department, April 2008, www.acphd.org/AXBYCZ/Admin/DataReports/unnatural_causes_exec_summ.pdf.

17. James J. Lynch, *The Broken Heart: The Medical Consequences of Loneliness* (New York: Basic Books, Inc., l979 ed.), p. 34. See also Friedman and Rosenman, op. cit., pp. 107–9.

18.   For a comprehensive report on this study, see Michele Dillon and Paul Wink, *In the Course of a Lifetime: Tracing Religious Belief, Practice, and Change* (Berkeley, CA: University of California Press, 2007).

19.   See Kenneth S. Kendler, MD, Xiao-Qing Liu, MD, MS, Charles O. Gardner, Ph.D., Michael E. McCullough, Ph.D., David Larson, MD, MSPH and Carol A. Prescott, Ph.D, 'Dimensions of Religiosity and Their Relationship to Lifetime Psychiatric and Substance Use Disorders', *American Journal of Psychiatry* 160 (March 2003):496-503.

20.   Dr Snowdon's very readable account of the project is detailed in David Snowdon, *Aging with Grace: What the Nun Study Teaches Us about Leading Longer, Healthier, and More Meaningful Lives* (New York and London: Bantam Books, 2001). Information about the results of the study can be found on its website, www.nunstudy.org.

21.   'Monks May Live Longer', CWNews.com: www.cwnews.com/news/viewstory.cfm?recnum=49891, 15 March 2007.

22.   Kevin J. Flannelly, Andrew J. Weaver, David B. Larson and Harold G. Koenig, 'A Review of Mortality Research on Clergy and Other Religious Professionals', *Journal of Religion and Health* 41 (March 2002) 1:57–68.

23.   A partial listing of highly professional, most often peer-reviewed journals, that have published reports on the religion-health connection over the last twenty years include the following: *Alternative Therapies in Health & Medicine, The American Family Physician, The American Journal of Drug & Alcohol Abuse, The American Journal of Medicine, The American Journal of Orthopsychiatry, The American Journal of Psychiatry, American Psychologist, The Annals of Internal Medicine, The Archives of Internal Medicine, Behavioral Medicine, The British Journal of Medical Psychology, The British Medical Journal, The Canadian Journal of Psychiatry, The Community Mental Health Journal, The Gerontologist, Health Psychology, Holistic Nursing Practice, The Journal for the Scientific Study of Religion, The Journal of Advanced Nursing, The Journal of Aging & Health, The Journal of Aging & Mental Health, The Journal of Alternative & Complementary Medicine, The Journal of the American Medical Association, The Journal of Clinical Ethics, The Journal of Clinical Psychology, The Journal of Family Practice, The Journal of Healthcare Management, The Journal of the National Medical Association, The Journal of Nervous and Mental Disease, The Journal of Personality and Social Psychology, The Journal of Reproductive Medicine, The Journal of Substance Abuse Treatment, The Lancet, The Mayo Clinic Proceedings, The New England Journal of Medicine, Pain Management Nursing, The Southern Medical Journal.*

24.   The first phrase is from F. Schleiermacher's great book, *On Religion: Speeches to its Cultured Despisers*. The second, of course, alludes to Christopher Hitchen's *God is Not Great: How Religion Poisons Everything.*

CHAPTER FOUR
WHAT THE DOCTOR ORDERED: RELIGION, SPIRITUALITY AND THE NURSING TRADITION

When he heard of Jesus, he sent to him elders of the Jews,
asking him to come and heal his slave.
Luke 7:3

Without doubt, religious warfare, intolerance and bigotry have added to the world's woes, although, as I shall contend later, the centuries-long toll on health, life and happiness taken by non-religious warfare and genocide vastly exceeds the worst aspects of religious depravity. It is also clearly evident that religion's harshest critics conveniently overlook the invaluable contributions made by religion to health, both individual and social, particularly the impact of nursing orders on human welfare throughout western history. The modern profession of nursing itself, like the institution of hospitals, and later, the hospice movement, owes its beginnings to Christians committed to the care of the sick and suffering.

The earliest ministry of nursing in the Christian tradition is traceable to the New Testament itself. In the Acts of the Apostles, the new order of 'ministers' or deacons, both male and female, had as their ministry the assistance of the sick as well as tending to the needs of the poor. 'The Deacons and Deaconesses were especially zealous in seeking out cases of need, and not only nursed the sick by a system of visiting, but brought them into their own homes to be cared for'.[1] Mary Elizabeth O'Brien notes that these refuges were called *diakonias* or 'Christrooms', forerunners of later hospitals.

In Romans 16:1-2 St Paul salutes the deaconess Phoebe, 'for she has been a helper of many and of myself as well'. Phoebe won renown for nursing the poor in their homes, a pattern that would prevail for centuries.[2] In later periods, noble Roman women organised themselves into groups or 'sodalities' to support the work of the Church in tending the ill, rescuing infants exposed on hillsides and exercising works of mercy toward the unfortunate.[3] St Lawrence, a deacon and martyr of the third century, was famed for his care of the crippled, blind, poor and sick, whom he claimed were the true 'treasures of the Church'.

From its inception, the monastic movement was also devoted to caring for the sick, especially as the common-life or coenobitic form took root in the desert area near Alexandria. Andrew Crislip has recently shown that the monastic development of a 'structured health care system was not only important for the growth of the early monastic movement, it was fundamentally transformative of Late Ancient health care as a whole'.[4] These early monastic health centres served as a template for the first hospitals to emerge toward the end of the fourth century, the *basileias* sponsored by St Basil and his associates, the 'Cappadocian Fathers'.[5] The specifically Christian tenor of these early hospitals was reflected in their expansion from the treatment of the sick to include care for lepers, the disabled, the elderly, orphans, refugees and the homeless. The Byzantine monastic tradition also achieved the remarkable feat of removing the traditional stigma from illness. In the *basileia*, those suffering from bodily infirmity and mental debility could receive expert medical care free and without carrying the additional weight of social opprobrium.[6]

A century after the fall of the Western Roman Empire, as western Benedictine monasteries began to proliferate in the sixth and seventh centuries, monastic hospitality, the characteristic welcome given to pilgrims, travellers and refugees, was similarly extended to the sick and suffering. Like 'hospitality', the words 'hospital' and 'hospice' derive in fact from the Latin *hospes*, which meant both 'host' and 'guest'.

Nursing care was not institutionalised in the West for several more centuries, but lay saints as well as monks gained fame for compassionate care for the sick, among them nobles and royalty as well as commoners. Queens such as St Clothilde, the wife of Clovis, and St Hildegard, Charlemagne's queen, were well known for their active care of the suffering poor. Churches later established charitable 'Lazar houses' for unfortunates suffering from leprosy (Hansen's disease), which spread widely throughout western Europe from the eleventh to the fifteenth century. (There were over 2,000 leprosaria in France in the twelfth century. Notable lepers of the period included King Baldwin IV of Jerusalem and King Robert Bruce of Scotland.)

Holy Healers: Medieval Saints

Although never formally canonised, St Hildegard of Bingen (1098–1179) represents an outstanding example of a medieval woman who was not only a mystic and writer, but a medical practitioner, scientist and highly capable administrator. (In 1165, she separated her community from the double Benedictine monastery at Disibodenberg in order to achieve greater autonomy and freedom for her nuns.) Born at Bingen in Hesse about 1098, she was a visionary from the age of three. Reared from her eighth year in the Benedictine convent in Bingen by the abbess, Jutta, in 1136 she succeeded her mentor as abbess. Two years later, guided by an interior voice, she began committing her visions to writing.

Her counsel was soon sought by bishops, priests, monks, nuns, and a variety of laypersons, including princes and the Emperor Frederick Barbarossa. Her replies to over three hundred letters are extant, and she left a major book, the *Scivias*, containing her visions and revelations. She also wrote scriptural commentaries and composed liturgical hymns. Perhaps most remarkably, Hildegard demonstrated an extraordinary interest in scientific observation and medicine.[7]

Her most important works in this regard are the *Physica*, consisting of *The Book of Simple Medicine*, in which she describes plants, herbs, trees, mammals, reptiles, fish, birds, metals, minerals and gems, 'each described with reference to its wholesome or toxic properties and its medicinal uses',[8] and *Causae et Curae* (*The Book of Compound Medicine*), which addressed both physical and mental diseases and the vagaries of human sexuality.[9]

Later medieval saints such as Francis of Assisi and Catherine of Siena were revered for their care of the sick and especially of lepers. In an era during which lepers were treated with scorn and often separated from society and actively persecuted, such care was not the norm.[10] Catherine also nursed those suffering from cancer and other then-mysterious and invariably fatal diseases. Following an outbreak of the Black Plague in 1372, she patrolled the sick wards of Siena night and day bringing solace and hope to the suffering, resting from her vigil only a few hours a day.

Beginning in the later Middle Ages, nursing orders were founded by religious men and women specifically for the care and treatment of the sick, almost always free of payment. The Catholic Church has, in fact, the oldest continuous tradition of medical care in Europe.[11] One of the earliest of these groups, the Alexian Brothers, had its origins in Flanders around the city of Mechlin in the thirteenth century. In Germany, the brothers, who were influenced by the teachings of Meister Eckhart and the Rhineland mystics, heroically tended victims of the Black Death in Cologne and surrounding areas, often at the cost of their own lives. These 'Cellites', so named for their simple dwellings, were later organised into a community of nurses who took St Alexius for their patron. (Alexius, who became a popular saint in the Middle Ages, was a fifth-century patrician who renounced his family and possessions and became an itinerant beggar and catechist. According to legend, he cared for the sick for some time in Edessa.)

Targeted for persecution later in the Middle Ages by over-zealous bishops, the Alexians were defended by several papal bulls and by popular demonstrations, particularly in Cologne. Having survived the Reformation, the Wars of Religion and the French Revolution, today the order operates hospitals in Germany, Belgium, the United States, England, Ireland, Hungary and the Philippines. They also provide acute and residential care for the sick and elderly, physically handicapped persons, the homeless and mentally ill, and operate centres for AIDS care and treatment.

It would be impossible in even a fairly lengthy account to detail the history of Christian nursing during and after the Middle Ages. But a few outstanding representatives can adequately exemplify the great cloud of witnesses that must remain unsung in these pages.

The Man of God

A Portuguese friar and patron of the sick, João Cidade (1495–1550) became one of Europe's favourite and most influential saints. After his family's fortunes suffered disaster, the young man worked as a shepherd, then became a soldier. Converted to a life of deeper spirituality by the preaching of St John of Avila, and after a period of hospitalisation for apparent madness, John decided to dedicate his life to the care of the poor and sick. He made Grenada the centre of his work and eventually gathered a band of disciples around him which was later confirmed as the Brothers Hospitaller of St John of God. Canonised in 1690, St John of God was proclaimed one of Europe's patron saints of hospitals, the sick and nurses, an honour he shares with St Catherine of Genoa. Today the Hospitaller Brothers operate hospitals and centres for the sick and suffering throughout the world as well as providing care for the mentally ill, the elderly and homeless.

A similar-sounding organisation, the Hospitallers of St John of Jerusalem, operate health and training centres as well as a valuable ambulance service in the United Kingdom and elsewhere in the English-speaking world, including Australia, New Zealand, Canada and the United States. These hospitallers derive from the Knights Hospitaller of Jerusalem, a military order that originated in the Holy Land after the First Crusade. Originally dedicated to providing care for the sick and protection for pilgrims at the end of the twelfth century, the Order had two distinct functions – nursing care and military protection. The latter devolved over the centuries into the Knights of Malta, while the nursing branch declined especially after the Reformation. Revived in England in 1877, the 'St John Ambulance', as it came to be known, provided battlefield assistance and homeland first aid and nurses training during the First and Second World Wars. In addition to providing ambulance service and health care training, the St John Ambulance engages in a number of charitable activities, including administering an eye hospital in Jerusalem.

From the Middle Ages to the present, numbers of nursing orders would be founded, and women and men of unimpeachable saintliness would be found ministering the poor, the sick, the suffering throughout Europe, and soon enough, the New World. One of them, Catherine of Genoa, became one of Europe's patron saints.

The Nurses

Against her will, Catherine Fieschi of Genoa (1449–1510) was married at the age of sixteen and for a number of years endured a life of misery with her young but dissolute husband, Giuliano Adorno. Converted some years later by a series of revelations, she began to mature spiritually, eventually aiding even her husband to undertake a commitment to Christ in the service of the poor. Both became actively involved in caring for the sick and in other works of mercy. After Adorno's death in 1497, Catherine plunged ever deeper into a life of service in the huge Hospital of Genoa, where she undertook the work of manager and treasurer.

Towards the end of her life, Catherine described many of her visionary experiences to her spiritual director and circle of friends. Edited and highly coloured by the religious attitudes of the time, these were published as her *Treatise on Purgatory*.[12] Beatified in 1675, Catherine was canonised in 1737. Because of her influence on nursing care, in 1944 St Catherine of Genoa was proclaimed patroness of Italian hospitals.

The foundation in France of the Daughters of Charity by St Vincent de Paul and St Louise de Marillac was another important milestone in the history of nursing in western Europe. The 'Ladies of Charity', like the Augustinian nuns they emulated, tended the 'poorest of the poor' in their own homes and worked, as had Catherine of Genoa, in the great hospital of the city, the Hotel-Dieu. The Daughters of Charity were formally approved in 1633, not as an order of nuns, but as an active congregation of religious sisters, the first in Catholic history. By breaking with tradition, St Vincent de

Paul and St Louise de Marillac established a solid foundation for subsequent Catholic nursing care.

Today the Daughters of Charity remains one of the largest international religious communities of women in the world. Health care continues to represent their central ministry. In addition to administering one of the largest systems of health care in the world, the Daughters continue 'to serve the sick poor in settings such as "free clinics in poor neighborhoods in the cities, in rural areas, with migrant workers in the deep south [of the United States], and in drug treatment centres"'.[13]

Modern Nursing: Continuing the Tradition

The example of past achievements in the development of nursing and hospitals continued after the Reformation and the beginning of the modern era in the seventeenth century. Now, however, laywomen and men were often moved by religious conviction to engage in often heroic efforts to tend the sick and, in an era of increasing and more violent warfare, the wounded.

The New World did not lack for religious nursing. In the youthful United States of America, a young Episcopalian widow, Elizabeth Bayley Seton (1774–1821), the daughter of a New York physician, determined to dedicate herself to educating children and the care of the sick. Initially she established a Protestant version of the Daughters of Charity, but after her conversion to Catholicism in 1805, 'Mother Seton' gradually gathered around herself a distinctive community of teaching and nursing sisters. Approved in 1809, the Sisters of Charity became the first religious community of apostolic women in the United States. After Seton's death in 1821, the main congregation sought affiliation with the French Daughters of Charity, but two groups, the Sisters of Charity of New York and those of Cincinnati, Ohio, separated to form independent American congregations. The Sisters of Charity continue to operate an extensive system of schools and health care centres throughout the United States.

Mother Seton was beatified on 17 March 1963, and canonised as the first native-born United States citizen saint on 14 September 1975.

Sisters of Mercy

In Ireland, a similar congregation was founded in Dublin by the heiress Catherine McAuley (1781–1841), who used her family inheritance to begin a 'House of Mercy' in 1827 to provide for destitute women and children. By 1831 the first sisters were professed. As the congregation grew, among their many ministries nursing the sick remained prominent in addition to operating orphanages and nursing homes in Ireland and England. During the Crimean War (1854–1856) twenty of Florence Nightingale's thirty-eight nurses came from the Mercy convent in London. The heroic efforts of the Sisters of Mercy had so impressed Nightingale that in 1852 she considered becoming Roman Catholic herself. Later, during the War, the custom within the British military of calling nurses 'sister' was born. Today the Sisters of Mercy continue their work in Ireland, the UK, South Africa, New Zealand, Australia, South America, Central America, the West Indies, Canada and the United States.[14]

Florence Nightingale (1820–1910) herself was motivated by profound religious conviction. Several times during her life, Nightingale experienced what she called a call from God to tend the sick, the first occurring in 1837 just before her seventeenth birthday. She became embroiled in the Poor Laws controversy in 1844, and the following year announced to the great dismay of her family that she intended to devote her life to nursing. Undaunted, she pressed ahead, and during a visit to Italy in 1847, following a period of great personal distress, she made a ten-day retreat at the convent of the Trinitá del Monti in Rome, during which her sense of religious destiny was greatly strengthened.[15]

Nightingale's religious sense was remarkably ecumenical. She was deeply impressed by the work of the Daughters of Charity of St Vincent de Paul in France, and in 1850 travelled to Germany to train under Pastor Theodor Fliedner at his Deaconess School in Kaiserswerth-am-Rhein, Westphalia, an experience that provided another turning point in her career. Although she briefly considered becoming Catholic, she remained within the Anglican Church, embracing Christian Universalism, much as did her near contemporary, Clara Barton.

After a period as superintendent of the Institute for the Care of Sick Gentlewomen in London, in 1854 Nightingale was sent with thirty-eight volunteer nurses, including the Mercy Sisters, to tend wounded soldiers during the Crimean War. After the war, she continued her mission of advocacy and education. Her work greatly influenced the treatment of the wounded during the American Civil War and was later recognised as the foundation of modern nursing method.[16]

Nightingale was decorated by Queen Victoria in 1883 with the Royal Red Cross and in 1907 received the Order of Merit, the first woman to be so honored. By 1896, worn out by years of tireless work, her health failed and she remained bedridden until her death in 1910.[17]

About the same time that Mother McAuley was establishing the Sisters of Mercy in Dublin, the Sisters of Bon Secours were founded in Paris in 1824 under the leadership of Josephine Potel to provide nursing care to the impoverished sick, especially those near death. 'The Sisters went out to the homes of those in need and "if the condition required extended care, the Sisters remained in the homes of the ill, often for long periods of time, always risking criticism from a public uncomfortable with such unconventional practices by religious women at that time."'[18] The Congregation gained official approval in France in 1827 and by the Vatican in 1875. In 1881 the sisters established a branch in Baltimore, Maryland. During the nineteenth and twentieth centuries they expanded their ministry to include the administration of hospitals, hospices, rehabilitation and women's health centres, community clinics and a variety of health facilities. Today the Sisters of Bon Secours minister to the sick and suffering in France, Ireland, England, Scotland, the United States and Peru.

In the United States, the work of Clara Barton (1821–1912) is justifiably famed for founding and organising the American Red Cross. Barton's parents had been instrumental in the founding of the Universalist Church in the United States, and Barton later identified herself as a Universalist. Her tireless volunteer work during the

American Civil War led to her being placed in charge of the front-line hospitals of the Army of the James. In 1865, Abraham Lincoln entrusted to her the charge of locating missing soldiers and later of identifying and marking graves. She became acquainted with the work of the International Committee of the Red Cross while travelling in Europe in 1870 and persuaded President Chester A. Arthur to establish an American branch in 1881. She served as its first president until 1904.

In 1895 Rose Hawthorne (1851–1926), the daughter of one of America's most famous early men of letters, Nathaniel Hawthorne, founded one of the most impressive American nursing orders, the Hawthorne Dominican Sisters or Servants for Relief of Incurable Cancer. From the beginning, Mother Alphonsa, as she was known, intended the congregation to care for those suffering from terminal cancer, especially the very poor. Like Mother Teresa of Calcutta, Mother Alphonsa regularly undertook nursing duties alongside the other sisters. Moreover, the services they offered were free, intended to provide those without means and often without hope a place of comfort and care where they could end their days in dignity. The Hawthorne Dominican sisters continue to operate homes for terminally ill cancer patients in six New England states.

The Return of Deaconesses
Except for the Celtic churches, the order of 'deaconesses' began to decline after the sixth century, and had all but disappeared by the Middle Ages. In the early nineteenth century, the ancient Christian order of women deacons was reinstituted in the Protestant and Anglican churches, particularly among German and Norwegian Lutherans. Like their sisters of old, the new deaconesses undertook a variety of active ministries, but became especially known for their work tending the sick.[19]

The first renewed community of deaconesses was founded by the Lutheran pastor, Theodor Fliedner, at Kaiserswerth in 1836. It was here that Florence Nightingale came in 1850 to observe and train. In 1849, Pastor Johann Löhe founded another community in Neuendettelsau, which, like Fliedner's institute, became a model for similar groups in Germany and abroad. In Norway, the deaconess movement was inaugurated in 1868 by Cathinka Guldberg (1840–1919), who was a professional nurse. Like Florence Nightingale, she studied for a time at Kaiserswerth. In 1915 Guldberg became the first non-royal woman to be decorated by reception into the Royal Norwegian Order of St Olav by King Haakon VII.

The first American deaconess community was instituted in Pittsburgh in 1849 by the Lutheran pastor, William Passavant, who also established the first Protestant hospital in the United States. Deaconess communities and hospitals were soon founded in Maryland, New York and Nebraska. Today a number of Deaconess hospitals, nursing homes and schools operate in Illinois, Indiana, Massachusetts, Minnesota, New Hampshire, Ohio, Oklahoma, Pennsylvania, Wisconsin and other parts of the United States, as well as in Germany, Norway and other countries.

By 1861, the first Anglican deaconesses were organised in London and in 1881 among Methodists. The movement had already reached the United States by 1845 with the founding of the Sisters of the Holy Communion by Anne Ayers, who was influenced by the Kaiserswerth deaconesses. By 1880, six Episcopalian communities were ministering in America.[20]

Many other Christian organisations and denominations such as the Seventh Day Adventists operate nursing homes, clinics and medical centres throughout the world. Jewish hospitals and medical schools also flourish in Israel, the United States, Iran, Morocco and elsewhere. Similarly, hospitals and medical schools operate under Muslim auspices in Egypt, Jordan, Yemen, Pakistan and other parts of the Islamic world, just as they did from the ninth to the thirteenth centuries in Baghdad, Egypt and Spain. Tracing them in an overview such as this would be impossible, but it can be said, I think, that despite religious differences, even major and sometimes dangerous fault lines, true health care can span even seemingly impassable boundaries. Within those boundaries, the roles of religion and health remain closely integrated.

Fellowships of Healing

A number of non-institutional Christian and other religious associations have developed in recent times which reflect and extend the healing ministries of the past. Some are closely associated with medical practice, others tend towards a predominantly religious activity such as faith healing, the relative distance between religion and medicine being a variable factor from group to group. At the far end of the religious spectrum, the boundary between 'natural' healing, whether facilitated or accelerated, and wholly inexplicable healing tends to become blurred and will be explored more fully in Chapter Twelve.

Among more traditional associations, the International Order of St Luke the Physician has a distinguished lineage. The Order had its origins in 1932 in San Diego, California, as an association of clergy and laywomen and men dedicated to the creation of an international Christian fellowship of healing. Founded by the Rev. John Gaynor Banks and his wife Ethel Tulloch Banks, the original organisation has spread internationally and ecumenically. The Order conducts healing missions, provides educational services, and engages in an apostolate of prayer for those suffering physically and mentally throughout the world.

The Florida-based charismatic Christian Healing Ministries, founded by Judith and Francis MacNutt, has recently allied itself with the Order of St Luke. Francis MacNutt, a former Dominican priest, is widely known for his ministry of healing and his many publications in the field.[21]

With these and similar, more explicitly religious ministries of healing, the realm of spirituality comes again to the fore. In later chapters, I will look more closely at the ministries of healing. At this point I would like to draw attention to several characteristics of healing that appear regularly in research lists such as the Life-Long Study and the Nun Study as well as informal healing networks that are taken as indices of good mental, spiritual and even physical health – gratitude and especially prayer – but not just any kind of prayer. Both figure prominently in world religious traditions as well as healing ministries – and with reason.

Giving Thanks

Several years ago, Oprah Winfrey's secretary called me with a request. 'Where,' she asked, 'can we find Oprah's favourite quotation in the writings of Meister Eckhart?' For those who are not regular viewers, that quote would be, 'If the only prayer you ever say is: "Thank you", that's enough'.

I pored over translations of Eckhart's sermons for a long time. He was, after all, a Dominican! Several other people had asked about the citation in the past, no doubt influenced by Oprah's frequent use of it. But I had not seen anything exactly like it in Eckhart's works. Then one day, I happened on a slightly different translation from German Sermon number 34: 'If a man had no more to do with God than to be thankful, that would suffice.'[22] However one translates it, thanksgiving or gratitude is one of the highest forms of prayer, as well as one of the noblest human acts we're capable of. Not surprisingly, gratefulness scores very highly on the scales of well-being.

Helping those in need without expecting reward foils the commercial mentality that blocks our freedom and makes us so unlike God. Spiritual healthiness consists not in expecting gratitude, but in expressing it in everything we do. Generosity of spirit *is* its own reward: 'When you give a banquet, invite the poor, the crippled, the lame and the blind. And you will be blessed, because they cannot repay you, for you will be repaid at the resurrection of the righteous' (Lk 14:13-14). So while it is easy to take God for granted in big as well as small things, true gratitude is attentive to every gift and unabashedly acknowledges their Source. Receptivity is only the beginning.

> Then one of them, when he saw that he was healed, turned back, praising God with a loud voice. He prostrated himself at Jesus' feet and thanked him. And he was a Samaritan. Then Jesus asked, 'Were not ten made clean? But the other nine, where are they? Was none of them found to return and give praise to God except this foreigner?' Then he said to him, 'Get up and go on your way; your faith has made you well' (Lk 17:11-19).

In his justifiably famous book *Gracias!*, a reflection on his travels in Bolivia and Peru, the late Henri Nouwen wrote: 'As long as someone feels that he or she is only an object of another person's generosity, no dialogue, no mutuality, and no authentic community can exist.'[23] Life unfolds healthily in thankful dialogue with God, with others, and in the interior solitude of the spirit. It makes little difference whether we call it grace or gratitude – it is communion that counts, effectively joining in love and good will with others. All others.

Prayer: Getting Good with God?

Understandably enough, prayer has a way of turning up in research studies on religion, spirituality and health. It is, after all, the usual way that people of all faiths employ when relating their lives to God and, most believe, opening themselves to divine blessing, chief among which is often better health.

It has frequently been observed that there's something a little mercenary about constantly petitioning God for favours, as if, as Meister Eckhart had it, God was a cow we turn to when we need milk or cheese or even steak. We're not concerned with the cow, but with ourselves. When we're finished with the cow, good-bye cow. And, Eckhart worried, when we finish that kind of prayer, good-bye God!

In times of distress and illth, it is admittedly tempting to turn prayer into a form of self-centeredness and God into some kind of wish-granting machine. It's against this kind of praying that Jesus ultimately warns us when he adds a proviso to his own prayer, 'Not my will be done, but yours'. In the end, every true prayer really asks that we get ourselves right with God – not that God get things right with us.

Some forms of prayer are traditionally (and according to research evidently) better than others – something we might remember from our catechism classes long ago. From a spiritual viewpoint, adoration, praising God out of gratitude or love, is a higher form of praying than wheedling.

Research indicates that disinterested prayer is good for us in general and, perhaps more importantly, good for others.[24]

' ... [T]he comfort and strength gained from religious prayer and spirituality can contribute to healing and a sense of well-being, and can help people cope when confronted with illness or death.'[25] A more recent study showed that in a carefully regulated experiment, people who were ill improved significantly more than a control group when they were prayed for, even if they did not know people were praying for them.[26] It also seems that people's happiness in life is related to the way they pray.

Four basic types of prayer were considered in the earlier study: *meditative prayer* – sensing the presence of God or thinking quietly about God; *talking things over with God*; *petitions*; and *ritual prayers* – reading them and reciting them in ceremonies and so on. Meditative prayer seems to be more closely related to a general sense of well-being. Conversational prayer, talking with God, is related positively to overall happiness. Strangely enough, petitions – asking for specific things – had no clear impact on people's lives, and ritual praying seemed to be related more to negative feelings than positive outcomes.[27]

What happens when people pray also suggests that it is less important how often a person prays than how well – happier people prayed less frequently, but more attentively. It also seems clear that they were more concerned about God and other people than with themselves. So should we pray for other people and help for ourselves when we need it? Of course. But we should do it in the right way. In Tennyson's *Idylls of the King*, Arthur famously says to Sir Bedivere:

> ... Pray for my soul. More things are wrought by prayer
> Than this world dreams of. Wherefore let thy voice
> Rise like a fountain for me night and day.

The social dimension of prayer, worship, also has a role in regard to health. Critics will no doubt object that attending religious services (whether church, synagogue, temple, mosque etc.) in order to promote health, lessen mortality, find solace in grief and sorrow, enjoy social support and achieve happiness somehow seems demeaning to the disinterested worship of God. Surely, however, attending services because they promote peace, joy, contentment, social support and health itself is not unworthy, self-serving behaviour, but a traditionally sanctioned benefit. If someone suffering from ill health attends church services in the hope of being healed or simply to find support and comfort, who could possibly object? This is one of the main purposes of religious observance, one specifically supported by the New Testament.

Finding the strength in prayer and worship to overcome alcohol and drug dependence, compulsive over-eating, loneliness, sorrow, aimlessness in life, or discouragement and hardship brings people to prayer and praise. 'Come to me, all who labour and are heavy laden, and I will give you rest.' (Mt 11:28) Should anyone really be surprised that increasing numbers of scientific studies of thousands of people throughout the world find that religious observance, from mere attendance to the heights of spiritual experience, does just that?

How Good is Religion for the World?

Despite occasional and sometimes significant demurrals, accumulated scientific evidence that religion in its various forms – historically and currently – is undeniably beneficial to individuals and also to the world seems conclusive. Physical and mental health have especially benefited from religious development, from the early therapeutic centres in temples, to monastic hospitality to the sick and dying, to the foundation of nursing orders and hospitals in the Middle Ages and afterwards, to the latest surveys that reveal a strong positive connection between religion and health. That is not to say that all religious activity is beneficial or even positive. In many instances, religious enthusiasm or extremism has led to disaster, as Kenneth Pargament has reminded us in his exhaustive survey. 'Some forms of religion are more helpful than others. Well-being has been linked positively to a religion that is internalised, intrinsically motivated, and based on a secure relationship with God and negatively to a religion that is imposed, unexamined, and reflective of a tenuous relationship with God and the world.'[28]

But as religion is capable of great good, so also, as history testifies, is it capable of great harm. But how harmful is religion, even at its worst?

Going to Extremes: Great Saints and Grievous Sinners

Late in 2007, *Time* magazine featured a study of moral heroes and their opposites, the good and evil 'geniuses' of our time.[29] Not surprisingly, the candidates for utter villainy were the usual suspects – Joseph Stalin, Adolf Hitler, Pol Pot, Augusto Pinochet and Osama Bin Laden, although more could surely be added. Hideki Tojo, Josef Mengele, Aribert Heim, Idi Amin and Saddam Hussein come to mind. Similarly, *Time*'s candidates for contemporary sainthood might at first glance seem the obvious choices – Mohandas Gandhi, Martin Luther King, Jr., Mother Teresa of Calcutta and the Dalai Lama, (one could also add Brother Roger of Taizé, Sr Helen Prejean and Jean Vanier, the founder of l'Arche, among others). What is striking about the selection, given the diatribes of Dawkins, Hitchens, et al., is that all the latter were explicitly religious leaders, and the former were not. In fact, they were largely anti-religious. Today's cultured despisers of religion could well remember that while Florence Nightingale and Clara Barton were founding the world's greatest nursing traditions out of religious conviction, the dedicated scientist Alfred Nobel invented dynamite and gelignite and the chemists Viktor Meyer, Hans Clarke and Emil Fischer were perfecting mustard gas.

To be sure, there have been wicked or at least bloody-minded religious leaders in the past and we shall likely see more. 'I've got a little list,' as the Lord High Executioner sings in *The Mikado*. It includes Pope Alexander VI, Tomás de Torquemada, Jan Bockleson, Jim Jones, and others of their ilk. But the most outrageous acts of mass murder in history were perpetrated not by religious leaders but by kings, emperors and generals. Admittedly some were influenced by religion, such as the massacres of Catherine de Medici and the Ottoman Empire. But the most lethal acts were carried out by an unholy alliance of politics, science and technology, from the Greek Fire of the Byzantines to mustard gas, Zyklon B and sarin gas, the firebombing of Hamburg, Dresden and Tokyo, and the nuclear incineration of Hiroshima and Nagasaki.

The most infamous of all such catastrophes is unarguably the mass murder of as many as ten million persons under Adolf Hitler and the German Nazi Party during the Second World War. (Scientific sophistication is not, of course, necessary: Stalin's mass murders were carried out by the crude if efficient employment of systematic starvation, although the death toll exceeded even that of the Nazis. Pol Pot's henchmen bludgeoned and starved over a million people to death in the hideous 'killing fields' of Cambodia in the 1960s and 1970s.) By way of contrast, all the executions carried out under the auspices of the Spanish Inquisition can be numbered in the hundreds rather than thousands.[30] Previous inquisitions culminated in the deaths of even fewer victims.[31] That, of course, does not excuse religious oppression and judicial murder, but places it in historical perspective. One can always insert the names of crazed individuals who led themselves and their followers to doom, such as Jim Jones, David Koresh and Shoko Asahara, who founded the lethal Aum Shinrikyo cult. But while undeniably tragic, the death toll from such misadventures is minuscule compared to the carnage wrought in the twentieth century alone by the political-military-scientific-industrial complex.

It is perhaps worth noting that after the Second World War numbers of doctors and scientists were indicted, tried and executed for crimes against humanity. Among the Nazis who escaped, however, were Josef Mengele and Aribert Heim, both physicians and both members of the dreaded SS who supervised ghastly experiments on the helpless inmates of concentration camps. Mengele was reported to have drowned off the coast of Brazil while swimming in 1979, but Heim is still at large – one of the most sought-after mass murderers in the world today. It is certainly no credit to the Catholic Church that many such Nazi war criminals were able to evade Allied arrest and by means of Vatican diplomatic channels escape to South America after the war.

By their Fruits You Shall Know Them

Given the very strong correlation between positive religious belief, behaviour and association with better physical and mental health, lower mortality rates, lower drug abuse and less domestic violence, the recent decline in religiosity in Europe, especially in traditionally Catholic countries such as Austria, Germany, Ireland, Spain and Poland, could be reflected in a proportionate rise and decline of these factors in those countries. It is too early to conclude much from the early statistical sampling that bears on this projection, but a variety of reports seem to indicate that over the past twenty years, as church attendance in particular and general confidence in the church have fallen, there have been significant shifts in public health, mortality rates, suicide (especially among the young), violence and drug abuse. Correlation, as the saying goes, does not establish causation – but it does leave many people wondering.

In the meantime, it seems clear enough from analyses of over a thousand scientific studies that religion and spirituality have historically and characteristically provided personal and social benefit over a wide range of human experience, including health in its many facets – overall well-being, improved bodily integrity, increased longevity, better psychological stability and strong social cohesion. How and why they do will concern us next.

NOTES

1. M.A. Nutting and L.L. Dock, *A History of Nursing* (New York: G.P. Putnam's Sons, 1935), Vol. 1, p. 118. Cited by Mary Elizabeth O'Brien, *Spirituality in Nursing: Standing on Holy Ground* (Sudbury, MA: Jones and Bartlett Publishing, 2003), p. 26.
2. O'Brien, ibid., p. 26.
3. See Rodney Stark, *The Rise of Christianity: How the Obscure, Marginal, Jesus Movement Became the Dominant Religious Force* (HarperSanFrancisco, 1997), pp. 73–94.
4. Andrew T. Crislip, *From Monastery to Hospital: Christian Monasticism and the Transformation of Health Care in Late Antiquity* (Ann Arbor, MI: University of Michigan Press, 2005), p. 8.
5. Ibid., p. 103.
6. Ibid., p. 142.

7. See Sabina Flanagan, *Hildegard of Bingen: A Visionary Life* (London and New York: Routledge, 1989), Barbara Newman, *Sisters of Wisdom: St Hildegard's Theory of the Feminine* (Berkeley, 1979) and 'The German Visionary: Hildegard of Bingen' by Kent Kraft in *Medieval Women Writers*, ed. by Katharina Wilson (Athens: The University of Georgia Press, 1984), pp. 109–30.

8. Newman, op. cit, p. 7.

9. Ibid., p. 7. See *Hildegard von Bingen's Physica: The Complete English Translation of Her Classic Work on Health and Healing*, trans. by Priscilla Throop (Rochester, VT: Healing Arts Press, 1998), and *Holistic Healing* [*Causae et Curae*], trans. by Manfred Pawlik and Patrick Madigan, SJ, ed. by Mary Palmquist and John Kulas, OSB (Collegeville, MN: Liturgical Press, 1994).

10. For a brief overview, see www2.kenyon.edu/projects/margin/lepers.htm. It should be noted that the treatment of lepers in Islamic nations of the time was much less harsh than that in the Christian West, which may reflect the fact that Islamic medicine was far more advanced during the Middle Ages.

11. For an exhaustive treatment of this aspect of Church history, see Erwin Gatz, ed., *Geschichte des kirchlichen Lebens in den deutschsprachigen Landern seit dem Ende des 18. Jahrhunderts: Die Katholische Kirche,* Vol. 5, *Caritas und soziale Dienste* (Freiburg, Switzerland: Herder, 1997).

12. See Catherine of Genoa, *Purgation and Purgatory, The Spiritual Dialogue*, trans. by Serge Hughes (New York: Paulist Press, 1979). The classic study of the spirituality of Catherine and her circle is the two-volume study by Baron Friedrich von Hügel, *The Mystical Element of Religion as Studied in St Catherine of Genoa and Her Friends* (London: J. M. Dent and Sons and James Clarke and Co., 2 vols., 1961 [1909]).

13. O'Brien, pp. 38–9, citing Daughters of Charity, 1995, p. 1. For the spiritual doctrine of Vincent de Paul and Louise de Marillac, see *Vincent De Paul and Louise De Marillac: Rules, Conferences, and Writings*, John E. Rybolt and Frances Ryan, eds. (New York: Paulist Press, 1995).

14. See Evelyn Bolster, *The Sisters of Mercy in the Crimean War* (Cork, Ireland: Mercier, 1964).

15. On Nightingale see Sioban Nelson, '*Say Little, Do Much: Nurses, Nuns and Hospitals in the Nineteenth Century*' (Philadelphia: The University of Pennsylvania Press, 2001), and especially Elizabeth O'Brien, *Spirituality in Nursing: Standing on Holy Ground* (Sudbury, MA: James and Bartlett Publishing, 2003) pp. 44–6. An excellent brief biography can be found at en.wikipedia.org/wiki/Florence_Nightingale.

16. Recent criticism concerning the high mortality among the invalids under her care in the Crimean War attributed to lack of hygienic rigour ignores the fact that mortality would have been far greater without the ministrations of Nightingale and her nurses. Undoubtedly, as Nightingale herself realised, many of the deaths resulted from infections contracted in hospital (not unlike the situation today with MRSA) from overcrowding and physical conditions over

which she had little or no control. It must also be remembered that the discoveries of Pasteur and Lister, and especially their implementation, would not occur for over a decade. It was not until 1881 that Carlos Finlay and Walter Reed established that yellow fever was spread by mosquitoes rather than human contact.

17. See G.L. Deloughery, ed., *Issues and Trends in Nursing*, (St Louis, MO: Mosby, 1995) and Cecil Woodham Smith, *Florence Nightingale* (London: Penguin, 1955).

18. O'Brien, op. cit., p. 47, quoting M.C. O'Sullivan, *Sisters of Bon Secours in the U.S. 1881–1991: Caring for God's Sake* (Marriottsville, MD: Sisters of Bon Secours, 1995), p. 4.

19. For a brief history of the deaconess movement, see O'Brien, pp. 42–4. See also Ann Doyle, 'Nursing by Religious Orders in the United States: Part IV: Lutheran Deaconesses, 1849–1928', *The American Journal of Nursing* 29 (Oct 1929) 10:1197–207, and Carolyn De Swarte Gifford, *The American Deaconess Movement in the Early Twentieth Century* (New York: Garland Pub., 1987).

20. See O'Brien, op. cit., 130f.

21. See his *Healing: The First Comprehensive Catholic Book on Healing* (Notre Dame, IN: Ave Maria Press, 1976 ed.) and *The Prayer That Heals: Praying for Healing in the Family* (Notre Dame, IN: Ave Maria Press, 2005).

22. Sermon 34, Walshe translation, in *Meister Eckhart, Sermons and Treatises* (Longmead, Shaftesbury, Dorset: Element Books, 1987) Vol. I, p. 209.

23. Henri Nouwen, *Gracias!* (New York: Orbis Books, 1993).

24. M.E. McCullough, 'Prayer and health: Conceptual issues, research review, and research agenda', *The Journal of Psychology and Theology* 23 (1995):15–29; M.M. Paloma and B.F. Pendleton, 'The effects of prayer and prayer experiences on measures of general well-being', *The Journal of Psychology and Theology* 19 (1991):71–83.

25. Gillian Friedman, MD, 'Religion & Health,' loc. lit.

26. See Stuart M. Butler, Harold Koenig, et al., 'Is Prayer Good for Your Health? A Critique of the Scientific Research', *Heritage Letters* 816 (Washington, DC: The Heritage Foundation, 2003): 1–24.

27. Consider in this regard Gillian Friedman's comment: 'One extensive survey of households in Ohio found that frequency of prayer was less important than individuals' subjective experiences of feeling an interaction with God, having prayers answered, or reaching a sense of peace. In general, people who seek connectedness with God while remaining open to the will of the divine derive greater benefit than for those who pray to change reality. Several studies have noted that people who prayed in their own words (used colloquial prayer) reported greater well-being than those who recited prayers by rote or read prescribed ritualistic prayers.' Gillian Friedman, MD, 'Religion & Health,' loc. lit.

28. Kenneth Pargament, 'The Bitter and the Sweet: An Evaluation of the Costs and Benefits of Religiousness', *Psychological Inquiry* 13 (2002) 3:168.
29. Jeffrey Kluger, 'What Makes Us Moral', *Time* Magazine, 3 Dec. 2007, pp. 54–60.
30. See Henry Kamen, *The Spanish Inquisition: A Historical Revision* (New Haven and London: Yale University Press, 1998).
31. See James Buchanan Given, *Inquisition and Medieval Society: Power, Discipline, and Resistance in Languedoc* (Ithaca and London: Cornell University Press, 1997); Mark Gregory Pegg, *Corruption of Angels: The Great Inquisition of 1245–1246* (Princeton and Oxford: Princeton University Press, 2001); Edward Peters, *Inquisition* (Berkeley and Los Angeles: University of California Press, 1988) and others.

CHAPTER FIVE

SPIRITUALITY AND THE BODY • I
AGEING, ILLTH AND HEALING

Glorify God with your body.
1 Corinthians 6:20

Exploring some of the ways in which 'religion is good for you' in the previous two chapters has necessarily taken a somewhat defensive route in the face of recent attacks on the personal and social value of religion by several prominent scientific writers and journalists. My main disagreement with these often strident critics concerns what they overlook in their preoccupation with real failures of organised religion and the sporadic disasters triggered by fanatics, both of which nevertheless pale when compared to the atrocities wrought just over the last century on humanity and the planet itself by an unholy alliance of politics, science and the 'military-industrial complex'. And *what* these cultured despisers of religion overlook is the personal and social health benefits conferred on the world through the individual and corporate endeavours of religiously motivated women and men, not least as illustrated by our brief history of nursing.

The 'fact of the matter' is that both religion and science, especially medical science, have befitted the human race just as both have inflicted harm. I submit, however, that the contributions of religion to health and healing far outweigh the harm caused by sectarianism and intolerance. And in that regard, nursing care very likely represents religion's chief physical boon, just as the gifts of hope, compassion and encouragement have so spiritually enriched the world.[1]

Depending on one's outlook, further argument along these lines would be either superfluous or irrelevant. It is time to look more closely at *how* the spiritual dimension of health care contributes to wholeness and healing. Even briefly considering the human life-span, especially the challenge of ageing well in the face of present and future health hazards, will provide a wide enough platform for exploring adjacent areas in later chapters – diet and nutrition, stress and exercise, sleep and dreams and the place of simply 'looking good', and the contributions of grooming and cosmetics.

As the German proverb goes, *Er ist was er est* – you are what you eat. While undeniably true, it is no less the case that you are what you drink, think, read, watch, work and wear (or 'accessorise' as today's bright young things would have it). You are also *where* you live, work, worship and play, a living testament to the power of place, geography, architecture and art in our lives. For while our genetic endowment provides the likely path of our growth and development, we are psychologically and spiritually as well as physically formed by our environment. This is true even of sleep, which is not only a physical requirement for replenishing our daily energies, but a psychological and spiritual necessity for good 'internal' health, particularly in regard to the role of dreaming.

But we do not only incorporate or 'internalise' our experiences and surroundings. Our bodies also *express* how we think, feel and in fact exist in a shared world. Body language is more eloquent than speech, but there is also hair language, clothing language, and even skin language, as witnessed by centuries of development throughout the world of the art of the tattoo. Considering all this is a very tall order, and here we can offer only a survey – but also an invitation for further exploration.

A Brief Guide for the Possibly Perplexed: Function, Symbol and Sacrament

Over the years I have come to recognise that in almost every area of life we organise the elements of daily experience in these three related but ascending orders of significance and value. I will have occasion to refer back to this pattern several times as we explore different subjects in spirituality and health in the following chapters. While a useful way to understand what, why and how we do some of the things that make life so interesting, it should be kept in mind that the functional, symbolic and sacramental dimensions of food and drink, exercise and the rest operate differently and hopefully appropriately with respect to age, gender, ethnic background and a host of other variables. They are, as will be very evident, based on the triadic model of the human person as and interdimensional whole of body-mind-spirit.

The most fundamental level of life is, of course, the body in all its physical complexity. I am convinced that *all spirituality begins with the body*, a notion that operates as a law of the spiritual life if there ever was one. Body, soul and spirit are not three 'parts' of a person, but aspects of the whole person in all the complexity that implies. The body is, however, the first and principle metaphor of the self and the chief 'handle' of human experience. Encountering the world, including nature and other people, must be done primarily through the body, whether well or badly.

We thus ignore or abuse our bodies at our spiritual peril. For example, we all eat to live and so we procure and prepare our food and drink functionally, for nourishment. The more health-producing and protective our diet, the better. But on a secondary, psychological and social level, food and drink have symbolic meaning. We do not enjoy birthday cakes and champagne because they are physically nourishing but because they are celebratory. But food and drink take on still 'higher' significance when they relate us to the transcendent order as both sacrifice and sacrament. In almost every religion on earth, sharing food and drink constitutes a communion with the Holy and with other worshippers.

Similarly, we dress to protect ourselves from the elements or physical danger, but we adorn ourselves with costumes, uniforms, party clothes and the latest fashions to express ourselves, to make a statement whether about the kind of occasion (e.g. a wedding or funeral), social identification (allegiance to a club, a state agency such as the judiciary, the police, the postal service, ambulance services, or even a street gang), or to evoke associations with historical events (the Battle of the Boyne, the signing of the Declaration of Independence). But dress also becomes sacramental when we design and wear ritual vestments or consecrate certain kinds of clothing for religious purposes, such as the ochre robes of Buddhist nuns and monks, the simple loincloth of a Hindu ascetic, or the odd headgear worn by popes and patriarchs.

Grooming, movement, even architecture, house cleaning and tool making, like many, maybe most, human activities, are perhaps instinctively organised into such patterns. How and why we do all this reveals our spirituality just as much as it shapes it. But in all of this, the 'ascending' purpose and 'dialectical' significance of *function, symbol* and *sacrament* are inclusive, cumulative and integrative. The 'higher' uses of food, clothing, shelter and so forth build upon and incorporate the 'lower' forms; they do not violate or abscind from them. Celebratory food such as wedding cakes may not be baked and 'iced' for their nutritional value, but they should not poison us, either! On the other hand, I well remember a nearly disastrous wedding reception when the well-intentioned and politically correct young couple opted for nutrition over celebration and ordered a two-storied carrot cake rather than the fluffy, frilly, sugary, many-tiered (and expensive as well as fattening) confectionary edifice that usually graces the nuptial sideboard. Unfortunately, although the resulting culinary creation was pretty enough, it collapsed under its own weight. And because it was so filling, most of it was left over after the reception was long concluded. But not even newly-weds can live on carrot cake alone!

The Span of Life

We have already seen how long-term 'life studies' have greatly enhanced our understanding of significant connections among religion, spirituality and health. Even more striking is the *absence* of studies showing that a life centred on faith, love and compassion for others can be harmful to individuals or to humanity. Concluding that *only* such a spiritually enriched life can enable people to live longer, happier and more socially valuable lives would be mistaken, however. Even so, life-time studies have shown many times over that religious involvement *even in the broadest sense* is more conducive to good health, longevity and happiness than the lack of religious engagement.

Such 'longitudinal' studies of human health and development have proved to be especially valuable because they reduce the tendency to draw premature conclusions from short-term investigations of religious involvement. For it is evident that religious life and spirituality change over the lifetime of a person – intense at the end of adolescence and early adulthood, diminished in the middle years, and prominent again toward the end of life. One thing is very clear in all of this: mortal beings are made of time as well as matter and spirit. It is ingredient in every sinew and fibre of our bodies.

Barring illness, accident, or premature death, human beings like all living creatures are born, flourish, then die, just as species themselves do. Even rocks weather. But the human ageing process is not mere change like the fall of leaves or the dawn of a new day or the tidal rhythms of the sea. It is a constantly *developing* story written on our bodies as much as it is in the invisible chambers of the mind. Perhaps the truth of our spiritual identity is also most poignantly revealed in the process of ageing. Not surprisingly, then, it is also toward the end of life that religion and spirituality would seem to have special benefits to offer.

Ageing Gracefully: The Art of Growing Older

Time is the framework, the canvas, the notepaper on which or in which all human beings fashion their individual character in the form of a work of art. Our bodies record this story, in some ways even more accurately than do our minds. As Ulysses claims in the famed poem of that name by Alfred Lord Tennyson:

> I am a part of all that I have met;
> Yet all experience is an arch wherethro'
> Gleams that untravell'd world, whose margin fades
> For ever and for ever when I move.

We *are* the sum of our experiences, but we are more than that – the whole is not only greater, but also revelatory. Experience is part of us, not all of us. And as temporary beings, the meaning of our life story is most clearly seen in hindsight.

From the middle decades of the last century, the path or trajectory of human life journeys have been studied from a variety of perspectives and expounded by a host of researchers, including Erik Erikson, Jean Piaget, Daniel Levinson, Gail Sheehy, Lawrence Kohlberg, James Fowler, Carol Gilligan and others.[2] It would be both unnecessary and distracting here to review the vast amount of information now available about the developmental patterns of the whole life process. Rather, I wish to focus on the culminating period of development, the passage toward final maturity. For it is here that the contributions of religion and spirituality become most evident.

In his valuable exploration of the 'golden years' of late adulthood, Eugene Bianchi noted several years ago that the developmental objective (in Erikson's sense of the phrase) of 'elderhood' is the enrichment of the contemplative dimension of life 'within the context of active, worldly endeavors'.[3] Throughout most of human history, elders were expected to manifest the wisdom that arises from a successful integration of the practical and the contemplative aspects of a life well-lived, turning their attention not only upwards, towards some transcendent, post-mortem existence, but outwards, toward the concerns of the tribe, the people, and humanity itself.

In a world that has grown to devalue old age and to relegate elders to nursing homes, the task can be thankless and in fact ignored. As Bianchi observes, 'These goals for mid-life and elderhood run against the grain of contemporary technological society, which tends to make contemplation impossible or unwanted among the middle-aged, and forces the old into individualistic pursuits at the periphery of the social order'.[4] Nevertheless, decades of research, most of it published after Bianchi's book appeared, have confirmed his thesis. 'Ageing gracefully' is of benefit not only to the elders themselves, but to society. The health connection is especially noteworthy in this regard.

Faith, frequent prayer and reliance on God have been shown to support and enhance mental health in particular. As a 2002 study of a group of elderly residents in a retirement complex concluded: 'Multiple regression analyses indicated [that the] importance of one's faith had the strongest association with positive mental health, even after controlling for the effect of other significant variables, age and education. The behavioural measure of prayer was a component of importance of faith to mental health, with no independent impact. This study highlights attitudes rather than practices as the stronger spiritual variables related to mental health in the elderly.[5]

As physical health declines, mental and spiritual health can, and ideally will, flourish, given the appropriate circumstances. According to Bianchi, 'Middle and late adulthood present opportunities for combining the physical descent or gradual organic diminution with a spiritual *ascent*. The latter, as we shall see, demands a delicate balance between a healthy acceptance of physical decline and a search for more satisfactory and humane experiences'.[6] It is important to bear in mind, moreover, that *social* benefits also arise from well-integrated maturation: 'The potential for this spiritual ascent, moreover, indicates more than individual development alone; it also promises a reform of social relationships toward a more sharing and just society.'[7]

The 'shape' of personality is not somehow fixed at an early age but simply continues to unfold by repeating the same patterns of engagement as people mature. Task management and organisation skills, acquired in young adulthood, continue to develop as we grow older, especially given the demands of work and family life. Similarly, social amiability improves with age, largely for the same reasons. On the other hand, worry and concern about the future do not diminish noticeably for males in western society, although it does for women. Similarly, the need for social support tends to diminish more for women than it does for men, while interest in novel experiences and interests (understandably) tends to decline for both genders.[8] Recent studies reinforce the growing conviction among medical researchers and psychologists that older persons are not only as healthy and in some cases healthier than people much younger, but on the whole (at least in modern western societies) tend to be happier.[9]

Needless to say, a host of countervailing events can interfere or entirely block the process of life enrichment. Perhaps chief among these, excepting unforeseen natural calamities, are illness, injury and the inevitability of suffering. How both women and men cope with diminishment toward the end of life thus becomes a measure of spiritual maturity.

Illth Revisited: Dis-integration and Re-integration

Another significant if overlooked 'developmental dialectic' operates within the human life process and its inter-dimensional body-mind-spirit wholeness. Long before Erik Erikson outlined the stages of human development as a series of 'epigenetic' or 'orthogenetic' ascents, crises and resolutions, it was evident to spiritual writers that the path was not a smooth one. Freud had already shown that severe challenges to emergent selfhood could blight full human healthiness for decades, and even an entire lifetime. But with Erikson and the next generation of students of human development, new groundwork was laid for a dynamic understanding of the ups and downs that characterise the process of maturation, including spiritual growth.[10]

In short, life process involves a recurring series of challenges and responses by which people acquire greater mastery of developmental objectives appropriate to age levels, perfecting their abilities and obtaining ever-greater satisfaction. Perhaps the simplest way to describe the process is as a dialectic of *integration, disintegration and reintegration*.[11] In this view, new behavioural objectives by which children (as well as adolescents and even adults) surmount successively more challenging tasks appear to be daunting and perhaps initially even impossible – arithmetic, grammar, spelling and the rules of deportment, which when mastered more or less well soon give way to higher maths, courtship rules, job interviews, financial setbacks, novel technologies, mid-life changes, retirement, illness and finally, death itself.

Crises of development often result as we face ever-higher levels of achievement goals, during which we experience a period of disintegration. Our tenuously integrated world threatens to crack and crumble before we succeed in mastering yet another series of tasks that can weld the world back together again, at least provisionally. But apart from developmental tasks, serious illness, injury, natural and social calamities can also shatter our sense of self. Ideally, in the normal course of life, reintegration follows as through sheer effort, assistance, or therapeutic intervention we achieve yet another level of achievement, or recovered health, fortune, or personal 'identity', gaining a standpoint probably just high enough to catch a glimpse of still further mountains to scale on the far horizon.

At this point in our exploration, it is the challenge of ill health that mainly comes to mind. To put it another way, preserving and restoring good health requires attending to the agents that threaten it. This, too, is part of the spirituality of health. According to Ben Sira:

> Better off is a poor man who is well and strong in constitution than a rich man who is severely afflicted in body. Health and soundness are better than all gold, and a robust body than countless riches. There is no wealth better than health of body, and there is no gladness above joy of heart. Death is better than a miserable life, and eternal rest than chronic sickness.
>
> (Sir 30:14-16)

Still, faced with the fragmentation of illth and injury, even the ancient world sought remedy, as we have seen, if the remedies were scant compared to the pharmaceutical cornucopia available to people today – at least those who can afford it. Today's world is hardly free of the ravages of disease, however. Thirty-nine new or 'emergent' diseases have been discovered since 1970, including AIDS, haemorrhagic fevers such as that caused by the Ebola virus, SARS (Severe Acute Respiratory Syndrome), 'Mad Cow Disease' (Bovine Spongiform Encephalopathy or BSE), Lassa fever, Lyme disease, Swine flu, different strains of Avian flu, Legionnaires disease, and new strains of tuberculosis and sexually transmitted diseases. Despite vaccines and antibiotics, in recent decades there has also been a resurgence of 'old' diseases, including tuberculosis, ME (myalgic encephalomyelitis), MRSA (Methicillin-resistant Staphylococcus aureus), which was identified only in 1961, Leishmaniasis, West Nile Virus, Rift Valley Fever (RVF), dengue fever, malaria (still the greatest killer in the world today), cholera, and various forms of measles (*rubeola* has killed as many as 200 million people over the last century and a half).[12] Cancer and heart disease have been increasing for decades, abetted by smoke from cigarettes and factories.

It is perhaps unnecessary to point out that the poor of the world, especially in the tropics, are the principal victims of disease, as they lack the means to obtain both preventive and curative medicines. Children constitute the majority of these unfortunates, especially in the case of malarial infections and other mosquito-borne illnesses. Addressing the overwhelming need for adequate medical care in the poorest nations of the world, also the most populous, is therefore an issue of grave importance for any spirituality for which social justice is an element. It is precisely here that the global situation is deteriorating despite sometimes incredible progress in the development of new medicines.[13] In parts of Sub-Saharan Africa, the AIDS virus has infected more than thirty per cent of the population, whereas in the United States, it never exceeded .5 per cent. Overall European rates are even lower.[14]

Chronic, non-contagious diseases are at least as worrisome to the health professions as are contagious diseases. Of particular concern with regard to the elderly is Alzheimer's Disease, a malady unknown before the twentieth century. Whether misdiagnosed or simply unrecognised in general practice, AD has now gained significant scientific attention as a neurodegenerative disease still of uncertain origin. Between 18 and 24 million people are presently believed to be afflicted with AD throughout the world, including as many as 5.2 million persons in the United States, 500,000 in Australia, over 40,000 in Ireland, and proportionate numbers in other European countries. Numbers are expected to increase over the next decade to about 34 million, over 60 per cent of whom will be in developing countries.[15]

Climate Change and Health
With each report of the Intergovernmental Panel on Climate Change, the seriousness of global climate change becomes more and more evident despite wishful thinking and denials on the part of government officials or the neighbours across the road. Clearly the

health implications of increasing climate instability are serious, and everyone can expect some nasty surprises over the next fifty to 100 years.[16] Warming in the northern latitudes will draw anopheles mosquitoes back to England, where malaria was a health hazard in the balmy High Middle Ages, before the 'Little Ice Age' lowered temperatures drastically at the beginning of the fourteenth century. Even Ireland and Scotland could be adversely affected.

During the lethal heat European wave during the summer of 2003, the hottest in over 400 years, tens of thousands of people died of hyperthermia, and the lesser emergencies of 2005 and 2006 most likely presage a trend rather than anomalous conditions. A rise of only one degree centigrade over the last quarter century was responsible for as many as 160,000 deaths and over five million years of healthy life according to the World Health Organisation. As global warming accelerates, both statistics will likely double by 2020. Heat waves will be longer and hotter, which after 41°c (106°f) temperatures in London in the summer of 2007 cannot be welcome news. (The London underground system reached a record temperature of 47°c, while temperatures in buses in the City of London climbed to an astonishing 52°c.)

Extreme heat in the west, southwest and southern United States in recent years have resulted in extreme drought and devastating forest and grass fires. Severe water shortages are projected for the coming decades. And although North Africa and southern Europe will continue to be adversely affected by ever-rising temperatures, the worst effects will occur in Africa, India and Southeast Asia. Cities are, moreover, about 5°c (9°f) warmer than surrounding countryside and tend not to lose heat at night. More than half the world's population now live in cities, and by 2050, approximately 32 per cent of those will be over 60 years of age – the group most endangered by excessive heat. The largest cities in the world are already located in developing nations, where air conditioning and medical relief is far less likely to be available than in the more affluent north.

Generally speaking, global climate change can be expected to create global health crises, a prospect of great concern to world health authorities already under enormous pressure to cope with present crises throughout the world, especially in developing countries. In an era of swift transportation and increasingly mobile populations, infectious diseases can spread with astonishing rapidity. No nation or group of persons, no matter how wealthy, powerful, or influential, is immune.

I am reminded in this regard of the great parable by Edgar Allen Poe, 'The Masque of the Red Death', in which he tells how Prince Prospero with 'a thousand hale and light-hearted friends from among the knights and dames of his court … retired to the deep seclusion of one of his castellated abbeys' to wait out a plague in luxurious idleness. Six months later, while the Red Death ravaged Prospero's realm, he held a magnificent masked ball. At midnight, a tolling bell arrested the attention of the revellers and they became aware of a presence none had noticed before. A shudder passed through the dancers as they recognised the stranger's mask as a likeness of the face of a corpse, daubed with the tell-tale emblems of the plague. One by one the revellers dropped, each dying in the despairing posture of their fall. 'And Darkness and Decay and the Red Death held illimitable dominion over all.'[17]

Hopefully, Poe's sobering story will not typify the situation of the world of the near future, either in terms of health or of the loss of human compassion. One thing is certainly evident, however. In coming decades, if not centuries, the quota of human and animal suffering will increase throughout the world because of the resurgence of old diseases, the emergence of new ones, and global climate change. How the inevitable pain and suffering arising from such menacing developments can be successfully integrated into life development will therefore become a proportionately more urgent issue for any spirituality that offers hope regardless of where people live, their age, social class, or economic condition.

I have no doubts that pioneering spirits will emerge from the relative darkness and distress of the coming decades just as they have in the past, forging new bonds of love and service adequate to meet the challenges involved in the promotion and maintenance of health even in the midst of possible catastrophe. It is, moreover, the age-old burden of religion to shoulder such a task. And as I review some of the leaders of the generation just behind us, I am reminded that advancing age is no barrier to insight, resourcefulness, or accomplishment. In fact, the wisdom of the elderly may well be our greatest asset as this generation and the next face an increasingly problematic future.

NOTES

1. I have recently received a copy of an important new book, *Who Speaks for Islam? What a Billion Muslims Really Think*, by John Esposito and Dalia Mogahed, published by the Gallup Poll Press (New York: 2007) which should be required reading for anyone compelled to make public statements about 'Islamic terrorists' or, for that matter, Islam.

2. The field is, of course, vast. But among foundational contributions in the field of human development, I would include Jean Piaget, *The Construction of Reality in the Child* (New York: Basic Books, 1954), *The Child's Conception of Time* (London: Routledge and Kegan Paul, 1969) and *The Moral Judgement of the Child* (New York: The Free Press, 1965); Erik Erikson, *Childhood and Society* (New York: W.W. Norton, 1970 ed.); Lawrence Kohlberg, 'Cognitive-Developmental Approach to Moral Education', *The Humanist* 32 (Nov–Dec 1972) 6:13–16; Daniel J. Levinson, *The Seasons of a Man's Life* (New York and Toronto: Ballantine Books, 1978); James Fowler, *Stages of Faith: The Psychology of Human Development* (New York: Harper, 1995); Sharon Parks, *The Critical Years: The Young Adult Search for a Faith to Live By* (San Francisco: Harper and Row, 1986); and Carol Gilligan, *In a Different Voice: Psychological Theory and Women's Development* (Cambridge: Harvard University Press, 1993).

3. Eugene C. Bianchi, *Aging as a Spiritual Journey* (New York: Crossroad, 1993), p. 2. Also see Andrew Weil, M.D., *Healthy Aging: A Lifelong Guide to Your Physical and Spiritual Well-being* (New York: Alfred A. Knopf), 2005, and H.G. Koenig, 'Religion, Spirituality and Aging', *Aging and Mental Health* 10 (Jan 2006) 1:1–3.

4. Ibid.

5. Janice Bell Meisenhelder and Emily N. Chandler, 'Spirituality and Health Outcomes in the Elderly', *Journal of Religion and Health* 41 (Sept 2002) 3:243–52. Correlations with physical health appeared to be less significant in this study. Other studies have shown a positive correlation, however. See

Maureen Benjamins, 'Predictors of Preventive Health Care Use among Middle-aged and Older Adults in Mexico: The Role of Religion', *Journal of Cross-Cultural Gerontology* 22 (June 2007) 2:221–34.

6. Bianchi, op. cit., p. 7.

7. Ibid.

8. See Sanjay Srivastava, Oliver P. John et al., 'Development of Personality in Early and Middle Adulthood: Set Like Plaster or Persistent Change?' *Journal of Personality and Social Psychology* 84 (May 2003) 5:1041–53, findings supported by research conducted by Daniel Mroczek, Brent Roberts and others reported in *Psychological Science* 18 (2007): 5. See also Sanjay Srivastava, Kelly M. McGonigal et al., 'Optimism in Close Relationships: How Seeing Things in a Positive Light Makes Them So', *Journal of Personality and Social Psychology* 91 (July 2006) 1:143–53.

9. In this regard, the short chapter in Norman Cousins' *Head First: The Biology of Hope and the Healing Power of the Human Spirit* (New York and London: Penguin Books, 1990), 'Functional Age', may still be read with profit. Recent studies indicate that elderly Americans are the happiest of all. See Yang Yang, 'Social Inequalities in Happiness in the United States, 1972 to 2004: An Age-Period-Cohort Analysis', *American Sociological Review* 73 (April 2008) 2:204–26.

10. It has been argued that perspective accounts for the fundamental difference between human development and spiritual development, which are in effect methodologically distinct ways of describing the same process. See Daniel A. Helminiak, *Spiritual Development: An Interdisciplinary Study* (Chicago: Loyola University Press, 1987), p. xii: 'spiritual development is nothing other than human development viewed from a particular perspective.'

11. The late Dr John Lilly characterised this process as one 'orthonoia', 'paranoia' and 'metanoia.' See the DVD interview recorded at the Bridge Psychedelic Conference at Stanford University, *Orthonoia Through Paranoia To Metanoia* in which he describes his research programme. Lilly's most accessible book is *The Center of the Cyclone: An Autobiography of Inner Space* (New York: Bantam Books, 1973). Other paradigms have been proposed, such as that by Evelyn Eaton Whitehead and James D. Whitehead: orientation, disorientation, reorientation. See *Christian Life Patterns: The Psychological Challenges and Religious Invitations of Adult Life* (New York: Crossroad, 1992 ed.), pp. 50–6.

12. See especially Laurie Garrett, *The Coming Plague: Newly Emerging Diseases in a World Out of Balance* (New York: Farrar, Straus and Giroux, 1994).

13. See in this regard Laurie Garrett, *Betrayal of Trust: The Collapse of Global Public Health* (New York: Hyperion, 2000).

14. For recent figures, see www.avert.org/worlstatinfo.htm and www.eurosurveillance.org/em/v08n03/0803-221.asp.

15. US numbers: www.annals.org/cgi/content/full/144/2/135 and www.alz.org/alzheimers_disease_facts_figures.asp.

Irish numbers: www.irishhealth.com/index.html?level=4&con=1.
Global statistics: family.jrank.org/pages/72/Alzheimer-s-Disease.html.

16. See especially John M. Balbus and Mark L. Wilson, 'Human Health and Global Climate Change, A Review of Potential Impacts in the United States', Pew Centre Report, www.pewclimate.org/docUploads/human_health.pdf.

17. Edgar Allan Poe, *The Complete Tales and Poems* (New York: Vantage Books ed., 1975), pp. 269–73.

CHAPTER SIX

SPIRITUALITY AND THE BODY · II
SUFFERING, HEALING AND THE CARE
OF PAIN

If one member suffers, all suffer together;
if one member is honored, all rejoice together.
1 Corinthians 12:26

In the summer of 1972, while visiting Leuven, Belgium, with friends, I found myself on my own for an afternoon, and while exploring the old city, pretty well lost and mapless. I was looking for a sign that would point me to the famous Béguinage, but came across one that pointed, rather, to 'Fr Damien's Tomb'. I wondered what that might be, because the only 'Fr Damien' I could think of was the leper-priest of Moloka'i, Hawai'i. I had been deeply impressed by his story even in high school, but I had always assumed that he was buried in Hawai'i, where he had worked and died.

I followed the signs and eventually found myself kneeling in front of a massive and modern stone tomb that was in fact the final resting place of the Venerable Damien of Moloka'i, whose body I learned had been returned to his native land in 1936 on a US Navy ship provided by President Franklin Roosevelt. I remained in the crypt of the church for well over an hour, overwhelmed by the thought that I was in the presence of the mortal remains of one of the great humanitarian martyrs of our times. (Although honored by the church, Fr Damien was not formally enrolled among the 'blessed' members of the church awaiting canonisation until 1995.)

The story of Fr Damien de Vreuster (1840–1889), like that of Mother Teresa of Calcutta, is both amazing and commonplace, for it exemplifies what is perhaps the greatest gift a human being is capable of offering, and yet he was just 'one of us', a young man who wanted to help the afflicted whom no one else seemed even to want to think about. It is a story about pain, suffering, sacrifice and healing. They all are, ultimately.

Looking back over the years before and after my visit to Leuven, three other names immediately come to mind in regard to my education in what might be called 'the spirituality and alleviation of suffering' – Ivan Illich, Cicely Saunders and Ursula Fleming.

I heard Fr Illich speak in the late 1960s when I was a student in the collegiate programme of the Dominican order just outside of Chicago. He was a remarkably charismatic man, deeply spiritual, a quality that never deserted him even after conflicts with Church authorities led to his resignation from the Catholic priesthood. He was no less controversial because of the work of his Intercultural Documentation Centre (CIDOC) in Cuernavaca, Mexico. Illich (1926–2002) had come to the attention of the world of radical politics, philosophy and cultural studies with his books *Deschooling Society*[1] and *Tools for Conviviality*.[2] But it was his daring, even if provisional critique of health systems that especially attracted my attention and continues to amaze me with its foresight and shrewdness – *Medical Nemesis: The Expropriation of Health*.[3] In large measure a direct assault on the emerging health care industry, on a much deeper level the little book was an appeal for a reassessment of the place of pain and suffering in modern society. Illich's message is perhaps more relevant today than it was thirty years ago.

First of all, it is important to bear in mind that how we regard pain and suffering in the highly industrialised First World not only differs significantly from earlier perceptions, even those of our great-grandparents. 'Pain has changed its position in relation to grief, guilt, sin, anguish, fear, hunger, impairment and discomfort,' Illich wrote. 'What we call pain in a surgical or cancer ward is something for which former generations had no special name.'[4]

Advances in medical theory and practice have greatly altered our understanding and treatment of pain over the last century, especially because of the tremendous development of pharmaceutical suppressants. According to Illich, 'Medical civilization tends to turn pain into a technical problem and thereby to deprive suffering of its inherent personal meaning'. He explained further:

> As long as pain was primarily an experience that had to be faced and suffered, its political function was to set limits to man-made abuses of man by man when these became intolerable. Now an increasing portion of all pain is man-made, a side effect of strategies for industrial expansion. Pain has ceased to be conceived as a 'natural' or 'metaphysical' evil. It is a social curse, and to stop the 'masses' from cursing society when they are pain-stricken, the industrial system responds by delivering them medical painkillers. Pain thus turns into a demand for more drugs, hospitals, medical services and other outputs of corporate, impersonal care and into political support for further corporate growth no matter what its human, social or economic cost.[5]

Ironically, as Laurie Garrett and others have argued, it is the growing inability of medical industries to deliver effective remedies to an ever-expanding global population that has led to an unprecedented awareness of the scope of pain and suffering throughout the world.

For Illich, human health, unlike the physiological balance of animals, is maintained, preserved and restored by a conjoined effort of 'self-awareness, self-discipline and inner resources by which each person regulates his own rhythm and actions, his diet, and his sex[uality]'.[6] Learned by example from peers and elders in a society, such personal activities are shaped and interpreted by culture. But a culture in which technological aspects of medical intervention are controlled by industrial and economic forces gives rise to that 'medical nemesis' which Illich sought to surface and identify as 'the experience of a people who are largely deprived of any autonomous ability to cope with nature, neighbour and dreams, and who are technically maintained within environmental, social and symbolic systems'.[7]

Illich proposed an entirely different approach. Reclaiming one's health, and one's people's health, from the health care industries, from the insurance industry, from government and from the assumptions of a consumer society, requires courage, education and access to resources of physical, psychological and spiritual reintegration precisely opposite to the questionable but costly benefits offered by a technologically oriented, consumerist society. From my viewpoint, such resourcefulness is the contribution of authentic spiritual traditions, a groundedness in nature recognised and celebrated as Creation, and an unswerving belief in the dignity and ultimate value of the human person.

Such an approach was brilliantly and humanely articulated for me by the work of Dr Cicely Saunders (1918–2005), who pioneered a far more humane approach to the treatment of chronic and terminal pain and by doing so inaugurated the modern hospice movement. While studying at Oxford in 1975 I was able to attend one of Dr Saunders' seminars at St Christopher's Hospice in Sydenham, a suburb of London. Although I was certainly impressed at the time, I did not anticipate that it would have a formative influence on my career.

Cicely Saunders and the Hospice Movement
Educated at Oxford University, and a practicing nurse, Dr Saunders began work in the 1940s among poor patients dying of cancer in London's hospitals. Eventually she entered medical school and in 1957 qualified as a physician. Her initial work with cancer patients gradually brought her to the conviction that conventional drug therapies undertaken to alleviate the severe and intractable pain associated with various forms of the disease achieved very little in enabling patients to live out their lives in dignity and a measure of comfort. At St Christopher's Hospice, which she founded in 1967, the infamous 'Brompton Cocktail' of morphine, cocaine and pure ethyl alcohol was considered particularly suspect, because in conventional treatment centres this potent combination of painkillers was administered to patients only when their suffering had become so intense that they were screaming in pain. The dosage had to be

extreme because of the overwhelming suffering, but it rendered the patient unconscious, then narcotised for many hours as the sedatives wore off and the terrible pain inexorably returned. When the patients' suffering again reached intolerable levels, the brutal 'cocktail' was readministered, starting the cycle over again.

Saunders realised that by administering a much lower level of sedatives before the onset of debilitating pain, the extremes of both suffering and dosage could be curtailed. Her patients were mildly sedated, having typically received only a third of the standard dosage of narcotics, but sufficiently comfortable to carry on ordinary life tasks with nearly full alertness. I was able to interview several of them at St Christopher's Hospice, and found them as responsive and engaging as anyone could reasonably expect. Even more surprising was the discovery that not only were many of the patients able to return to their homes to live out their lives amid family and friends, but a number of them actually recovered.

The movement inspired by Dr Saunders' work in England grew slowly. It was not until 1979 that the first institutional hospice in the United States was founded in Branford, Connecticut. But by 1992, US hospice programmes were providing services to almost 250,000 people. Within a decade, that number would triple. By 2008, more than one third of all Americans who died were in hospice care in some 3,000 hospice units.

Almost three decades after first visiting St Christopher's, I met Dr Saunders again at a conference in London. She was quite elderly then and in fact would not live much longer. Although suffering from cancer herself, she was aglow with a spiritual radiance I have only rarely seen so manifest. And by then, her work had been fully recognised by the British government. Already a Fellow of the Royal College of Physicians, the Royal College of Nursing and the Royal College of Surgeons, in 1979 she was honored as a Dame of the British Empire, and received the Order of Merit in 1989. Dame Cicely was awarded the Templeton Prize in 1981, and in 2001 the Conrad N. Hilton Humanitarian Prize. Three months before her death her portrait was unveiled at the National Portrait Gallery.

Given the honors that surrounded her at the time of her death, it is well to recall that her work was initially resisted by the medical establishment and it took many years for it to be accepted. It is perhaps also too easy to pass over the simple fact that her life's work was guided by a profound Christian attitude toward suffering and a resolute compassion that succeeded in transforming palliative care. She claimed that at the beginning of her major work, her guiding star had been a quotation from Psalm 37: 'Commit your way to the Lord; trust also in him; and he shall bring it to pass.'[8]

Ursula Fleming and the Control of Pain

A decade after first meeting Dr Saunders, I met Ursula Fleming (1930–1992), another pioneer who offered therapy, taught courses and wrote in the area of pain management. In the late 1980s, I came to know her much better in view of her work with the Eckhart Society, which she had founded in 1987 and to which she attracted me very early in its history. In her book of readings and passages from and about Meister Eckhart she wrote: 'Most of what I know and teach about pain control comes from the study of Eckhart.'[9] As I was to discover, that was not pious exaggeration.

Ursula was the daughter of doctors and came to the study and practice of pain management because of her own battle with suffering. Although she had anticipated a career in music, a nervous condition prevented her from continuing piano studies. She turned to the therapist Gertrud Heller for guidance and went on to develop her own technique of managing pain by focused relaxation. She worked for years in Oxford, then at London's Royal Free Hospital as a therapist, while conducting workshops and lecturing throughout England and Scotland. Her most famous device was a broom handle, which she employed to teach her clients how to endure discomfort by lying on it positioned next to their spine for progressively longer periods of time. She also taught them how to balance the broom handle on their fingers while walking. Some of her workshop participants developed remarkable emotional associations with their broom handles through all of this – not always of the positive kind. (Some became very angry with them, ever growing to hate them after a time.)

Drawn to Eckhart's mystical spirituality by her Buddhist friend and mentor, Marco Pallis, Ursula found in his doctrine a complement to her own approach to pain and suffering. Appalled by the neglect of Eckhart in the Catholic Church, she founded the Eckhart Society with the purpose of securing exoneration for the mistaken condemnation of some points of his teaching in 1329. She succeeded in nudging the Dominican Order to undertake a decade-long examination of Eckhart's teaching which resulted in a petition to the Congregation of the Doctrine of the Faith for his exoneration. While that has not been acted upon, Eckhart studies in the English-speaking world experienced a quantum leap forward. The Society survived her untimely death in 1992 and continues to grow in England and abroad. Ursula's approach to pain management also survived her, thanks to the work of her sister, Anne Fleming, and Carol Horrigan and the Albertus Magnus Trust, which was established for that purpose.[10]

The Promise in Pain

After Ursula's death, I began delving more deeply into Eckhart's works to see what she had found there that spoke so clearly and deeply to her mind and heart. Ministering to those in pain was not entirely a new experience for me. In addition to my illuminating encounter with Cicely Saunders, I had undergone training as a biofeedback therapist at the Menninger Clinic in Topeka, Kansas, with regard to the alleviation of migraine, and had a brief, part-time practice in Chicago just prior to the development of the now famous Diamond Headache Clinic. Treating pain was not a primary focus in my ministry or teaching, however. My clinical practice over the next twenty-five years would be in the area of sexual dysfunction at Loyola University Medical School where I trained as a therapist under the watchful eye of Dr Domeena Renshaw and was occasional lecturer in the Department of Psychiatry. Not that there isn't a lot of pain in that area, too. But my interest in pain and suffering had more to do with understanding human experience and helping people cope with and even overcome bodily, mental and spiritual disintegration.

I learned far more about pain and suffering from my several mentors and their writings, including Dr Renshaw, than I can begin to treat with justice here. Fortunately, their books and essays are still available, even if one has to dig around a bit in libraries and on-line resources. Several points come to mind, however, that bear on present concerns.

Like other dimensions of human experience, pain and suffering can be understood in terms of the physical, psychological and spiritual coordinates that locate them in a hierarchy of meaning and value, both personally and socially. (By 'hierarchy' here I mean 'holy order' in the sense that Dionysios the Areopagite first used the term in the sixth century.) *Physiologically*, for all sentient creatures pain warns of danger. In that regard it is not evil, but good. Without it, life on earth would indeed be short, nasty and brutish, for pain instructively prompts us to take appropriate action to avoid serious injury or death. A life without dis-comfort would be life without contact in the real world, which is to say, no life at all. Consequently, pain is to a greater or lesser degree inescapable. In this regard, it is worth recalling the story of the young Buddha, whose royal father attempted to rear him in complete ignorance of pain, illness, suffering and death. But as he would learn to the world's great benefit, the possibility of painlessness is the first and, perhaps, the greatest of illusions.

Pain also has a profound *psychological* dimension in higher animals, proportionately so. Expectation, fear and attempts to avoid it considerably amplify the perception of pain. Generally speaking, it has been estimated that even acute physiological distress accounts for only about 20 per cent of experienced pain. The remainder can be usefully described as 'suffering' – how we register pain, especially when it is inescapable, and particularly within a framework of shared hopes, values and goals. The psychological factor in experiencing pain also makes it easy enough to induce pain artificially, particularly by suggestion and more formally through hypnosis. Conversely, the magic penny that becomes mysteriously hot has long since occupied a hallowed position in the family doctor's pharmacopoeia as a sovereign cure for common warts.

Pain and suffering have psychological uses and meanings that transcend immediate threat, however. Afflicting enemies with sometimes excruciating suffering as a form of punishment has been practiced globally from humankind's earliest days. But undertaking voluntary or involuntary pain and suffering for political or social purposes has also characterised human interaction since the dawn of history. People express serious protest, for example, by inflicting pain on themselves as in the case of hunger strikers. Remorse, shame and mourning are signified by a range of gestures from breast-beating to scourging, mutilation and, ultimately, public suicide, as in the case of *seppuku* in Japan.

Pain and suffering may also have a *sacramental* dimension, whether self-inflicted or accepted at the hands of others. In religious experience and even ritual, such suffering can serve to express fidelity to God or one's religious group, or may even unite worshippers in a holy communion of shared witness, protest and solidarity. Undergoing persecution and ultimately martyrdom thus acquires a range of religious meaning and value from atonement and expiation to redemption, especially by substitution. This was strikingly exemplified in the case of Fr Maximilian Kolbe, the Polish priest who volunteered himself for painful execution at the hands of his Nazi jailers in order to save the live of a younger, married man with children, for 'Greater love has no one than to lay down his life for his friends' (Jn 15:13).

We recognise the redemptive power of suffering in the life and death of martyrs throughout history and the world – Jesus himself and most of his earliest followers; the Muslim mystic Mansur Al-Hallaj; the Czech reformer Jan Hus; Joan of Arc; Thomas Cranmer; Mohandas Gandhi; Martin Luther King, Jr.; Archbishop Oscar Romero, shot dead at mass in 1980; Jean Donovan and three sisters, Maura Clarke, Dorothy Kazel and Ita Ford, also martyred in El Salvador in 1980; the six Jesuit martyrs of El Salvador, assassinated with their housekeeper and her daughter in 1989; and more recently Bishop Pierre Claverie of Algeria, who alongside his Muslim driver was killed by a bomb in 1996; Margaret Hassan, the Irish-born director of CARE, abducted and killed in Iraq in 2004; and Archbishop Paulos Rahho of Mosul, who with Fr Ragheed Ganni and three deacons were martyred in Iraq in March, 2008. Environmental martyrs such as Dian Fossey, Sr Dorothy Stang and Chico Mendez have now added a new dimension to the range of causes that evoke heroic sacrifice in order to preserve Creation and materially powerless creatures, human and other, in the face of industrial might, money and ruthlessness.

Multitudes of nurses, doctors, relief workers, police personnel, firefighters and soldiers also expose themselves daily to disease, physical violence and death, risking pain and suffering to fulfill a sense of duty, solidarity, or service that can be understood and explained only in religious or spiritual terms. The kidnapping ordeals of Terry Waite, Fr Lawrence Jenco, Terry Anderson and other aid workers during the Lebanese crisis of the late 1980s remain in mind as vivid witness to the indomitable spirit of religiously motivated, self-sacrificing men and women in the midst of turmoil and violence.[11]

So how could I not think in this respect of the saintly leper priest of Moloka'i, who as a handsome young missionary offered his life as a ransom for the all-but-forgotten victims of the most dreaded disease of the tropics? Perhaps not surprisingly, Fr Damien was vilified by some after his own death from Hansen's disease at an early age. But his sacrificial care for outcasts and oppressed men and women earned him the admiration first of Robert Louis Stevenson, then Mohandas Gandhi, and eventually the entire world, leading to beatification by the Catholic Church. Fr Damien's confession to his parishioners as he began his homily one day, 'We lepers … ', has found place among the simplest if most noble statements of all time.[12]

To such heroic and sometimes celebrated self-sacrifice must be added the daily and often invisible sacrifices of parents, spouses, caregivers and adult children who faithfully undertake the strenuous and demanding service of those who look to them for assistance. Saints matter because after all they are also 'one of us'. They open the way of human transcendence to us by scattering the darkness of disillusionment and despair.

Ultimately, as Buddha the Jesus, Meister Eckhart and Ivan Illich were right to insist, in this life, pain and suffering represent an inescapable portion of the human condition. But if we can never completely escape their reach, they can be transformed and their tyranny overcome, as the examples cited above illustrate. But suffering acquires redemptive meaning and value only because it can be *made* creative by being willingly accepted as a sign of solidarity and compassion. That is as much to say that only a profound *love* can make suffering creative and redemptive. For Christians, this is the ultimate mystery revealed in the life and death of Jesus of Nazareth and made effective in his resurrection.

Suffering must be gone *through* – not around. No pill or potion will ever remove the burden of pain and suffering from the living world. That is not to deny that the alleviation of both ranks among the most noble of all human enterprises, but it would be foolhardy to assume, as did the Buddha's father, that life can be devoid of all affliction. Pain and suffering must be transformed when they cannot be lightened or removed. 'And he called to him the multitude with his disciples, and said to them, "If any man would come after me, let him deny himself and take up his cross and follow me"' (Mk 8:34). Resurrection promises that on the other side of suffering willingly undergone as a sign of our solidarity with all men and women there awaits eternal joy and peace. In the meantime, the healing of life's daily hurts and vast catastrophes remains a task, a calling and a very real achievement.

Traditional Care and the Treatment of Pain

How people managed chronic illness, injury, pain and suffering before the era of industrialised medicine and pharmaceuticals, especially the over-the-counter variety, is perhaps best summed up under the rubric of 'traditional' medicine or healing. (I'll return to the religious role of healing shrines, wells and other extraordinary traditional remedies in a later chapter). *Traditional* in this regard means only 'handed down', presumably over generations within societies lacking academically trained practitioners and especially industrialised medicines and procedures.

It should be borne in mind that informal, sometimes merely fanciful or superstitious remedies can be transmitted alongside modern medicines and therapies, providing, as many 'traditional' beliefs and practices tend to, a 'default' or back-up system of redress when more scientific avenues are either unavailable or seem to be unavailing. Unfortunately, not only are some of these approaches valueless or even harmful in themselves, when combined with modern medicines in particular, they can sometimes amplify, accelerate, or nullify their effectiveness.

Medical science and arts have developed immensely over the past century. Diagnosis and treatment, especially surgery and pharmacology, aided by rapid progress in the growth of medical technology, have transformed the field of professional healing. But there have been losses as well. Perhaps the greatest of these in the view of many medical practitioners themselves is the care of the patient in view of the wholeness of life – body, mind and spirit, in the midst of family and social relations. Professor Seán Ó Súilleabháin observes in this regard that:

> The healer's diagnosis of the ailment and of the cause of it was one of the main parts of his functions. The ceremonial attempt at curing the sick person followed and immediately restored to him the will to recover his health and to live. Just as in modern scientific medicine, the placebo-effect of the medication was to activate the patient's faith. In the olden days, if the ritual curing happened to fail and the patient did not recover, the belief was that a new type of ailment had come into being and the healer was again called in to cope with that. Thus, it may be said that the folk-healer had a social, as well as a medical, function to fulfill – not only those who were ill, but the whole population-group as well, depended on him for advice and help.[13]

We shall have cause to return to the placebo effect later on. At the moment, it is enough to note that in the realm of pharmacology, the connection between the diverse worlds of traditional remedies and contemporary practice remains in many instances the source of healing substances common to both. Although often synthesised in laboratories today, the chemical basis of drugs and other 'medicines' remains naturally occurring compounds in plants, fungi and sometimes animal tissues. Many were known to the ancients in their raw and sometimes refined forms – morphia, salicylates, penicillin-like moulds, etc. Ó Súilleabháin comments:

> African medicine-men have for a long time used the bark of a certain type of willow to cure rheumatism with salicyl; the Hottentots knew of aspirin; the natives of the Amazon River basin used cocillana as an effective cough-mixture, and curare, which they applied to arrow-tips to stun their enemies, is now used as an anaesthetic; the Incas have left us cocaine; ephedrine reached the Western World from China; cascara was known to the North American Indians; from the juice of the foxglove was derived digitalin for heart-ailments; and finally, here in Ireland, moulds from which penicillin has been derived were traditionally used for septic wounds. Also, early peoples used compresses, scarification, hot baths (*tithe alluis*), even vaccination; and, if the old saga is to be believed, some kind of trepanning (with a mixture of lime and brain-matter) was tried out on Conchobhar Mac Neasa when his skull had been injured in battle almost two thousand years ago.[14]

In rural Ireland in particular, but also in other parts of the world, including urban areas where rural migrants had gathered, traditional healers were (and still are) called upon to cure a wide variety of ills, pains and problems – asthma and bronchitis, bites and stings, boils and ulcers, broken bones, burns and scalds, bursitis, chicken pox, diarrhoea, eczema and other skin problems, fevers, influenza, kidney stones, measles, shingles, sties, thrush, toothache, tumours, warts, whooping cough, wounds, and many other ailments. That healers who 'had the cure', often a procedure passed down for generations within families, were able to alleviate a percentage of those who repaired to them is something of a wonder.

It didn't always succeed, of course. Traditional medicine, particularly 'country cures' such as those recounted by Dr Logan, also had limitations, sometimes severely so. Misdiagnosis and faulty treatment could result in scarring, permanent injury, or even death. Sometimes the cures had no effect at all other than to provide time enough for natural healing processes to work. And there were a range of diseases clearly beyond their capacity to deal with.[15] But sometimes they did work.

The Holy Herbal – Hildegard's legacy

For the most part, 'herbs' (generally plants that do not develop wood in their stems and branches and die down after flowering) have constituted the medical arsenal for most traditional healers throughout history and all over the world. The power of herbs and other plants to heal evoked expressions of gratitude and praise wherever spirituality provided insight into the benevolent providence of the Creator. As we read in the Book of Wisdom, 'For God created all things so that they might exist; the generative forces of the world are wholesome, and there is no destructive poison in them, and the dominion of Hades is not on earth' (Wis 1:14-15).

As noted earlier, the twelfth-century saint and mystic Hildegard of Bingen typifies this aspect of holy healing at its best. In her writings, she describes and recommends an amazing array of medicinal herbs and ordinary kitchen spices such as aloe, cumin, fennel, fenugreek galangal ('catarrh root'), licorice, pellitory, sage and wild ginger for a variety of simple complaints (bad breath, dry skin, lank hair) as well as chronic illness, accident and disease, including heart disease and even cancer. Although astonishing for her erudition and encompassing breadth of interests, Hildegard's concern for health was not unusual in the Benedictine monastic tradition. In later centuries, even as the medical arts were being developed in Muslim and Christian universities, the monastery herb garden continued to offer remedies for the monks, nuns and friars as well as members of the laity who had recourse to them for treatment. (A paradoxical example can be found in Shakespeare's lovable but bumbling Friar Lawrence or the more positive image of Ellis Peter's Brother Cadfael.)[16]

Today, holy herbalists still ply their trade, whether in the guise of urban practitioners, medical researchers searching out the secrets of plants from the Amazon rainforest and other remote parts of the world, a Chinese 'barefoot doctor', or an old curandera in a village somewhere in Mexico, Chicago, or Limerick. They share a common truth: plants heal because in some mysterious way they are meant to. As gifts, they are a grace.

It would be impossible in a work of this nature even to list the most important medicinal herbs, holy or otherwise. (Some herbs do in fact betray their religious disposition in their names, among them Blessed Thistle or St Benedict's Thistle or Holy Thistle as it is variously called, Holy Basil, St John's Wort, St John's Girdle (*Cingulum Sancti Johannis*), St James' Wort – which is also known as Stinking Billy or common ragwort, and Cascara Sagrada.) Fortunately, catalogues of healing herbs can be found in libraries, book stores and even on the internet. Dried herbs and even potted herbs can be found in shops everywhere, and some are so common they can be found growing in just about any garden or along the roadside. A few of them are worth a brief mention, but it is well to bear in mind that resorting to herbal remedies and supplements should be undertaken with the advice of competent medical authority, especially if one is taking conventional medicines for serious illness.[17]

Ashwaganda (*Withania somnifera*) is well-known in Ayurvedic medicine and has recently gained considerable attention in Europe and North America for benefits as an anti-inflammatory, analgesic, sedative, skin ointment, diuretic, fertility enhancement, sedative and utility in treating memory loss.

Blessed thistle (*Cnicus benedictus*) seems to contain anti-inflammatory and anti-cancer compounds.

Chinchona or cinchona, a species of evergreen shrubs from South America (also known as Jesuits' bark), was for a time the principal source of quinine. Grown today in Sri Lanka, India and Java, Chinchona is valued in the treatment of malaria, among many other uses as an antiseptic, astringent, anti-inflammatory, anti-spasmodic, analgesic and calmative.

Hawthorn (*Crataegus oxycantha*), according to some ancient Christian legends, was the wood from which the soldiers plaited Jesus' crown of thorns and was subsequently possessed of curative potency. Traditional healers used the berries to concoct remedies for heart ailments, a practice later confirmed by laboratory research. Hawthorn is valued today as an antispasmodic, cardiac, sedative and vasodilator, regulating and even lowering blood pressure. Hawthorn tea is recommended for stress and insomnia. (Once again, persons taking medications for heart conditions should not supplement them with hawthorn without consultation with their physician.)

Mugwort (*Artemisia vulgaris*), long used to flavour drinks, has also found use medicinally to treat a variety of ills as a stimulant and tonic, diuretic, diaphoretic and emmenagogue. There are over 180 species of artemisia, including the common artemisia or Wormwood (*Artemisia absinthium*), which is used in many beverages and gained an undeservedly infamous reputation a century ago for its use in the popular intoxicant absinthe. The beneficial and popular spice tarragon (*artemisia dracunculus*) is another form.

St John's Wort (*Hypericum perforatum*) has been used for centuries to treat mild depression and anxiety, as has valerian and a little yellow flowering plant known as *rhodiola rosea* which grows in colder, more northerly regions from Canada to Iceland and Ireland to Siberia. Also useful as an antibacterial agent, St John's Wort is under study with regard to its ability in a highly concentrated form to destroy Methicillin-resistant *Staphylococcus aureus* (MRSA).

For all its aggravation to gardeners, stinging nettle (*Urtica diotica*), both root and leaves, is a cornucopeia of healing chemicals which alleviate allergies, anemia, arthritis, asthma, diabetes, hay fever, hypertension, kidney problems, pleurisy, rheumatism, and a variety of aches and pains. Considerable research is being conducted on its value in treating benign prostatic hyperplasia. It is also used as a diuretic. The compound that gives nettle its sting contains formic acid, choline, histamine and serotonin, among other things. The plant itself contains over forty different chemicals. Not surprisingly, stinging nettle is only one of a huge number of types of urtica. Hung briefly by the stem or root, it loses it sting and makes a good tea as well as an excellent salad. Horses like it, too.

Ashwaganda, rhodiola and similar plants are known as *adaptogens*, because they help people adapt to changing, often stressful conditions, reducing anxiety and fatigue without the harmful effects of artificial stimulants and concentrated medicines. Among them are also found astragalus, cordyceps sinensis, ginseng, licorice, holy basil and schisandra.[18]

Roots, stems, leaves and bark can all contain near-miraculous substances that ward off or cure disease. Willow bark was used in China, Europe, and by native peoples in North America for a variety of complaints, and since it contains salicin, the parent form of aspirin, that is not so amazing. The bark of the Pacific yew (*Taxus brevifolia*), long considered a junk tree by timber companies and consequently cleared from the forests, was shown in 1964 to contain a potent anti-carcinogenic compound, taxol.[19] Regrettably, for a yew to reach maturity may require a century or more.

Ordinary household herbs and culinary spices also have healing properties, and many are listed in Hildegard's pharmacy, among them cinnamon, rosemary, oregano, sage and tumeric. For many centuries they have been used therapeutically in India, China, Greece and Rome, as well as western Europe.[20] A few of the more common include the following:

Asafoetida is a cooking spice extracted from the giant fennel that alleviates indigestion, toothache and irritable bowel syndrome. It is also used to treat asthma and bronchitis.

Common cinnamon (*Cinnamomum aromaticum*) or cassia has been found to regulate blood sugar and may prove to be of value in the treatment of diabetes.[21] In Traditional Chinese Medicine, cassia is considered one of the fifty fundamental herbs. It contains a powerful compound called coumarin, however, and should not be consumed especially in large quantities by anyone using the prescription drug Coumadin (warfarin).

Ordinary rosemary has long been celebrated for its many virtues: 'Take the flowers and put them in a lynen clothe, and so boyle them in fayre cleane water to the halfe and cole it, and drynke it for it is much worth against all evyls in the body,' according to Anthony Askham's 1550 *Lytel Herball*. More a shrub than a true herb, rosemary is used to combat rheumatism, heart disease, paralysis, headache, vertigo, colic, colds and weakness of the limbs, besides being very good on roast potatoes and in most meat and vegetable dishes.

Turmeric, an Indian spice used traditionally in curries, appears to be another potent preventative and curative. Research in India and Japan, and most recently at Rutgers University in the US, indicates that the compound curcumin, which gives both turmeric and mustard their distinctive colour, is useful in treating multiple myeloma and other types of cancer.[22] Also an antioxidant and anti-inflammatory, curcumin may find use in treating Alzheimer's disease and multiple sclerosis. It has no apparent side effects.

That people living in regions where curries are popular and even staple items in the diet show a much lower incidence of cancer is not surprising. The southern Mediterranean diet has been shown, similarly, to prevent a range of heart diseases. Diet and health are very strongly correlated, not least because of the herbs and spices that most of us probably regard as mere incidental flavourings. The remarkable connection between health, healing and nutrition deserves additional consideration, of course, and it is to the subject of what Jean Carper, the *New York Times*' nutritionist, called 'The Food Pharmacy',[23] that we turn next.

NOTES

1. New York: Harper and Row, 1971.
2. London: Calder and Boyars, 1973.
3. Ivan Illich, *Medical Nemesis: The Expropriation of Health* (London: Calder and Boyars, 1975).
4. Ibid., p. 97.
5. Ibid., pp. 93–4.
6. Ibid., p. 168.
7. Ibid., p. 166.
8. Dr Saunder's major published works include *Living with Dying: The Management of Terminal Disease* (Oxford University Press, 1983), *Hospice: The Living Idea* (Philadelphia: W. B. Saunders Co., 1981), *Watch With Me: Inspiration for a Life in Hospice Care* (Rockford: Mortal Press, 2003) and *Cicely Saunders: Selected Writings* 1958–2004 (Oxford University Press, 2006).
9. *Meister Eckhart, The Man from Whom God Hid Nothing* (London: Collins, 1988), p. 52. A new edition was published by Gracewing in 1995.
10. In addition to her book on Eckhart, the major collection of Fleming's writings on pain management have been republished: *Grasping the Nettle: A Positive Approach to Pain*, ed. by Carol Horrigan and Anne Fleming (Cuckfield, Sussex: The Old Forge Press, 2002). Fleming's *The Desert and the Market Place: Writings, Letters, Journals* was published by Gracewing in 1995. Fleming's tapes on pain management can also be obtained in care of ursulafleming@hotmail.com.
11. See Terry Waite, *Taken on Trust* (London: Coronet Books, 1994 ed.), and Lawrence Jenco, OSM, *Bound to Forgive: The Pilgrimage to Reconciliation of a Beirut Hostage* (Notre Dame, IN: Ave Maria Press, 1995).
12. See Richard Stewart, *Leper Priest of Moloka'i: The Father Damien* Story (Honolulu: The University of Hawai'i Press, 2001).
13. Patrick Logan, *Irish Country Cures* (Belfast: Appletree Press, 1981), Foreword, pp. ix–x.
14. Ibid., p. ix.
15. Logan remarks in this regard: 'Folk medicine provides treatment for all the ordinary and obvious diseases, but it does not deal with certain parts of

medicine. Treatments for internal cancers are very rare, and disorders of the central nervous system are almost never treated.' Ibid., p. 4.

16. See Jany Fournier-Rosset, *From Saint Hildegard's Kitchen: Foods of Health, Foods of Joy* (Ligouri, MO: Liguori Publications, 1999) and Hildegard Von Bingen, *Hildegard's Healing Plants: From Her Medieval Classic Physica*, ed. and trans. by Bruce W. Hozecki (Boston: Beacon Press, 2002).

17. For a useful guide to the use of herbs with reference to side effects and possible interactions with other drugs, see Chris D. Meletis, N.D., *Complete Guide to Safe Herbs* (London and New York: DK Publishing, 2002).

18. For a thorough study, see David Winston and Steven Maimes, *Adaptogens: Herbs for Strength, Stamina, and Stress Relief* (Rochester, VT: Healing Arts Press, 2007).

19. See Rudolf Fritz Weiss and Volker Fintelmann, *Herbal Medicine* (New York: Thieme Medical Publishers, 2000 ed.), p. 376.

20. For an excellent guide to the curative power of plants, see James A. Duke, *The Green Pharmacy* (Emmaus, PA: Rodale Press, 1997).

21. Clinical studies have demonstrated the effectiveness of cassia in reducing blood glucose, total cholesterol and triglycerides in subjects with type 2 diabetes, but have not indicated its effectiveness in treating type 1 diabetes in adolescents. See Steve M. Blevins, Misti J. Leyva, Joshua Brown et al., 'Effect of Cinnamon on Glucose and Lipid Levels in Non-Insulin-Dependent Type 2 Diabetes,' *Diabetes Care* 30 (2007):2236–7, published online 11 June 2007; Justin A. Altschuler, Samuel J. Casella, Todd A. MacKenzie and Kevin M. Curtis, 'The Effect of Cinnamon on A1C among Adolescents with Type 1 Diabetes,' *Diabetes Care* 30 (2007):813-816; and Alam Khan, Mahpara Safdar, Mohammad Muzaffar Ali Khan, et al., 'Cinnamon Improves Glucose and Lipids of People With Type 2 Diabetes,' *Diabetes Care* 26 (2003):3215–3218.

22. See Ah-Ng Tony Kong, Tin Oo Khor, Young-Sam Keum et al., 'Combined Inhibitory Effects of Curcumin and Phenethyl Isothiocyanate on the Growth of Human PC-3 Prostate Xenografts in Immunodeficient Mice', *Cancer Research* 66 (15 Jan 2006) 2:613–21.

23. Jean Carper, *The Food Pharmacy* (New York: Bantam, 1988).

CHAPTER SEVEN
SPIRITUALITY AND THE BODY • III
NUTRITION, STRESS, EXERCISE AND
GROOMING

... whether you eat or drink or whatever you do,
do all to the glory of God.
1 Corinthians 10:31

Physical care for our bodies has been an index of spiritual health (and illth) for thousands of years, including practices and regulations regarding food and drink, work, play, rest, exercise, hygiene and 'grooming'. (Sleep and dreams; sex, love and friendship; and death are also part of the overall pattern, but will be treated later on.) Food and drink come first, both in importance and probably chronologically, since next to air, they are the most fundamental requirements for just staying alive. But all are important and each dimension of concern has found its way into functional, symbolic and sacramental niches in the cultures and religions of the world.

Food customs are possibly the most interesting of all these areas to study if only because so much attention has been given to the production, preparation, consumption and disposal of food waste in the religious classics of the human race. Proportionately, the food laws of Israel take up a sizable portion of the Pentateuch, from the categorisation of edible animals to the disposition of leftovers.[1] But if eating and drinking were considered important, so were their opposites – fasting and abstinence, which have been enshrined in practices still observed in Judaism, Christianity, and Islam. Other world religions have similar histories. Hindus, Buddhists, Sikhs, Jainists, even the ancient Greeks and Romans conscientiously integrated food into their religious life-ways – more often for symbolic and sacramental purposes than for nutritional or economic reasons.

Today, while the affluent Christian West has all but eliminated food asceticism such as fasting and abstinence, in Islamic nations and wherever devout Muslims live, Ramadan – the month of fasting – is observed perhaps even more strenuously today than in past eras. Among some Christian denominations specific practices have survived, as in the vegetarian regimen of Seventh Day Adventists, who also avoid all forms of drugs, including alcohol, coffee, tea and cigarettes. Mormons are similarly sensitive to the place of food and drink in their lives. But overall, during the last century Catholic and Protestant Christians seem to have abandoned an explicit emphasis on the connections between food and spirituality, even in monasteries and convents, which have generally adapted to the prevailing food customs of the dominant culture surrounding them. Unfortunately, the prevalence of nutritional malfeasance in modern industrial society, from fast food to junk food, has led to the development of eating disorders within groups that once thrived on fasting and abstinence and the avoidance of luxury items in the diet. Friar Tuck has returned to haunt us.

In the meantime, nutritionists have also risen to the task of recalling affluent, westernised nations to the dangers of processed foods, over-eating and unbalanced diets, with their often dire consequences – morbid obesity, adult and childhood diabetes, heart disease and reactive disorders such as anorexia nervosa, bulimia and bingeing. Even more promising, nutritional scientists and medical researchers have rediscovered the many health benefits, even the medicinal contributions, of good nutritional practice. It is certainly true that we are what we eat, as the proverb claims. But is no less true that what functions to make us stronger shouldn't kill us.

Nutrition, Diet and Health

All animals (and some plants) consume nutrients to support life processes, which is to say to provide the raw materials for providing energy, replacing cellular tissue, repairing nerves, replenishing hormones, enzymes, neurotransmitters, bone structure and blood cell count, as well as providing fluids for respiration, digestion, the elimination of toxins, and dozens of other functions, none of which we need to know about for the whole system to work properly. Many animals instinctively recognise foods that are nutritious and even curative, while others can be poisoned by ingesting the wrong kind of food or contaminated food sources. Humans are unusual, if not exactly unique, in that we have learned how to improve food preparation and consumption by sometimes elaborate technological means, not least of which is cooking. In fact, cooking skills and the development of civilization are very closely linked.[2]

The publication of Jean Carper's *The Food Pharmacy* in 1988 came as a revelation to many nutritionists and dieticians, not to mention cooks, although the connection between diet and both the maintenance and restoration of health was recognised medically from the days of Hippocrates. But Carper focused on how the specific medicinal effects of foods, as distinct from medicinal herbs and minerals, added immensely to our knowledge of both the sources and remedies of disease as well as the remarkable, almost miraculous potency of ordinary food and drink. As we have seen, heart diseases had already been linked to a diet high in cholesterol (low-density lipoprotein), and maladies such as gout (metabolic arthritis) were associated with certain kinds of meat and vegetable produce – rightly or wrongly. Much of the evidence for medicinal diets was based solely on anecdote. Now, however, the full panoply of medical research was being brought to bear on what was in many respects an undiscovered country.

Purposefully and wisely eating for health and longevity has become a passion for many people today, which if elevated to compulsive heights can eclipse the noble benefits of celebration and worship, although in my own experience the threat seems to be minimal compared to the lethal allure of junk food, fast food and processed foods in general. But foods can also harm health not only because of contamination by bacteria or pollutants such as lead and mercury and the chemical residue of pesticides, herbicides and fertilisers, or even overindulgence, but because of their 'natural' chemical components. Food allergies, which are basically a radical incompatibility, often protein-related, between certain foods and one's immune system, can in fact become life-threatening, leading to anaphylactic or toxic shock. (More common allergic reactions involve milk, eggs, peanuts, tree nuts, fish and shellfish.) Our diet should not only be properly balanced, it must also be biologically compatible.

More ordinary hazards involve eating disorders such as compulsive overeating, self-starvation (anorexia nervosa), bulimia and bingeing. In terms of our daily food and drink, it is entirely possible to have too much of a good thing. Not surprisingly, in world religious traditions, the spirituality of food has usually tended to emphasise the value of moderation, first of all, and of deprivation for medicinal as well as psychological and social ends – fasting and abstinence. Gluttony, drunkenness and hoarding were all discouraged and often severely sanctioned. Ultimately, the employment of food and drink in sacrifice and worship builds upon the perceived and manifold blessings of nutrition and celebration, both positive and negative.

Global Indigestion: Fast Food and Junk Food

Widespread starvation and the increasing depletion of sources of clean drinking water in many parts of the world today stand in sharp contrast to the excesses of industrialised food production, preparation, consumption and waste disposal in Europe, North America, and other regions of the 'rich nations' of the earth. Ironically, the 'general enrichment' of the western diet has led to the highest rates of coronary disease in the world. The proportion of heart attacks in the United States has doubled every twenty years since 1900. Obesity and diabetes are rapidly increasing as well, even and perhaps especially among the very young. Vitamin and mineral deficiencies are also acute in many forms of the 'affluent Western diet'.[3]

Coping with food problems, including eating disorders, is hardly an easy task, whether individually or socially. Popular diets come and go rapidly, promoted by the press, publishers and the electronic media. But physicians and nutritionists agree that for the most part 'fad' diets do not work despite initial enthusiasm and even noticeable weight loss. For once off the diet, people tend to pack the weight back on by way of their general lifestyle. The 'diet' that works is a joint product of patient endurance and a simple but effective regimen – reducing dietary fat, reducing the quantities of food consumed (which may mean more but smaller meals), eliminating high-caloric snack foods and drinks, and adopting a consistent programme of exercise, which may mean no more than walking briskly, climbing stairs and otherwise avoiding labour-saving devices (but more of this later).

Traditional religious strategies to bring diet under control, specifically fasting and total or partial abstinence, can contribute positively to health, as can an effort at nutrition education, even on a small scale. Knowing what to eat, as well as when, how, how much, and why, will take anyone a long way toward nutritional wisdom. Diversity is likewise helpful. Ethnic foods are often more beneficial than the traditional meat-and-potatoes-with-one vegetable (usually overcooked) salty diet typical of the western industrial diet favoured in Germany, Poland, England, Ireland, Canada, the United States and Australia. The Southern Italian or Mediterranean diet, with its reliance on vegetables, wheat, tomato sauce, seafood and a wide range of leafy greens, is considered by many nutritionists to be the healthiest in the world. Despite some problems with overly refined ingredients, Asian diets are generally healthier than their European counterparts in regard to excessive carbohydrates, empty calories and high-density cholesterol. As a general rule, whole foods should be preferred to processed foods whenever possible.

Balancing Act

The ideal diet for providing support for brain and nerve support is a combination of protein (30 per cent), complex carbohydrates (40 per cent) and fats (30 per cent). The easiest way to obtain the right proportions is to eat meals that consist mainly of whole grains, fruits and vegetables. For protein, fish, poultry, lean meats, legumes, nuts and a variety of seeds are next in the order of priority. Healthy fats can be found in fish oils, olive oil, avocados and nuts such as almonds and walnuts. Of less utility for adults, despite the insistent claims of agri-businesses, are most dairy products (yogurt excepted) and packaged and processed foods, such as refined white bread, rice and pasta, and especially sugar, which are basically simple carbohydrates that boost blood glucose levels and may contribute to diabetes, cardio-vascular disease and even dementia.

Red meats, especially beef, are of little real value in the diet, despite the savoury and ubiquitous hamburger and the conspicuous consumption of roasts and hefty steaks, once considered to be a talisman of wealth and power. In addition to contributing to a variety of health problems such as arteriosclerosis, cancer of the breast, colon and prostate, osteoporosis and rheumatoid arthritis,[4] beef is particularly hard on planetary health as millions of hectares of rain forest and rich agricultural land are sacrificed to pasture vast herds of cattle or millions of tons of wheat and corn are diverted to vast feedlots where cattle are fattened in congested mobs before slaughter. White meats (poultry and pork) are a much healthier alternative. Lamb and veal are not.

The Food Pharmacy

On the positive side, sometimes quite ordinary ingredients, even those we might avoid because of their pungency, contain powerful health-producing substances. For instance, the humble garlic, much loved in southern Italian cooking, contains allicin, which makes it aromatically challenging but also endows it with potent health benefits. In addition to warding off vampires (which may reflect metaphorical folk wisdom), garlic has been recommended for centuries for its cardiological benefits. Allicin enables garlic to improve red blood cell flow, cell-signalling, vascular relaxation (important with regard to hypertension) and oxygen supply. It appears to lower cholesterol and reduce blood clotting. Garlic is also a natural antioxidant, broad-spectrum antibiotic and viricide. It has anti-fungal properties and reduces yeast infections. Some claim that it is a useful treatment for acne and arthritis as well.

Another humble fruit of the earth, the grapefruit, has been shown to have a number of potent medicinal properties. (I always thought that *pampelmuse* or *pamplemousse* or even *pompelmo* was a better name for this marvellous produce. It doesn't look at all like a grape.) Some of these properties are significant enough to warrant caution with regard to combining grapefruit and its juice with medications such as cholesterol-lowering drugs ('statins') and a number of antidepressants and immunosuppressants since they mimic their effect and can in fact accelerate it.[5] Naringin, the active ingredient in grapefruit responsible for its bitter taste, is metabolised into an antioxidant which is known to lower blood cholesterol levels. Grapefruit may also prevent Hepatitis C infection.[6]

Other foods and beverages are known to be heart-healthy by reducing coronary artery disease (CAD). Consumed in moderation, wine, beer and mixed alcoholic drinks have been shown to reduce CAD by as much as 30 per cent and they also keep brain membranes more flexible. ('Moderation' here means one glass of wine or beer per day for women, two for men. More alcohol intake per day begins to have the reverse effect, damaging brain tissues and impairing memory. Moderation in all things is still the best prescription.)

Among the nutrient-rich vegetables and fruits that will benefit any diet are leafy greens such as Swiss chard, kale and spinach; legumes such as peas and lentils; sweet potatoes; tomatoes; and a variety of vegetables – asparagus, avocados, broccoli, cabbage, carrots, cauliflower, peppers, pumpkin and courgette among them. Five helpings of vegetables and fruits should be consumed as a daily minimum. Among fruits, the most health-friendly are apples, apricots, bananas, berries of all kinds, cantaloupe, guava, kiwi fruit, melons, pineapple and pomegranate.

Some fruits and vegetables are particularly rich in one or another element which makes them highly useful when deficiencies are identified or supplementation is warranted. In recent times for instance, folic acid has been shown to be especially valuable for pregnant mothers in order to prevent a host of developmental problems in their infant. Fruits and vegetables rich in folic acid include asparagus, chickpeas, kidney beans, lentils, lima beans, parsley, peas, romaine lettuce, spinach, brown rice, fortified cereals and wheat germ. Similarly, bilberries and other dark, especially blue and black berries, contain vitamins and anthocyanin pigments linked to vision improvement and, according to legend, remedy 'night blindness'. In some clinical tests bilberry extract, which has antioxidant properties, has in fact been shown to improve visual accuracy, and may be useful in treating eye diseases such as pigmentosa, retinitis and glaucoma. Other substances such as lutein and zeaxanthin, carotenoids found in spinach, kale and egg yolk, also aid in vision health, whether preventing disorders such as macular degeneration or strengthening vision itself.

Not to be forgotten, the fungi (which are neither fruit nor vegetable), especially mushrooms such as Asian forms including chaga, maitake, shiitake and reishi, and traditional western portabellas and even the humble white mushroom, are fairly good sources of protein, but especially high in niacin and riboflavin, pantothenic acid and potassium – more so even than bananas – as well as rich in selenium and copper. Mushrooms are also low in calories and contain no fat or cholesterol.

The recent trend toward organic farming of fruits, vegetables and mushrooms (as well as animal products) may increase the price of all these commodities, but for those who can afford the slight extra cost, the reduction in pesticide and fertiliser residue, preservatives and flavour and colour enhancers is worth the sacrifice when it comes to personal and global health.

The Water of Life
If 'solid' food is necessary to sustain and enhance life, fluids, especially water, are even more so. Water is the mother of life. Next to the air we breathe, the water and other fluids we drink (and they are mostly water) represent the major exchange we and other living inhabitants of the Earth experience with the world of Nature. It is vital to survival.

All animals (including human ones) will die within minutes if deprived of air, and in weeks if deprived of food. But without water, or its equivalent, tissue dehydration produces debility and death within a few days as the biological systems that keep us alive simply shut down. Water is absolutely essential to good health, from the replenishment of blood cells to the wonders of digestion and respiration. The removal of toxic wastes from cells, the digestive and respiratory systems depends utterly on water. It is hardly surprising that so many biblical allusions to grace and salvation employ its image, especially in the Gospel of John (see especially Jn 4:14).

Physically, water is lost through urination, breathing, perspiration, bleeding and the emission of other body fluids, especially in cases of diarrhoea and worst of all, dysentery. The rate at which we lose water depends on activity, humidity, ambient temperature, and other factors. Consequently, we all need to replace water more or less frequently throughout the daily cycle. A normally active adult will, on the average, need to replenish about two litres (approximately four pints) per day, which converts to the classic eight glasses of water. In extreme conditions, one could require eight times as much, however.

Having grown up in a desert environment, I was acutely aware of the importance of water for as long as I can remember. I recall water rationing during periods of drought, long before it was possible to buy plastic containers of distilled and 'pure mountain spring water' in the grocery stores and supermarkets. When I went hiking with my friends or on camping trips with the Boy Scouts, having a well-filled canteen was not merely a part of our normal routine; it was a necessity.

Moving to the great American Midwest in the 1960s and then living in England and Ireland after the 1970s, I gradually became accustomed to having plenty of water around – too much sometimes. Seeing the Mississippi River for the first time in flood stage and working for days filling and placing sandbags to keep it at bay from the streets of Dubuque, Iowa, was as fascinating to me as it was exhausting. Three events stand out in memory as even more unforgettable – the first time I saw the vast blue Pacific Ocean from the Oregon coast in 1960, my initiation to the cold, fresh water of

Lake Michigan on a sailboat in 1963 and my first glimpse of the restless Atlantic ocean five miles below as I first flew to Ireland in 1972. The salvation of the world may well have been prepared in the wilderness, but the human race lives on a water planet!

How strange now to see it wasted, polluted and sold in plastic bottles, even in Ireland, where agricultural runoff and industrial pollution have made much of the ground water increasingly undrinkable. Plain water may be a miracle of divine proportions, but as beverages go, it is only the beginning. The use of additives and alterations for celebration and worship did not begin at Cana!

In Vino Veritas

The history of alcoholic drinks seems to be as old as humankind itself, at least according to the biblical account, which traces the origins of wine back to Noah himself, and it is not an entirely happy tale (Gen 9:20-27). Beer kegs have been uncovered in the ruins of ancient Egypt as well. The art of distillation came much later, developed by Babylonian, Greek and, later, Persian ingenuity. But Arabic alchemists gave us the name 'alcohol' from *al-guwl*, meaning 'the spirit'.

Wine, beer, mead, fermented milk and other alcoholic beverages have long been used in ceremonial occasions to express solidarity and benevolence.[7] In religion, wine was and is a principal accompaniment of the Jewish *seder* and from there came into Christian usage as a sacramental drink. Although St Brigit of Ireland wanted to host 'a great ale-feast for Christ', and Benjamin Franklin is supposed to have observed, 'Beer is living proof that God loves us and wants us to be happy', in recent decades the health benefits (as well as the harmful effects) of beer, wine and 'spirits' have attracted increasing scientific and medical attention. For the ingredients 'added' to water to create such beverages contain nutrients (and sometimes poisons) that bear significantly on human health and illth.

Both beer and wine are not only foods in that sense, but have medicinal properties as well. The novelist Dorothy Sayers was right when she quipped back in the 1930s that 'Guinness is good for you'. I recall accounts of doctors in Ireland prescribing 'the porther', which is rich in protein as well as carbohydrates, to nursing mothers despite its alcoholic content. (Breeders also tipped a bottle of 'the Guinness' into a bucket of mash to aid an ailing horse.) Beer is 92 per cent water. Significantly, it contains no fat or cholesterol and few calories but is rich in magnesium, selenium, potassium, phosphorus, Vitamin B3 (niacin), B5 (pantothenic acid), B6 (pyridoxin), and B9 (folate), with smaller amounts of B1 (thiamine), B2 (riboflavin), B12 inotisol and choline.[8]

The health benefits of wine match and in some respects outstrip those of beer, especially in the case of red wines. In both regards, the freer they are from artificial additives such as colouring and preservatives (especially sulfites with regard to wine), the healthier. Red wines have anti-microbial potency, reduce cholesterol, and may be effective in reducing tumours.[9] Other recent studies show that resveratrol, a compound found in grapes and red wines made from them, helps prevent inflammation and cancer and offset some of the deficiencies associated with ageing. A study of 12,500 nurses indicated that those who drank one glass of wine daily had greater cognitive clarity over several years than did women who abstained. Moderate alcohol consumption also appears to prevent heart disease and stroke. Drinking more than a glass or two of wine did not improve cognitive abilities or cardiovascular health, however.[10] In fact, increased consumption has proportionately harmful effects.

Inebriation and Intoxication: the Dangers in Drink

The biblical story of the origin of wine ends with inebriation and shame. It is not by accident that over-consumption of alcohol is called 'intoxication'. In quantity, alcohol can be a deadly poison. In even less than lethal doses, alcoholic poisoning can destroy brain cells, interfere with digestion and cause serious damage to the liver and cardiovascular system. When habitual, compulsive drinking or alcoholism can be a personal disaster and a social scourge leading to family tragedy, social detriment and premature death.

For all that, moderate alcohol consumption can be healthy and in fact medicinal. It figures prominently in social gatherings, from toasts at banquets and New Year's celebrations, to the ceremonial launch of ships. Silenus, the drunken Greek sage, and the drunken kung fu master, are not mere comic figures, but embody an insight into the role that altered consciousness plays in wisdom and skill. The symposia described by Plato during which Socrates imparted his teaching as his young companions celebrated and quarrelled over their cups of wine is an illustration of the old axiom, *in vino veritas*. It is not unrelated that Jesus and his disciples were accused of laxity in their consumption of wine, nor should it be forgotten that in John's Gospel, Jesus' first great sign involved transforming great jars of water into choice wine. At Pentecost, the Disciples were scorned by the throng as being 'filled with new wine' (Acts 2:13).

The Dominican poet and professor, Paul Murray, has traced the notion of spiritual intoxication in the lives of some of the Order's greatest saints – Blessed Jordan of Saxony, St Thomas Aquinas and St Catherine of Siena.[11] Although possibly distinctive, Dominicans are hardly isolated in their spiritual intoxication. It is a catholic image found in Hinduism, Buddhism and even the otherwise abstinent Muslim tradition of Sufism.

The Cup of Salvation

The spiritual elevation of alcohol to a metaphor of inspiration and revelation leads, not surprisingly, to the sacramental dimension of wine consumption. The use of wine for the Christian Eucharist, with its multi-layered valence in the Passover meal, the cup of friendship, the cup of suffering, and finally the very life's blood of the Saviour, is so well-known that its startling, even provocative meaning can be too easily taken for granted. All the resonance of the place of wine in Judaism and many of the religions of humankind find their apotheosis in the Cup of Christ. (The cup alone became the most potent religious symbol of the Christian West during and after the Middle Ages, in the legend of the Holy Grail.) 'The one who eats my flesh and drinks my blood has eternal life, and I will raise him up at the last day.' (Jn 6:54)[12]

Sharing in the cup of Christ is both a communion with all who drink throughout time and space, but simultaneously a physical communion with Christ and through Christ with God. The Eucharist was thus the primary 'sacrament' or, for the early Christians, the Mystery of personal, social and cosmic salvation, ultimately divinizing.

Essential nutrition is fundamental to physical, mental and emotional health, and it provides a wide and substantial base. From the beginning of human civilization food and drink served to create community, commemorate important occasions and provide the currency of social and religious celebrations of all kinds. It should not be forgotten, however, that while alcohol may function as the 'mysticism of the poor', as William James regarded it, alcoholism has blighted the spiritual life of many a sincere seeker, not least among the clergy and religious. Metaphors, like life, can be hazardous.

Food, Drink and Asceticism

The ascetical principle in Christianity and other religious traditions was linked to health as much as to moral and spiritual strengthening. Even in the colder northern climes, the early Irish monastic diet was spare, consisting mainly of bread, cereals, vegetables and water. Beer, fish, honey, milk and butter were sometimes permitted, but in the more rigorous monasteries of Comgall at Bangor and Mel Ruain at Tallaght, only on suitable and infrequent occasions. One account relates how Mel Ruain instructed the cook to take the butter out of the monks' porridge if they looked too hearty, and when they became wan and weak, to put it back in. It's unlikely that obesity was a problem at Tallaght.[13]

The monastic diet ranked spiritual health above that of the body, but the saints did not, for the most part, lose sight of the interrelated dimensions of the holiness and beauty of food as God's creative gifts, the disciplinary role of voluntary fasting and abstinence, and the religious importance of sacrifice. These dimensions are still noted today. Recent research indicates that fasting and abstinence, whether periodic, or perpetual, has remarkable health benefits, not least of which seems to be increased longevity in both experimental animals and humans. Deepak Chopra relates, for instance, that 'In India there is a tradition, centuries old, that longevity can result from taking little or no food one day a week (in the form of fruit juice, warm water with honey, or low-fat milk). The principle at work is simple: 'The digestive system is allowed to take a rest, to recover its balance and flush out accumulated impurities.'[14]

As the world faces very probable food shortages in the coming decades, actively preparing for both scarcity and increased artificiality will require attitudes that can be described as elements of a true spiritual discipline. Unlearning bad food habits and acquiring more positive approaches will involve the entire range of human interests – bodily, mental, emotional and spiritual. Such a new food ethic will, moreover, reflect social as well as particular implications for each of us, and on both nutritional and symbolic as well as economic levels of concern. While new in some respects, a contemporary spirituality of food will also embody some of the early ascetical practices of the Christian people.[15]

Fasting is a reminder that we are made of matter and yet that we are not wholly determined by our material dimension. It reminds us, moreover, that we are obligated to organise and direct our material embodiedness and environmental situation, to exert control, lest we do in fact lose our spiritual freedom to the dominating forces of the material realm.

In the future, fasting as a discipline will play a greater role in environmental spirituality for all these reasons, and not least for the symbolic function of relating us to billions of people on this planet who will not eat a full meal in their entire lifetime. The ascetical principle involves both a negative and a positive dimension, however. Detachment from food on a periodic basis or for special reasons, private or social, can and should lead to reattachment on a more developed level of awareness and involvement for those blessed with an abundance or even a sufficiency of food and drink. The social correlative of a new consciousness of creation in all its beauty, power and goodness is a recommitment to working for a more just society for all, especially those who hunger and thirst for food and drink as well as for righteousness and the Kingdom of God.

Food, Poverty and Social Justice
Poverty plays an important role in how and when, as well as what, people eat. Food shortages and outright famine, so distressingly frequent today, necessarily inhibit the celebratory and sacramental character of food and meals, further impoverishing the spiritual and social life of millions of human beings. That affluent, highly industrialised nations waste food prodigiously and now increasingly divert agriculture to the production of biomass for conversion to fuel thus becomes a serious matter of social ethics. Starvation was commonly used in ancient times to reduce enemies to submission. In the twentieth century, the dictator Joseph Stalin used mass starvation to consolidate his power over resistant 'Kulaks' in the Ukraine in the 1930s, and food deprivation has been used as a weapon of mass destruction in more recent times, whether under the UN sanctions imposed on Iraq in the 1990s, or the ethnic cleansing practiced in Darfur in the first decades of the 21st century. 'Accidental' starvation, such as that created by astronomical inflation and social collapse in Zimbabwe in 2007–2008, has had obvious political utility for the ruling party. 'Ordinary' famine, whether caused by crop failure, insects, or climate change, is no less lethal, as millions of children, women and men slowly starve to death in various poverty-stricken parts of the world.

Simultaneous with global climate change and the prospect of the displacement of millions of environmental refugees in the coming decades, world-wide hunger and thirst will, in all likelihood, remain a major problem for decades to come. They likewise represent a challenge and a call for human enterprise and outreach on what will undoubtedly be an unprecedented scale. How fitting that in the great religious traditions, sharing bread and wine was chosen to symbolise and realise the most ardent longings of the human heart for community and communion, both nurturing and healing as an effective sign of human equality and divine friendship.[16]

Other aspects of bodily spirituality affect our daily lives and warrant at least a brief overview. In the remaining pages of this chapter, I will look briefly at the effect of stress in our lives, the role of exercise, and finally, the place of hygiene and grooming in caring for and with our bodies as 'temples of the Holy Spirit' and instruments of praise and glory (see 1 Cor 10:31; 2 Cor 6:16; Eph 2:21).

Stress, Fitness and Exercise

Physical and especially social stresses in the home and workplace change our body biologically and in serious cases can increase the risk of heart disease and death. Workers tracked over decades of experience who reported high levels of stress showed both a much higher risk of developing heart conditions and actual heart disease than those reporting less stress. In particular, continuous release of the stress hormone cortisol leads to changes in heartbeat and ultimately to heart disease and even death. A recent study indicated that both male and female workers under the age of fifty showed the strongest link between stress and heart disease, possibly because older workers are healthier than those who retire early over health concerns.[17]

Stress has already found mention as one of the triggers of illth, not only among adults, but even among youngsters.[18] Most would agree that people today live in a more stressful world than at any time in history, a development not unrelated to the fact that more than half the world's population now live in cities. Stress itself is a relatively new term in the health field. Dr Hans Selye, often considered to be the 'father of psychosomatic medicine', imported the notion from engineering dynamics, where it refers to the effect of load upon material. Although slow in finding acceptance, Selye's work succeeded in revolutionising both the popular and medical understanding of the connection between social factors and mental as well as physical health.[19]

Selye's accomplishment came not long after hundreds of British and Commonwealth recruits were executed during the First World

War because, suffering from what was initially derided as 'shell shock', they had retreated from the front lines. In fact, they were so stressed that they could no longer function normally at all, much less fight. Thanks to Selye and his legacy, 'Post-Traumatic Stress Disorder' (PTSD) is now recognised as a true psychological and medical condition requiring skilled treatment.

Stress, now defined as a non-specific physiological response to change, pervades all of modern life. Selye distinguished 'good' stress ('eustress') from harmful stress (distress), but the impact on health from sudden good fortune – a wedding, or a promotion at work – can be as harmful to health as accident, misfortune, or being fired at work. 'Hyperstress' refers to extreme forms of bodily change, which would include battle fatigue and the effects of terrorist attacks, major natural disasters and so forth. Such major demands on our physical, mental, emotional and spiritual resources, especially if prolonged, can seriously injure health and even shorten life.

Reducing the harmful effects of stress (distress) has become a major item in the health care agenda, especially as it bears on cardiovascular disease and cancer, the two major 'killer diseases' in the western world. Because of the stressful potential of global climate change in the coming decades, that agenda has become even more crowded. The role of religion and spirituality in stress reduction is therefore both significant and noteworthy.

Stress and the New Asceticism

As the integrating principle which gives meaning and direction to our life, the human spirit encompasses both body and soul or mind. As a psychosomatic response to life events, stress is thus a spiritual concern as much as it is an issue for physical and mental health. Learning to cope physically, mentally and spiritually with stress will require learning how to insulate ourselves as much as possible from distress-related events. That is, we will have either to eliminate detrimental patterns of behaviour, values, ideas and beliefs from our lives or to at least reduce their toll as much as possible when they are inescapable. Neither task will be easy.

Even recognising distressing factors is difficult in today's fast and furious world. Developing healthful alternatives will require insight and patient practice, in short a new kind of ascetical ideal. Finding ways to relax, reducing the relentless pace of work-related assignments, following a balanced diet, getting sufficient exercise and simply taking the time to get a full night's sleep instead of relying on caffeinated drinks to stay alert during ever-longer work periods will allow the natural healing powers of the body and mind to refresh and re-create us day by day. The alterative, as Hans Selye warned decades ago, is to tap into our vital reserves of energy, thereby imperiling our health and probably shortening our lives.

Recent reports published in the United States predict that it is very likely that the children of the present generation will have shorter life spans than their parents and grandparents. Although mainly the result of childhood obesity caused by today's high-fat diet and lack of exercise, other stress factors contribute to the problem.[20] The same pattern is found in other parts of the world as well. One way or another, in the coming decades stress factors are likely to increase in intensity and scope, whether as overload or deprivation, 'eustress' or distress. Finding ways to mitigate the harmful effects of such pressures will become an ever-greater necessity in personal and social spiritualities. As all spirituality begins with the body, physical de-stressing should concern us first, but we should attend as well to psychological and spiritual stress.

As we are living in an increasingly indolent society, ordinary physical exercise has been displaced by a wide range of 'labour-saving' devices and opportunities. For many urbanites, recourse takes the form of memberships in gymnasiums (or 'health clubs') of one kind or another, many of which feature machines that duplicate calorie-burning, muscle-building activities that were once just part of daily life. It is darkly amusing, especially in a university setting, to see undergraduates ascending one or two storeys in lifts that are adjacent to a staircase. The irony is not reduced by finding youngsters later working out on 'stair machines' or treadmills in the exercise room.

It is possible (and much less expensive) to get a good-enough workout by 'ordinary exercise' – walking, climbing stairs, housekeeping, gardening and engaging in recreational or competitive sports such as hiking, swimming, running, bicycling, tennis and ball games. Twenty or thirty minutes a day of brisk walking (or climbing stairs, for that matter) burns calories and can provide a good cardio-vascular workout. One way or the other, sufficient physical exercise, a healthy diet and (as we shall see) some application of 'mental hygienics' and spiritual care can offset many of the detrimental effects of stress. Mental and spiritual health 'exercises' will be considered at greater length in later chapters.

Closely allied to rest, exercise and good nutrition in the quest for a healthy 'spirituality of the body' are the necessities and, sometimes, the indulgences associated with grooming and cosmetics. Here too, body care encompasses much more than physiological fitness. How we look 'skin-deep' is both psychologically and spiritually significant.

Looking Good: Grooming, Health and Hygiene

Our skin is the largest organ of our bodies. Much more than the flexible container that keeps our insides inside, it is part of the respiratory system, the peripheral and central nervous system, the circulatory system, the reproductive system and the immune system. Skin care is thus of immense importance for health. Regrettably, it tends to be overlooked or even discounted as a source of vanity and self-indulgence. Among classical spiritual writers, 'looking good' has never ranked as high as has being good and doing good. Cosmetics and couture, especially *haute couture*, were usually regarded as dangerous if not sinful. According to the apocryphal but nevertheless influential pre-Christian Book of Enoch, the arts of cosmetology (and other arts) were in fact given to the human race by the demon Azazel to lure them from the path of righteousness.[21] This attitude of distrust is echoed in the First Epistles of Peter and Timothy and was conveyed eventually to Clement of Alexandria, the early Christian teacher.

According to the author of 1 Peter: 'Let not yours be the outward adorning with braiding of hair, decoration of gold, and wearing of fine clothing, but let it be the hidden person of the heart with the imperishable jewel of a gentle and quiet spirit, which in God's sight is very precious' (3:3). The later epistle reads: 'I desire then that in every place the men should pray, lifting holy hands without anger or quarrelling; also that women should adorn themselves modestly and sensibly in seemly apparel, not with braided hair or gold or pearls or costly attire but by good deeds, as befits women who profess religion' (1 Tim 2:8-10).

Rather than a passing caution, Clement devoted an entire chapter of one of his great books to the lure and danger of cosmetology:

> So those women who wear gold, occupying themselves in curling their locks, and engaged in anointing their cheeks, painting their eyes, and dyeing their hair, and practising the other pernicious arts of luxury, decking the covering of flesh – in truth, imitate the Egyptians, in order to attract their infatuated lovers.[22]

In more recent times, William Stringfellow (1929–1985) gave a sobering if stern interpretation that is not far removed from that of Clement:

> Where the uses of cosmetics are not corrupted (as they are in America) they serve to indicate some sort of position in society or to enhance the beauty of the human body. Of course opinions vary in different societies as to what enhances the beauty of the body. In some societies what would be thought attractive might in another be thought ugly or mutilating. But in our society cosmetics are increasingly used by both women and men to serve the ideal of mass conformity; to make everybody look like everybody else. Usually the standards of conformity in such matters are identified with some public idol such as a movie star or other public figure, and therefore they tend to create a deception.[23]

Despite such cautions, which especially in a historical context are not as extreme as they might sound (Roman matrons sometimes spent entire days as well as fortunes having themselves made up for evening parties), grooming and hygiene are essential elements of health – cleansing, skin care, hair care, attention to nails and cuticles, and the ordinary tasks of keeping 'fit' are not only expressive of how we feel about ourselves but also how we regard others. Self-presentation is communication. Conversely, bodily disfigurement and ill-treatment, sometimes associated with religious asceticism, also indicates psychological distress and, in many cultures, social distress, as when people scratch, scar, mutilate and brand themselves, shave off their hair, beat themselves bloody, put dirt and ashes on themselves, and otherwise deface their bodies whether as part of ritual expressions of grief, guilt, or repentance, or in the case of pathology, a disordered mind. Sometimes it is not easy to distinguish between them.

Despite Jesus' injunction not to disfigure our faces when we fast, for over a thousand years Christians have resolutely rubbed ashes onto their foreheads at the beginning of Lent. It's a curiously Catholic custom, but not exclusively so. I am told that even non-Christians sometimes present themselves on Ash Wednesday to receive their ashes and be told that they are dust and will return to dust. *Memento mori*.

The temptation of pursuing the thread of religious customs of bodily decoration and disfigurement into the labyrinth of the history of religions will have to wait another day. Here, I wish only to sketch a few parameters of spirituality and health care as they concern taking care of our bodies externally as an expression of reverence and compassion – for ourselves as well as for others. If, dear reader, you cannot remember the last time someone anointed your hair or feet with oil, read on (perhaps after reading Mark 14:3 and John 12:1-8).[24]

The Oil of Gladness
Enoch notwithstanding, in the biblical tradition moderation rather than severity was the norm and, ideally, the practice, as we saw in the instructions to Timothy: 'I desire ... that women should adorn themselves modestly and sensibly in seemly apparel ... as befits women who profess religion' (1 Tim 2:8-10). Older traditions arose from life in

desert conditions, where grooming was not mere adornment, but life-preserving. Oil was necessary to prevent desiccation of the skin and hair. But like other aspects of life, the oil of gladness was more than functional – it was used to welcome and celebrate, to heal, and in ritual gestures to initiate prophets, priests and kings. (It still is, at least in the latter instances.) It is not beside the point to recall that 'Christ' comes from the same root as 'chrism', the oil of anointing.

The so-called 'Royal' psalms frequently mention oil and anointing:

> Your divine throne endures for ever and ever.
>
> Your royal scepter is a scepter of equity;
> you love righteousness and hate wickedness.
>
> Therefore God, your God, has anointed you with the oil of gladness above your fellows;
> your robes are all fragrant with myrrh and aloes and cassia.
>
> (Ps 45:6-8)

In the Book of Isaiah, the messianic character of anointing is used to great effect, a point notable in Jesus' citation of this passage in his own inaugural sermon:

> The Spirit of the Lord God is upon me,
> because the Lord has anointed me to bring good tidings to the afflicted;
> he has sent me to bind up the brokenhearted,
> to proclaim liberty to the captives,
> and the opening of the prison to those who are bound;
> to proclaim the year of the Lord's favour, and the day of vengeance of our God;
> to comfort all who mourn;
> to grant to those who mourn in Zion –
> to give them a garland instead of ashes,
> the oil of gladness instead of mourning,
> the mantle of praise instead of a faint spirit;
> that they may be called oaks of righteousness,
> the planting of the Lord, that he may be glorified.
>
> (Isa 61:1-3)

Today, aided by recent discoveries about the effects of sunlight on skin cells, the risk of cancer and just the process of accelerated ageing because of exposure to wind, weather and the aridity of indoor air, the use of moisturisers, oils, unguents and emollients has become more or less necessary for basic skin health. The art of massage has hygienic as well as therapeutic uses, not to say personal and social ones, and fragrant oils are often associated with the custom and practice.

The multiple connections among body image, self-concept, spirituality and both psychological and sociological health are tight. As St Thomas Aquinas affirmed centuries ago, our bodies are the manifestation of our souls – in many respects, what you see is indeed what you get. Body language is more eloquent than speech and communicates more effectively, and thus has an important social dimension. Like our clothing, the way we look, our 'grooming' announces us to the world. It informs others of how we feel about ourselves and how we feel about them. That language can, moreover, have many dialects – scarification and tattooing (culturally much more important today than at any time in the recent past) were highly developed in ancient cultures, just as branding was used to indicate the status of a slave or prisoner.

The spirituality of grooming is nowhere more evident than in its lack. Those in ill health cannot tend to their physical appearance, which may well increase their discomfort. I remember visiting my aged mother in a nursing home where she was recuperating from a leg fracture. When I asked what I could get for her to make her stay more comfortable, she said, 'I want to have my hair washed and done up'. Those suffering from mental distress or 'illness' are prone to disregard even the most basic conventions concerning grooming and dress. The more serious their condition, the more likely they are to regress to very primitive forms of hygiene and self-care.

Social distress and dis-ease, such as extreme poverty and alienation, also announce themselves in rags and disfigurement. (Of course, even wealth may become manifest in bizarre forms of dress and cosmetics, as seen in the late Roman Empire, the Byzantine court, the late Middle Ages, and the last gasps of eighteenth-century aristocratic excess.) Conversely, therapeutic intervention may well begin with what is, in fact, most obvious – redirecting attention to self-care in hygiene, grooming and dress. Looking good does help people to feel good. In turn, increased self-confidence and self-appreciation can lead to greater integration at all levels of personal and social interaction.

In extreme cases, cosmetic surgery, far from being the extravagant and desperate attempt of the socially hyper-conscious to ward off visible signs of ageing, is a medical art that can restore dignity, wholeness and the possibility of happiness to persons who have been disfigured by accident at birth or physical misadventure. One of the most deeply impressive encounters I had when visiting the orphanage of the Missionaries of Charity in Baghdad in 2001 was learning about their programme of sending facially disfigured Iraqi babies to Australia for corrective surgery, something their impoverished and embattled parents could never afford. One of most deserving of charities is surely the Smile Train, an organisation that provides corrective surgery for impoverished children throughout the world who were born with facial clefts.[25]

Our public, 'daytime' experience constitutes only a part of our physical, psychological and spiritual health (or, for that matter, illth). We also devote a third of our life to behaviour that on first consideration must seem odd and even wasteful. Yet sleep and dreams are intimately connected to all these areas of health and holiness and it is to the realm of rest and the 'visions of the night' that we turn next.

NOTES

1. See in particular Leviticus 1-3, 6-7, 11, 17, 19; Numbers 28; Deuteronomy 14. Much of this material focuses on appropriate sacrifice, but overall forms the basis of the food laws of Israel.

2. The observations of anthropologist Claude Lévi-Strauss in *The Raw and the Cooked* (London: Jonathan Cape, 1970 and Chicago: University of Chicago Press, 1983), like those of Mircea Eliade, *The Sacred and the Profane: The Nature of Religion* (London: Harcourt, Brace, and Jovanovich, 1959), and Piero Camporesi in regard to the development of the Italian diet, *The Magic Harvest:*

Food, Folklore and Society (Cambridge: Polity Press, 1994) are especially illuminating in this regard.

3. For recent explorations of this theme as it pertains to the United States, see especially Eric Schlosser, *Fast Food Nation* (New York: Harper Perennial, 2005 ed.) and Morgan Spurlock, *Don't Eat This Book: Fast Food and the Supersizing of America* (New York: Berkley Books, 2005).

4. See Dorothy J. Pattison, Deborah P.M. Symmons et al., 'Dietary Risk Factors for the Development of Inflammatory Polyarthritis: Evidence for a Role of High Level of Red Meat Consumption', *Arthritis & Rheumatism* 50 (December 2004) 12:3804–12.

5. In 2006, a class of chemicals found in grapefruit known as furanocoumarins was identified as the cause of the interaction with medications. See Mary F. Paine, Wilbur W. Widmer, Heather L. Hart et al., 'A furanocoumarin-free grapefruit juice establishes furanocoumarins as the mediators of the grapefruit juice–felodipine interaction 1,2,3', *American Journal of Clinical Nutrition* 83 (May 2006) 5:1097–105.

6. The results of research related to hepatitis C conducted by Dr Raymond Chung, Associate Professor of Medicine at Harvard Medical School and Director of Hepatology at Massachusetts General Hospital, where he is also Director of the Liver Transplant unit, will be published shortly in the journal *Hepatology*.

7. The expansive effects of alcohol with regard to religion were eloquently noted by William James, himself a physician, in his famed study of religion, *The Varieties of Religious Experience*: 'The sway of alcohol over mankind is unquestionably due to its power to stimulate the mystical faculties of human nature, usually crushed to earth by the cold facts and dry criticisms of the sober hour. Sobriety diminishes, discriminates, and says no; drunkenness expands, unites, and says yes. To the poor and the unlettered it stands in the place of symphony concerts and of literature.' William James, *The Varieties of Religious Experience*, foreword by Jacques Barzun (New York: New American Library, 1958 ed., p. 297).

8. For a bountiful review of the healthful properties of beer, see the on-line resource www.myubrew.ca/Health%20and%20Beer.htm.

9. 'Red wines may defend against food-borne pathogens', *Medical Research News*, Sunday, 14 Oct 2007. www.news-medical.net/?id=31114.

10. Meir J. Stampfer, MD, Jae Hee Kang, Sc.D. et al., 'Effects of Moderate Alcohol Consumption on Cognitive Function in Women', *New England Journal of Medicine* 352 (January 20, 2005) 3:245–53.

11. Paul Murray, OP, *The New Wine of Dominican Spirituality: A Drink Called Happiness* (London and New York: Burns & Oates, 2006).

12. The motif is much earlier, of course. In his first Letter to the Corinthians, St Paul writes: 'The cup of blessing which we bless, is it not a participation in the blood of Christ? The bread which we break, is it not a participation in the body

of Christ?' (1 Cor 10:16); and again: 'In the same way also the cup, after supper, saying, "This cup is the new covenant in my blood. Do this, as often as you drink it, in remembrance of me". For as often as you eat this bread and drink the cup, you proclaim the Lord's death until he comes' (1 Cor 11:25-26).

13.	For the fasts of Mel Ruain and the discipline of the Célí Dé, 'the Friends of God', see Peter O'Dwyer, O.Carm., *Célí Dé: Spiritual Reform in Ireland 750–900* (Dublin: Editions Tailliura, 1981 ed.), p. 80 *et passim*.

14.	Deepak Chopra, *Ageless Body, Timeless Mind: The Quantum Alternative to Growing Old* (New York: Harmony Books, 1993), pp. 130–4.

15.	Portions of the following reflections stem from reviewing my 1983 book, *Symbion: Spirituality for a Possible Future* in which I tried to anticipate the problems and possibilities of food futures. It is mildly deflating to note how little things seem to have changed.

16.	The physical, social and religious dimensions of food and drink are explored from a variety of spiritual perspectives in Michael Schut's remarkable anthology *Food and Faith: Justice, Joy and Daily Bread* (Denver: Living the Good News, 2002).

17.	Tarani Chandola, Annie Britton, Eric Brunner, et al., 'Work stress and coronary heart disease: what are the mechanisms?' *European Heart Journal* 29, 5:640–8, first published online on 23 Jan 2008.

18.	See above, Chapter 3, note 10.

19.	On Selye's contributions to psychosomatic medicine and the role of stress in health and disease, see Anne Harrington, op. cit., pp. 148–54 *et passim*. Many of Selye's seminal works are still widely available: *Stress without Distress* (New York: Signet, 1975), *The Stress of Life* (New York: McGraw Hill, 1956) and 'Stress: The Basis of Illness', in *Inner Balance*, ed. by Elliott Goldwag (New York: Prentice-Hall, 1979).

20.	See David S. Ludwig, MD, Ph.D., 'Childhood Obesity – The Shape of Things to Come', *The New England Journal of Medicine* 357 (6 Dec 2007) 23:2325–7, and S. Jay Olshansky, Ph.D., Douglas J. Passaro, MD, Ronald C. Hershow, MD, et al., 'A Potential Decline in Life Expectancy in the United States in the 21st Century', *The New England Journal of Medicine* 352 (17 Mar 2005) 11:1138–45.

21.	The first part of 1 Enoch, known as 'The Book of Watchers', relates that 'Azazel taught men to make swords, and knives, and shields, and breastplates, and made known to them metals and the art of working them, and bracelets, and ornaments, and the use of antimony, and the beautifying of the eyelids, and all kinds of costly stones, and all colouring tinctures. And there arose much godlessness, and they committed fornication, and they were led astray, and became corrupt in all their ways' (1 Enoch 2, 8:1-2).

22.	*The Pedagogue*, Book III, ch. 2, 'Against Embellishing the Body'. The comparatively liberal Alexandrian goes on to lament, 'But if one withdraw the veil of the temple, I mean the head-dress, the dye, the clothes, the gold, the paint, the cosmetics – that is, the web consisting of them, the veil, with the view of finding within the true beauty, he will be disgusted, I know well. For he will not find the image of God dwelling within, as is meet; but instead of it a fornicator and adulteress has occupied the shrine of the soul. And the true beast will thus be detected – an ape smeared with white paint. And that deceitful serpent, devouring the understanding part of man through vanity, has the soul as its hole, filling all with deadly poisons; and injecting his own venom of deception, this pander of a dragon has changed women into harlots. For love of display is not for a lady, but a courtesan.'

23. William Stringfellow, *Instead of Death* (New York: Seabury Press, 1976 ed.), p. 48.

24. These accounts are also found in Matthew 26:7-12 and Luke 7:36-50, indicating their rootedness in the tradition.

25. For information, contact The Smile Train, 245 Fifth Ave., Suite 2201, New York, NY 10016. www.SmileTrain.org.

CHAPTER EIGHT
THE NIGHT WORLD
THE SPIRITUALITY OF SLEEP
AND DREAMS

I will both lie down and sleep in peace; for you alone,
O Lord , make me lie down in safety.
Psalm 4:8

Sleep and dreams have both fascinated and worried spiritual seekers from the beginnings of recorded history. In almost every culture, dreams in particular were believed to reveal not only our inner selves but the directives of God and other spirits, as the Bible itself amply testifies. But they were also the source of temptation and a symbol of vanity and the evanescence of life. 'As when a hungry man dreams he is eating and awakes with his hunger not satisfied, or as when a thirsty man dreams he is drinking and awakes faint, with his thirst not quenched, so shall the multitude of all the nations be that fight against Mount Zion' (Isa 29:8).[1]

Today, sleep has gained greater attention among health researchers than perhaps at any time in history, and dreams continue to fascinate and worry us, not least because of the pioneering work of Sigmund Freud and the decades of dream research that followed.[2] We now recognise sleep, a good eight hours of it, as a necessary component of physical and mental health. But in the classical 'desert spirituality' of Christian antiquity, sleep was often regarded as the enemy of progress. The 'old men' devoted considerable energy to resisting the onset of sleep and depriving themselves of as much sleep as possible.

To be sure, sleep deprivation can heighten awareness and produce altered states of consciousness, sometimes highly exalted ones.

Among other saints, Catherine of Siena is noteworthy for having slept little and toward the end of her short life, some scholars believe, not at all. In our own era, Thomas Edison and John F. Kennedy slept very little at night, preferring to obtain rest by catching 'cat naps' during the day. (Cats sleep more than many animals, as much as sixteen hours a day, but not all at once. Like dogs, but unlike teenaged humans, they also possess the uncanny ability of instant arousal. Bats and opossums sleep even more than cats, up to twenty hours a day, while horses, elephants and giraffes sleep very little – only about two to four hours a day.)[3]

The saints had their reasons for despising sleep, but as a rule, getting sufficient sleep is, by contemporary standards, not only beneficial for physical and psychological health, but spiritual well-being also. Prolonged sleep deprivation is both useless and harmful. So is excessive sleep, of course. But the pressures of modern urban life prod people toward sleep reduction, a trend that is worrisome for several reasons. Overall, it is as true of sleep and dreams as any other dimension of our life experience that functional, symbolic and sacramental levels reveal their place and value in a spirituality of wellness.

Resting
In Shakespeare's great Scottish play, Macbeth and Lady Macbeth both suffer the loss of sleep over their bloody acts, but it is Macbeth himself who utters the great tribute:

> Sleep that knits up the ravell'd sleeve of care,
> The death of each day's life, sore labour's bath,
> Balm of hurt minds, great nature's second course,
> Chief nourisher in life's feast,– [4]

Clinical studies have in fact revealed that several hours of deep night sleep is especially health-protective. The production of melatonin, a hormone secreted by the pineal gland that regulates sleep, is stimulated by darkness. Night-shift workers who lack melatonin seem to show an increased susceptibility to cancer, which argues that sleep may protect us in unsuspected ways beyond getting simple rest and recuperation.[5]

Sleep may be even more important to us psychologically and spiritually, for as Sigmund Freud came to realise a century ago, sleep is rather the guardian of dreams than the other way around, as he first thought. Dreams are even more mentally, emotionally and spiritually beneficial or, I suggest, necessary for optimum health than the fundamental physical rest we derive from sleep. And while sleep deprivation is physically harmful, dream deprivation can be even more injurious. Experiments have shown that over a period of days subjects deprived of dream-sleep, but allowed to get sufficient non-dream sleep, soon develop signs of distress – agitation, anxiety, depression and even disorders such as hallucinations. (Thus the common practice of forcing young duty doctors to remain awake for twenty-four to forty-eight hours at a stretch is, one can argue, simply insane. I know of several instances in which interns became dependent on amphetamines and other drugs in a desperate effort to remain awake, and other cases in which they were virtually sleep walking.)[6]

Sleep Patterns
Sleep needs and patterns vary by age and physical condition. Newborn babies and infants sleep not so much irregularly as very frequently and relatively briefly, but the short periods gradually coalesce into progressively longer periods of wakefulness and sleep. By the age of three or four, a regular pattern of approximately eight hours of sleep tends to predominate, although sleep needs continue to vary from person to person. Adolescents also need more sleep than adults and it is the last sleep of the night that is most productive of healthy growth. Forcing teenagers to rise early to suit the schedules of school administrators thus does more harm than good. The adolescent's physiological need for that early morning sleep also explains why it is so difficult to awaken them on time for a good breakfast and the bus. (It should be noted that Japanese researchers have concluded from long-term studies that rising before 5 a.m. seems to be unhealthy in general.)[7]

If infants and adolescents need proportionately more sleep during periods of rapid growth, the elderly need proportionately less. But on the whole, adult humans need to sleep about eight hours per night. We are diurnal animals, after all. And it should be noted that despite individual differences, sleeping significantly more or less than eight hours can be a sign or even a cause of illth. Recent studies conducted at University College London indicate that persons who regularly sleep less than the standard eight hours tend to die at an earlier age from heart-related illness than those who sleep more. But those who slept over nine hours a night were also likely to die from both cardio-vascular disease and other causes.[8]

Among other benefits of getting a good night's sleep, cognitive abilities in general and memory in particular are enhanced by good sleep habits.[9] Even napping, which can be a heart-healthy remedy for job-related stresses, tends to improve the retention of learned information according to researchers.[10] Like Guinness, both sleep and siestas are good for you – physically, psychologically and, as we shall see, spiritually.

Sleep Aids
For those who find it difficult to get to sleep or stay asleep, help is available, other than reliance on stupefying sedatives and soporifics, which can interfere not only with dreaming but memory, as well as producing a host of side effects, including confusion and lethargy. More natural remedies include diet, exercise, appropriate music and relaxation techniques.

Most helpful among foods that induce and maintain sleep are milk products and poultry, which contain tryptophan, an amino acid from which melatonin is synthesised. For many people, a turkey sandwich and a glass of milk (it need not be warm) can assist in falling asleep, although a hefty snack immediately before retiring is probably less helpful than an earlier one. Other sleep-inducing foods include bananas, honey, oatmeal, potatoes and nuts, especially almonds. Carbohydrates such as those found in whole-grain bread, pasta, beans and some seafood – tuna, salmon and other fish – can also help.

Coffee, tea and soft drinks containing caffeine should, of course, be avoided.

Being too rested can actually interfere with sleep, so a brisk walk after dinner or a swim later on can set the scene for a good night's sleep. Vigorous exercise immediately before bedtime has the opposite effect. But gentle breathing exercises and progressive muscle relaxation dispose the body for rest. Reading in bed may or may not help, but it is not advisable to keep a light on in the bedroom during sleep, as melatonin is produced when it is dark. So having a television on is more likely to interfere than assist in falling asleep.

Music can assist, however – provided it is the right kind of music. Some experiments have shown that the regular rhythms of baroque music (Bach, Buxtehude, Haydn, Handel and Mozart, for instance) are more relaxing than later classical music, jazz, or (not surprisingly) rock 'n' roll.[11] (I'm told that hens also prefer Mozart as an accompaniment to their egg-laying efforts. If there's a connection there, it may have to do with rhythms of relaxation.)[12]

Commercially available and inexpensive melatonin tablets can also be of help in falling asleep and staying asleep, especially to older people whose pineal gland does not produce as much of the sleep-regulating hormone as it does for younger folks. Herbal remedies such as teas or capsules can also enhance sleep and if taken in moderation have few if any side effects – among them valerian and chamomile (although as it belongs to the same family as ragwort, it can trigger allergic reactions in some people).

It may well be, and scientific study seems to indicate that it is the case, that, if fundamentally healthy, we do not ordinarily need a full eight hours to get the bodily rest and recuperation required for the next day's tasks. Rather, it is the psychological and (I would add) the spiritual benefits of sleep that make longer sleep periods helpful and even necessary. For it is in the later hours of sleep especially that we enter the realm of dreams.

Perchance to Dream: Psychological and Spiritual Reintegration

Sleep has a manifest physiological function: to gain rest and allow the body to regenerate its energies, to grow and to heal. But the psychological and spiritual benefits of sleep are not only important but deeply fascinating – fundamentally, in the form of those 'visions of the night' that help us reintegrate our experience with regard to the social and spiritual worlds we inhabit by day. Thus, like so many aspects of life, sleep, and especially dreams, have the familiar dialectical pattern of cumulatively ascending value – function, symbol and sacrament.

Everyone dreams, whether they recall having them or not, and we dream in stages, usually having four or five dream periods each night, separated by periods of deeper, dreamless sleep. As the night progresses, the length of the dream period increases, from about ten or fifteen minutes to as long as forty-five minutes or an hour. The dreamless periods of intervening sleep become progressively lighter and shorter as well, thus permitting easier recall after awakening.

Significantly, the earliest dreams of the night tend to focus on recent physical experience, while the later dreams turn on more coherent and psychologically relevant experiences that may have happened some time before.[13] The last period of sleep, when our dreams are longer and, because sleep is lighter, more easily remembered, tends to focus on more profound dimensions of life experience, ranging back to early childhood experience and possibly future or anticipated experience.[14] Such dreams are more coherent and often seem very real, as well as deeply meaningful and emotionally intense. (Some of the creative breakthroughs and spiritual insights gained in dream experience tend to occur during these later periods, which is a good reason not to shorten the sleep cycle unnecessarily.) But dreams during this period can also be profoundly disturbing. If we awake in fear, we regard the distressing dreams we were having as a 'nightmare', a felt danger or threat, when it is in fact a necessary moment in our personality development.[15]

Thus the physiological function of dreams helps to integrate experience by enabling us to process physical leftovers of daily experience, especially stressful events, including hormones and enzymes such as adrenalin and noradrenalin. Psychological integration can take place during the middle stages of dream-sleep as we incorporate new learnings into our repertoire of behavioural assets symbolically, disclosing and possibly enhancing our infra-psychic needs and interpersonal relationships. Spiritual meaning, even revelation, can occur in the final dreams of the sleep cycle, which makes them in some respects the most valuable sleep experiences of all. As the Bible itself testifies, such dreams can have truly sacramental efficacy, as we receive inspiration or guidance and even gain some sense of the presence of God symbolised by material signs.

What is a Dream?
Etymologically, 'dream' is a Middle English word that arose from the Old Saxon word *drôm* and the Old High German *troum* (modern *traum*). Scholars conjecture that the root meaning, from *dreug* or *draug*, is 'to deceive' or 'delude', as reflected in the Old Norse *draugr*, 'ghost'. In short, the original meaning of dream suggested deceptive appearance or illusion.[16]

The biblical tradition also often regarded dreams as ephemeral, even misleading phantasms of the night. (Some of the more negative citations include the following: Gen 37:19; Deut 13:1-5, 18:10; Ps 73:20; Eccl 5:3 -7; Isa 29:7 -8; and Jer 23:27-32.) Litanies of such quotations can be marshalled today to disparage dreamwork, but only at the expense of the more positive view of dreams that emerges in both Hebrew scripture and Christian writings. (Some of the passages that regard dreams favourably include Gen 20:3, 28:12, 31:10-11, 37:5-10, 46:2; Num 12:6; 1 Sam 3:2ff; 1 Kings 3:5; and Job 33:13-17. Christian references include Mt 1:20, 27:19; and Acts 16: 9). Two of the most famous dreamers of the Bible were both named Joseph, and each was guided by dreams to save their people (and both were instructed to journey to Egypt and back) – Gen 41:1-15, 42:9; and Mt 1:20; 2:12-22. Another great dreamer was the prophet Daniel (Dan 1:17, 2:1-3, 7:7-8:23), and the prophecy of Joel is cited in the Acts of the Apostles as a sign of fulfillment of the ages: 'your old men shall dream dreams and your young men shall see visions' (Joel 2:28; and Acts 2:17).

In later Christian periods, despite the ascetical suspicion that sleep deprived spiritual seekers time to devote to prayer and good works, dreams and dream interpretation were favoured in both the Eastern and Western churches.[17] However, caution was normally urged lest misunderstanding or deception distort the meaning that could be derived from their study and interpretation. Guides modelled on the *oneirokritica* (dream-interpretation manuals) of the ancient Greeks were therefore devised by Christian writers. A fifth-century Christian bishop, Synesius of Cyrene, wrote his book *De Insomniis* ('Concerning Dreams') before he was baptised, but he never recanted it. It deals with the causes and meaning of dreams, and still represents a deeply Christian and spiritual attitude toward the world of our dreams:

> Intellectual application is the most incisive weapon against those things which combine to injure the *pneuma*, for this mysteriously refines it and raises it towards God; and when it has become adapted to it, draws the divine *pneuma* by its kindred nature to association with the soul.
>
> We, therefore, have set ourselves to speak of divination through dreams, that men should not despise it, but rather cultivate it, seeing that it fulfils a service to life; and it is to this end that we have so much occupied ourselves with the imaginative nature. ... [A] better fruit of a sane spirit is the uplifting of the soul, a really sacred gain; so that it becomes a sort of cult of piety to endeavour that this form of divination should be ours.[18]

The ninth-century Patriarch Nicephorus of Constantinople, who is considered a saint by the Orthodox Church because of his courage during the iconoclast controversy, also penned a volume on the interpretation of dreams, including the following advice:

> Before you can even hope for the future to be revealed to you in dreams, you must learn to know yourself and to dominate your passions and carnal appetites. When you are master of yourself, if you go to sleep, first having prayed to God, you may see some symbolic images representing future events. But if your belly is loaded with meat, if you have drunk more wine than is fitting,

you will be obsessed by trivial fantasies, and your spirit will be lost in the realm of darkness.[19]

One of the most telling remarks about the spiritual potency of dreams came from someone who might be expected to be an unfriendly witness (as Morton Kelsey erroneously claims): St Thomas Aquinas. Concerning the possibility of experiencing revelation in our dreams, this most rational of theologians wrote: 'the more our soul is abstracted from physical things, the more it is capable of receiving abstract intelligible things. Hence in dreams and alienation of the bodily senses, divine revelations and foresight of future events are perceived the more clearly' (*Summa Theologiae* I, Q. 12, A. 11).

Even in regard to knowledge of future events, Thomas reckoned that aided by impressions of superior spiritual or physical causes, it was at least possible:

> The soul is naturally more inclined to receive these impressions of spiritual causes when it is withdrawn from the senses, as it is then nearer the spiritual world, and freer from external distractions. The same may be said for physical causes ... such as the influence of heavenly bodies, which operate on the imagination just as they do on future events (*Summa Theologiae* I, Q. 86, A. 4, ad 2).

Importantly, the images produced 'are perceived more at night while we are asleep than in the daytime and while we are awake ...'

Creative Dreaming

Today, medical science has turned to the study of sleep and dreams from a wide range of perspectives, from basic physiology to psychiatry. Sigmund Freud was not the first healer to employ dreams as an aid in the diagnosis and treatment of physical and mental illth, but he revolutionised the study of dreams in what he called 'psychoanalysis' as 'the royal road to the unconscious'. He rightly foresaw that his great book *On the Interpretation of Dreams* would be one of the most important works of the early twentieth century and delayed its publication until 1901 to underscore his point.

Our understanding of dreams has developed immensely over the last century, needless to say. Among modern researchers, William C. Dement, Ernest Hartmann and Robert Van de Castle have devoted considerable study to the relationship of dreams, creativity and problem-solving, an aspect of dreaming that was recognised much earlier but left largely alone as a curiosity or anomaly. Quite clearly, however, the creative function of dreaming has had very practical consequences in the arts and sciences.

The evidence is there in some of the greater and lesser discoveries of the modern world. Elias Howe's invention of the lockstitch sewing machine in 1845 was facilitated by a dream, while August Kekulé solved the problem of the structure of the benzene molecule in 1865 by dreaming about snakes. In 1868 Dmitry Mendeleyev recognised the logic of the periodic table because of a dream. In 1896, Herman Helprecht dreamed up the true identity of Babylonian votive cylinders. In 1903, Otto Loewi dreamed about an experiment which he later developed to establish the chemical nature of nerve transmission, a discovery that won him the Nobel Prize in 1936. In 1915 Niels Bohr drew on a dream of the solar system in formulating his model of the structure of the atom for which he won the Nobel Prize in physics in 1922.

Philosophers, artists and literary figures often drew on dreams for their works. René Descartes' choice of a philosophical career hung on a dream, and Gottfried Leibniz also paid close attention to his dreams. The great violin virtuosi Giuseppe Tartini and Niccolo Paganini were both inspired by dreams, and the works they produced were considered so diabolically difficult they were dubbed the 'Devil's Trill' and the 'Devil's Sonata'. Richard Wagner used dream imagery in his great operatic works. Significantly, even nightmares were summoned into service, as Ernest Hartmann recounts:

> Robert Louis Stevenson is well known to have had frequent nightmares and reported using them in his work. *Dr Jekyll and Mr Hyde* was based on a nightmare in which Stevenson saw a man change from a good-looking, upper-class Englishman into a hideous monster ... Mary Shelley is reported to have had

nightmares frequently and to have based her best-known work, *Frankenstein*, on a nightmare.[20]

Among other notable figures whose creative works were influenced by dreams can be counted John Milton, William Blake, Samuel Taylor Coleridge, Bram Stoker, Theodore Dreiser and André Gide. Sir Basil Spence's innovative design for Coventry cathedral was inspired by a dream induced by a dental anaesthetic. Undocumented accounts exist as well for Nathaniel Hawthorne, Goya, Edgar Allen Poe, Tchaikovsky, Mark Twain, Arthur Rimbaud, Dostoevsky, Henry James and Jack Keroac.[21]

Political decisions and critical historical moments often turned on dreams as well, including Hannibal's decision to cross the Alps, Julius Caesar's decision to cross the Rubicon, and Constantine's dream before the battle of the Milvian Bridge that led to the emancipation of Christianity. Abraham Lincoln dreamed of his own assassination and described in detail the scene of his laying in state under the great rotunda.

Holy Dreaming

The explicitly religious and spiritual aspects of dreams and dreaming can be found in many accounts of the lives of saints and holy sages, both East and West, as well as in their writings. One of the most common elements in biographical accounts of great religious figures is a dream experienced by their mothers before their birth, as in the case of the Buddha and Queen Maya. The birth of Jesus was heralded by a number of dreams involving St Joseph according to the Gospel of Matthew, and a puzzling dream by Pilate's wife is mentioned at the end of his life (Mt 27:19).

The prophetic maternal dream became commonplace in medieval saints' lives, being found in the story of St Bernard of Clairvaux and St Dominic, among many others.[22] Dreams also served to guide the paths of missionaries in particular, as we read in the story of St Paul's mission to Macedonia (Acts 16:9) and later, the great mission of St Patrick to the people of Ireland.[23] Similarly, Muhammad, the prophet of Islam, was guided by visions and dreams, as recorded in the Qu'ran (Surah 48:27-28).

One of the most paradigmatic of dreams is that described by Sulpicius Severus in his life of St Martin of Tours who in 335, while still a catechumen according to the well-known story, divided his cloak with his sword at the gate of the city of Amiens to clothe a shivering beggar. That night, Martin dreamed that Jesus appeared to him wrapped in the cloak, an event that led to his baptism that year and his assuming leadership of the church in Gaul.[24] In later periods, dreams proliferate in the stories of saints and mystics, including St Anselm, St Gertrude the Great, Meister Eckhart, St Teresa of Avila and St Thérèse of Lisieux. Clearly, far from being a hindrance to the spiritual life, dreams can become a resource and an avenue of inspiration.

Spiritual Dreamwork

Excellent resources can be found in almost any good bookstore for approaching dreams responsibly and with spiritual profit.[25] Occasionally, a classic source turns up that can be surprisingly apt decades later, as I discovered in flipping through the pages of the classic 1947 work on the intellectual life by the French Dominican scholar A.D. Sertillanges:

> ... sleep itself is a worker, a partner of the daily toil; we can make its forces serve us, utilise its laws, profit by that filtering-process, that clarification which takes place during the self-surrender of the night ... When you wake, you find the collaboration of sleep all performed and recorded. The work of the previous day appears to you in a clearer light; a new path, a virgin region lies before you; some relationship of ideas, of facts, of expressions, some happy comparison or illuminating image, a whole passage perhaps or a plan ready to be realised, will have surged into your consciousness. The whole is there, clear and distinct; you will only need at the right moment to utilise what Hypnos has condescended to do for you.[26]

Sertillanges was, of course, referring to dreams, although, curiously, he never uses the term. But he insightfully suggested that a person of study 'have at hand a scribbling-block or box of slips. Make a note without waking up too fully, without turning on the light, if possible ...' Like modern dreamwork coaches, Sertillanges realised that dreams are evanescent, quickly vanishing from memory as the mind turns to the work of the day. Having a notepad and a pencil nearby for jotting down the insights we receive in dreams remains wise counsel, if today we are more inclined to keep a dream journal as well, collecting and interpreting our dream life on an on-going basis. Sertillanges also realised that arising and fumbling for the light switch, in addition to searching for a pad and pencil, would probably drive the dream out of mind. As I found to my consternation, trying to write in the dark can be self-defeating. Having a penlight or a nearby lamp for necessary illumination is a very good idea. Today, dream-workers are also able to use voice-activated digital or tape recorders, an electronic blessing that Sertillanges never envisioned.

Sertillanges' approach was admittedly intellectual, as befit his theme. But a purely functional, intellectual, problem-solving approach to dreams would keep dreamwork at a very elementary if nevertheless profitable level. Allowing the creative imagination and mind to rise to artistic and spiritual heights reveals the full scope of our night-time experience, one that, as we recognised at the beginning, is also a time of blessing and growth.

Truly integrative spirituality is, first of all, our embodied response to the wonder and mystery of life. Food and drink, exercise and recreation, hygiene, grooming, even sleep and dreams, are not mere components of physical, mental and spiritual wellness, but the ways and means by which we balance and integrate our lives, the expression of our personal identity and place in the world. Having considered a few of the ways in which we incorporate these primarily physical dimensions into our spiritual lives, we turn next to some of the mental and emotional aspects of health and illth.

NOTES

1. See also Ecclesiastes 5:3, 7: 'For dreams come with many cares, and a fool's voice with many words ... For when dreams increase, empty words grow many: but do you fear God.'

2. Among many excellent resources available today I especially recommend William C. Dement and Christopher Vaughan, *The Promise of Sleep: A Pioneer in Sleep Medicine Explores the Vital Connection Between Health, Happiness, and a Good Night's Sleep* (New York: Dell, 2000) and Robert L. Van de Castle, *Our Dreaming Mind* (New York: Ballantine, 1994).

3. For an excellent article on animals and sleep, see Jessica Marshall, 'To Sleep, Perchance to Dream', *Zoogoer*, Nov–Dec 2007, Smithsonian National Zoological Park. nationalzoo.si.edu/Publications/ZooGoer/2007/6/To_Sleep_Perchance_to_Dream.cfm.

4. *Macbeth*, I, ii, 38–42.

5. See, among other resources, Vijayalaxmi, Charles R. Thomas, Jr., Russel J. Reiter, Terence S. Herman, 'Melatonin: From Basic Research to Cancer Treatment Clinics', *Journal of Clinical Oncology* 20 (May 2002) 10:2575–601, and A.N. Viswanathan, S.E. Hankinson and E.S. Schernhammer, 'Night Shift Work and the Risk of Endometrial Cancer', *Cancer Research* 67 (1 Nov 2007) 21:10618–22.

6. Norman Cousins rightly called for major reform of what is by any humane or professional standard a punitive and pointless hazing of young doctors during their internship in *Head First*, op. cit., pp. 41–2.

7. See 'The Early Bird Gets Heart Disease', *Heartzine* Magazine 36 (11 Sept 2007) 1. www.heartzine.com/660-The-Early-Bird-Gets-Heart-Disease.html

8. See Jane E. Ferrie, Martin J. Shipley, Francesco P. Cappuccio et al., 'A Prospective Study of Change in Sleep Duration: Associations with Mortality in the Whitehall II Cohort University London Sleep', *Sleep* 30 (2007)12:1659–66.

9. See Jeffrey Ellenbogen, 'Cognitive benefits of sleep and their loss due to sleep deprivation', *Neurology* 64 (2005):25–7.

10. Maria Korman, Avi Karni et al., 'Daytime sleep condenses the time course of motor memory consolidation', *Nature Neuroscience* 10 (2007):1206–13. Published online: 12 August 2007. www.nature.com/neuro/journal/v10/n9/abs/nn1959.html

11. See, for instance, Hui-Ling Lai and Marion Good, 'Music improves sleep quality in older adults', *Journal of Advanced Nursing* 49 (2005) 3:234–44, and László Harmat, Johanna Takács and Róbert Bódizs, 'Music improves sleep quality in students', *Journal of Advanced Nursing* 62 (2008) 3:327–35.

12. For a useful on-line resource, see www.peaceful-sleep.com, especially the page on sound and music.

13. 'Dream contents of awakenings during the first REM-period (say one to five minutes after the start of the period) are predominantly straightforward material referring to events that took place the day of the dream or the few days before. Dream contents of awakenings later during the night and later during a REM-period are more "dream-like" and contain elements from earlier in the dreamer's life – often from childhood …' Ernest Hartmann, *The Nightmare* (New York: Basic Books, 1984), p. 174.

14. Ibid., p. 248.

15. 'The typical nightmare … occurs late during the night (4:00 to 7:00 a.m.) and from a long REM-period – in my experience, the awakening is often twenty to forty minutes or more after the start of a REM-period. Thus, the last part of the nightmare, which is almost always the frightening part just before awakening, comes exactly when one would expect the elements from the dreamer's childhood to emerge.' Hartmann, op. cit., p. 174.

16. See the *Oxford English Dictionary*, Vol. 3, p. 651. It is interesting that the Old English word *drëam* also meant 'joy','pleasure','noise' and 'music'. Although linguistic scholars generally believe that this *drëam* was a different word, it is difficult to account for the fact that the spelling is identical. Could it be that the same word conveyed the sense of pleasure and music as well as deception much as modern usage embraces both meanings – the insubstantial or illusory as well as the unattainably ideal?

17. For an excellent historical study of dreams in early Christian life, see Patricia Cox Miller, *Dreams in Late Antiquity: Studies in the Imagination of a Culture* (Princeton and Chichester: Princeton University Press, 1994).

18. Translation by Augustine Fitzgerald from T*he Essays and Hymns of Synesius of Cyrene* (London: Oxford University Press, 1930). Selections have been included in the appendix of Morton T. Kelsey's *God, Dreams, and Revelation: A Christian Interpretation of Dreams* (Minneapolis: Augsburg Fortress, 1991), pp. 266–78.

19. Cited by Paul Christian in *The History and Practice of Magic* (Whitefish, MT: Kessinger Publishing, 1994 ed.), p. 377–8. Whether the work is authentic remains doubtful, but the Greek manuscript is from the early medieval period.

20. Hartmann, op. cit., p. 122.

21. Ibid.

22. For a sobering account of this tradition, see Simon Tugwell, ed., *Early Dominicans: Selected Writings* (New York and London: Paulist Press, 1982), pp. 53, 104, n. 2; cf. also p. 138.

23. For an excellent discussion of Patrick's prophetic dreams, see Máire B. de Paor, PBVM, ed. and trans., *Patrick the Pilgrim Apostle of Ireland: St Patrick's Confessio and Epistola* (Dublin: Veritas, 1998), pp. 80–4. Also see Noel Dermot O'Donoghue, ODC, *Aristocracy of Soul: Patrick of Ireland* (Wilmington, DE: Michael Glazier, 1987), p. 105 and especially p. 107.

24. See Régine Pernoud, *Martin of Tours: Soldier, Bishop, Saint*, trans. by Michael J. Miller (San Francisco: Ignatius Press, 2006), pp. 27–8.

25. Doubtful souls with a strong biblical background might start by reading Lois Hendricks' fine volume *Discovering My Biblical Dream Heritage* (San Jose, CA: Resource Publications, 1989). Other valuable resources include Kelly Bulkeley, *Spiritual Dreaming: A Cross-Cultural and Historical Journey* (New York: Paulist Press, 1995); James A. Hall, *The Unconscious Christian: Images of God in Dreams*, ed. by Daniel J. Meckel (New York: Paulist Press, 1993); and Jeremy Taylor, *Dream Work: Techniques for Discovering the Creative Power in Dreams* (New York: Paulist Press, 1994).
26. A.D. Sertillanges, OP, *The Intellectual Life*, trans. by Mary Ryan (Cork: Mercier Press, 1962 ed.), pp. 82–3.

CHAPTER NINE
MINDFULNESS
SPIRITUALITY AND MENTAL HEALTH

For nature, crescent, does not grow alone
In thews and bulk; but, as this temple waxes,
The inward service of the mind and soul
Grows wide withal.
Hamlet, Prince of Denmark, I. iii. 16–19

'Optimism, cheerfulness and a positive outlook on life generally help heal and undoubtedly protect us from some of the worst ravages of disease.' Whether this was my own observation or something I quickly jotted down in my notes one day without bothering to identify the source, it summarises not only my personal and professional view but also that of a substantial amount of writing on the subject. How it all came to that takes a bit of explaining, however.

As we have already seen, decades of research have demonstrated the physical health benefits of religious involvement from affiliation to very active participation which are frequently claimed to be associated also with good mental, social and spiritual health. This does not refute the contention of Richard Dawkins and other learned despisers of religion that for some people religious allegiance can foster delusion, mania, intolerance and persecution. But so evidently can politics, commerce, police work, military life, science and even medicine. All these vocations, avocations and professions (and many others) have populated history with villains and monsters, especially it seems when new, unsettling and especially threatening ideas or approaches are afoot. Perhaps we rightly expect more sanity and sheer benevolence, or at least less villainy, from religion than from commerce, science, military occupation and industry, so it is not idle to raise the question more pointedly: is religion also healthy for our mental and emotional life? Or does it inevitably lead to confusion, delusion and unhappiness as Dawkins, Hitchens, Harris, Dennett and other critics claim?

It should be evident at this point that I strongly believe that a contemporary, holistic approach to health encompasses every dimension of human personal and social existence in terms of well-being, traditionally represented by the body-mind-spirit triad. These are only 'tags', however, for enormously complex, interactive systems that are 'mutually entailed', as the expression goes. They are certainly not separate 'parts' of a person or of life. From William James' endorsement of 'psychophysiological parallelism' to Hans Selye's 'psychosomatic medicine', and the latest research in 'psycho-socio-neuro-immunology', the testimony of medical research in particular supports the assertion cited earlier of William Stringfellow with regard to spirituality – pre-eminently so:

> spiritual maturity or spiritual fulfillment necessarily involves the *whole* person – body, mind, soul, place, relationships – in connection with the whole of creation throughout the era of time. Biblical spirituality encompasses the whole person in the totality of existence in the world, not some fragment or scrap or incident of a person.[1]

The holistic nature of Christian spirituality is not a new feature tacked on in response to recent secular trends. It is a perennial characteristic of Christian spirituality as such, one succinctly expressed fifty years ago by a traditionally classic Dominican theologian, Reginald Garrigou-Lagrange (in language regrettably reflecting the sexist bias of the time): 'The interior life is lived in the depths of the soul; it is the life of the whole man, not merely of one or other of his faculties.'[2] Even if we grant all that, the question remains, does religion foster or hinder mental and moral health?

To begin with, wondering how an institution that has been part of the human world since the dawn of history could be physically beneficial to countless persons without being socially and spiritually beneficial and still endure, much less flourish, may just beg the question. But it still poses a problem that warrants exploration. Is religion just another social mechanism for assuring conformity and adaptation? Or is it possible that at least part of the function of religion and spirituality is to disrupt our social complacency, perhaps even inciting mental discomfort by disengaging people from their social base? Could authentic religious experience actually lead to social upheaval?

Mental Illth

The study and treatment of mental dis-ease, whether cognitive disorder or emotional dysfunction, has figured in the theory and practice of healing, particularly within religious traditions, since medicine began. The physical causes and possible cures of psychological disorders were sought by Hippocrates, Aristotle, Galen, and the healers of China, India and the Americas. To alleviate mental or spiritual suffering, primitive if sometimes apparently effective brain surgery was practiced in Egypt and Peru, while what can surely be described as early forms of psychodrama found expression in the rites of healing and alleviation of ancient Judaism and other traditions in the form of exorcism. At the end of the nineteenth century, Sigmund Freud advanced the art of psychiatry immeasurably but not definitively by seizing upon unconscious factors, the role of which was plainly perceived by St Augustine and other writers of antiquity, not least of them St Paul:

> I do not understand my own actions. For I do not do what I want, but I do the very thing I hate. Now if I do what I do not want, I agree that the law is good. But in fact it is no longer I that do it, but sin that dwells within me. For I know that nothing good dwells within me, that is, in my flesh. I can will what is right, but I cannot do it. For I do not do the good I want, but the evil I do not want is what I do. Now if I do what I do not want, it is no longer I that do it, but sin which dwells within me. ... but I see in my members another law at war with the law of my mind and making me captive to the law of sin which dwells in my members (Rom 7:15-20, 23).

What Freud instinctively realised as a doctor is that the likely cause of real mental illth (as distinct from spiritual anguish) lay in the physiology and chemistry of the brain, not in some secret chamber of the mind. But because of the limitations of medical research at the time, he could neither identify nor treat these causes and approached mental disease as if it were the result of culture and behaviour, especially traumatic early childhood experience. And despite his Jewish family background, he came to feel that religion itself was one of the factors productive of mental disorder, both individually and socially.[3]

Debates over Freud, religion and psychoanalysis will no doubt rage on for years to come. From my perspective, I am convinced that Freud not only failed to make his case, which was already substantially demolished by the work of William James, but over the last century, an impressive body of clinical information has continued to accumulate that more than suggests that a healthy religious life generally contributes to a healthy mental and emotional life. Recent studies indicate that positive religious attitudes benefit people suffering from a variety of persistent mental illnesses and that both research and treatment could profitably address this area.[4] And as the treatment of mental illness has advanced astonishingly with the development of drugs that balance the chemical elements in the brain, the positive role played by faith has begun to emerge even more clearly. This was evident a generation ago from the findings of the longitudinal study of religious women, the now-famous 'nun study'.

In regard to anxiety and dementia among the very elderly, religious faith clearly provided positive benefits in maintaining mental balance and coping skills.[5] By incorporating a holistic approach to a person's history, especially their spiritual or religious background, distress from progressive communication disability and mental confusion can be greatly diminished.[6] But are spiritual soundness and mental health truly reciprocal? Can a saint also be neurotic?

The Perils of Piety

Some years ago, a devout and scholarly Jesuit colleague insisted to me that holiness has nothing whatever to do with wholeness. We were discussing the relation between spirituality and health – both mental and physical. I had observed that proponents of the holistic movement had been proposing for decades that health is an integral (and integrating) quality of life as a whole – mind, body and spirit. Imbalance in one dimension has repercussions in the other, while improvements are likewise reciprocal, as Fr Josef Goldbrunner eloquently proposed over fifty years ago in his long out-of-print little classic, *Holiness is Wholeness*.[7]

Not so, claimed my colleague. Sickness and even neuroticism are not incompatible with sanctity and may actually promote it, as Freud had claimed in a rather different sense, and was evident in the lives of many saints such as Paul of Tarsus, Ignatius Loyola, Teresa of Avila, and more recently Cardinal Joseph Bernardin, Pope John Paul II and Mother Teresa of Calcutta.[8] For illness and injury can and have led to conversion, and psychological as well as physical suffering can temper and strengthen the spirit. Conversely, as the English poet and mystic Caryll Houselander wondered in her still-stunning masterpiece of spiritual discernment, *Guilt*,[9] could sanctity itself cause at least temporary neurosis? Some years later, the venerable Jesuit spiritual writer Bernard Bassett penned a superb and still-relevant little book to that effect entitled *We Neurotics: A Handbook for the Half-Mad*.[10]

On the other hand, a serious objection to the compatibility thesis, and much more to the view that holiness fosters physical or mental unhealthiness (and vice versa), is found in the simple fact that Jesus himself was a healer, as have been so many saints in every religious tradition. If either physical or mental illth promotes holiness, why discourage it, much less cure it? Yet, as we have seen, not only did Jesus heal peoples' bodies, minds and spirits, his followers have always done so, or at least attempted to. In addition to a vast chorus of physicians and nurses, scores of patron saints have also been invoked for centuries against entire litanies of diseases and health woes, while healing shrines from the Pool of Bethesda to the Spring at Lourdes still testify to the hope that faith will facilitate healing. Christian, as well as Muslim and Jewish hospitals and medical schools now encompass the globe.

Personally I have no doubt that many emotionally and mentally unwell persons have scaled the heights of sanctity despite their illth and perhaps even because of it. But I likewise believe that the tendency of life and faith urge us all toward the fullness of health, however much it may elude us till the end. 'Have I any pleasure in the death of the wicked, says the Lord God, and not rather that he should turn from his way and live? ... I have no pleasure in the death of any one, says the Lord God, so turn, and live' (Ezk 18:23, 32). And, as Jesus himself has it in the Gospel of John, 'I came that they may have life, and have it abundantly' (Jn 10:10).

Mental and Emotional Wellness: The Miracle of Mental Health[11]
A miracle is something that causes people to wonder. And not only is real mental health wonderful, sometimes I think that its persistence in the modern world transcends the power of science and medicine to explain. For despite the popularity of books on positive thinking, many of us probably have a sneaking suspicion that most of us are in fact a pretty sick bunch, a notion reinforced by what seems to be an ever greater number of books and articles excoriating the manifold ills of married life, politics, finance and even the challenges of childhood. (The doleful and comically calamitous histories of children in the stories of *Lemony Snickett* (David Handler) and other writers, and perhaps even the 'dark materials' of Philip Pullman are more than cautionary tales: they are, in effect, apocalyptic horror stories about life in the adult world.)

The production of a veritable library trained on various kinds of addiction has tended to reinforce the notion that real mental health, never mind perfect mental health, is uncommon, hard to attain, and may in the end be an impossible dream. The Freudian vision in particular tends to be downright bleak, trapped as we are in his view in the neuroticism, narcissism, infantile projections, illusions and other discontents that constitute the price of admission to civilization itself.

Still, mental 'healthiness' has been the Holy Grail of the psychiatric arts since the late nineteenth century. (It is worth mentioning that the word 'psychiatry' comes from the Greek *psyche* and *iatros*, 'mind-healer'.) School after school has itemised the elements of sanity, largely in terms of avoiding or curing the mental discontents that beset civilized humanity. In this, psychotherapy, psychiatry and psychoanalysis took physical medicine as their methodological model and mentor. Hence the creation of 'mental illness'.

But what is it that constitutes sanity or mental healthiness? Freedom from anxiety, guilt, the power of the negative emotions of anger, fear, sorrow and resentment, and especially the thralldom of suppressed or otherwise unconscious motives and instincts, obsessions, compulsions, and now, addictions – all have had their day. In some measure, all are accurate descriptions of mental illth. But mental health is not the absence of mental disease any more than physical health is merely the absence of physical disease, or virtue is the absence of vice, or grace the absence of sin.

It is nevertheless very difficult to describe good mental health positively and precisely, just as it is hard to describe physical or spiritual health accurately, not least because all health varies according to the constitution of the individual as well as the perception of the community. Some might argue that is because there *is* no Holy Grail, that mental health, if not actually a chimera, simply indicates the good fortune not to be considered insane by one's community and society.

Let me suggest, however, that there is such a thing as positive mental health, something we used to call wisdom. It escapes precise definition, but can be recognised. Simply put, good mental health involves the ability to think independently, to choose freely, to love deeply, to act responsibly and to enjoy life fully despite inevitable setbacks and failures. Prescriptive lists such as this are only approximate, of course, and they all suffer the limitations of cultural assumptions, history and economic conditioning. Furthermore, they are not recipes, but if anything, descriptions of ideal modifications of attitude and behaviour. They represent goals. But they at least succeed in pointing to something concrete and even measurable.

Common to most such prescriptions is an assumption that most people aspire to these goals, but never realise them perfectly. The reason is, we can't and we shouldn't expect to. Full and lasting happiness is necessarily a recessive phenomenon, not a mirage, but a horizon. The beginning of wisdom is not only the fear of God, but also the acceptance of human imperfectibility. This is true not only psychologically, but physically and spiritually as well.

Paradoxically, once freed from the illusion of perfectibility, including the alluring siren of perfect mental health, people are able to develop into rather excellent specimens of sanity and sanctity. Thus, the common origins of the words 'holy', 'health' and 'whole' point to a widespread perception of an intrinsic and positive relationship among actual holiness, health and wholeness. Moreover, despite the fact that even saints experience illness, pain and suffering, the language of holiness suggests that people grow closer to God not because of illness or injury, but in spite of them. For evidence abounds that sickness of mind or body can just as likely lead to self-pity, despair, moral disintegration and even self-destruction as it can to transcendence and ultimate integrity. However, scripture, theology and pastoral experience all testify that the grace of healing moves the human organism individually and corporately towards integrity and abundance of life, not away from them.

My friend was certainly right about one thing: the life experience and writings of mystics such as St Teresa of Avila, St Thérèse of Lisieux, Caryll Houselander, Simone Weil and most recently Mother Teresa of Calcutta have eloquently taught us that mental anguish and emotional suffering are not incompatible with sanctity. Indeed, what St John of the Cross called 'the active and passive purifications of the intellect, memory and will', otherwise known as 'the dark night of the soul', may be a necessary if culminating step in reaching full spiritual maturity. Distinguishing spiritual suffering from clinical depression is hardly easy in practice and may even be impossible because of the likelihood of coincidence.[12] But as William James had argued over a century ago, it is the outcome of the experience, not its origin or even its progress, that reveals its true nature.[13]

In the practical order, a number of activities present themselves for consideration as allies in the quest for Grail-like spirituality of mental health and healing – prayer and meditation, and some perhaps surprisingly normal abilities that are still underestimated: crying and laughing.

Praying Yourself Well

It is hardly surprising that people would pray when they feel mental distress, as is evident throughout the Bible as well as countless stories of saints' lives and the experience of ordinary people. The very word 'prayer' comes from an ancient Indo-European root that means 'to ask' or 'call for help'. But does prayer really help? Later, we will consider whether prayer for others can be a healing power. But what of those, like Jesus himself, who pray in their own hour of need? Can medical science provide any assistance here?

As noted above in chapter four, research over the last two decades has in fact shown that prayer, both public and private, has demonstrably beneficial effects on mood, emotional state, mental balance and overall well-being.[14] Should people pray therefore to achieve better mental and physical health? Undoubtedly some spiritual writers would consider such petitioning to be egocentric and mercantile – turning to God for benefits rather than offering disinterested praise and thankfulness for favours received.

In the biblical tradition, however, believers are explicitly urged to pray for health and healing, for happiness, peace and even prosperity, for deliverance from natural calamity and the threats and violence of enemies. Praying for help in time of distress was certainly modelled by Jesus himself (Mt 14:23, 26:36-44; Mk 1:35, 6:46, 14:32-39; Lk 5:16, 6:12, 9:28, 22:41-44, etc.). That is not to say that silent communion with God in selfless adoration is not a 'higher' form of prayer, nor is it to deny that the same or even greater benefit may likely result from such contemplative worship. It is to say that prayer by its very nature is an appeal to God for help. (The Latin word *precor*, which is the root from which our English word springs, means 'to beg or appeal'. It also sprouted the words 'precarious', which points to the typical human predicament out of which prayer often arises, and 'imprecation', which reverses the polarity and asks God to shower calamity on someone. Regrettably, many psalms involve imprecations, which cannot help but grate against the Christian ear.)

In regard to mental health, recent research indicates that using a variety of measurements of perceived well-being submitted to a large number of people in multiple studies, praying is an effective 'coping' behaviour. Saying formal ('rote') prayers or attending worship services is not necessary, however, and may even be less effective than spontaneous prayer. What helps appears to be the petitioners' ability to situate themselves consciously in a receptive and grateful frame of mind, confidently expecting assistance from a 'higher power'. In conventional spiritual language, this amounts to 'practicing the presence of God'. Consolation and strength appear to be the twin towers of support that are reinforced by personal prayer.[15]

Related practices traditionally known as meditation and contemplation have also been subject to rigorous medical examination to determine whether and how they can assist in developing mental stability and integrity. Both Asian and Western forms have been studied, and the results from both sides of the religious spectrum have been not only positive but complementary.

Meditation and Contemplation

Volumes have been published on the benefits of meditative practice and its more developed form, generally referred to in the West as contemplation. Here, space permits only a few remarks, not unlike the problem of briefly evaluating the efficacy of prayer.

Clearly, the stabilising potential of meditative practice has been demonstrated many times over, most recently among Tibetan Buddhist monks.[16] Accumulating evidence appears to show that meditation not only alters brain wave patterns, producing calmness and compassion, but actually alters the structure of the brain, more or less permanently adapting it to induce higher and more comprehensive experiences of tranquility and consideration for others. Regular practice may also slow the thinning of the frontal cortex area of the brain which has been associated with advancing age.[17] In addition, skilled practitioners have demonstrated the ability to monitor and regulate their heart rate, breathing and other autonomous or semi-autonomous functions. The use of guided imagery has been shown to increase white blood-cell count.[18]

The practice of similar forms of meditation in all monastic traditions, Asian and European, and similar practices among indigenous peoples in the Americas and Africa, are almost always associated with spirituality and even formal religious training. The connection is hardly adventitious and despite the possibility of disengaging doctrinal elements from both practices and results, as seen in the work of Herbert Benson, meditation training and contemplative prayer are likely to remain important factors in the life and health of monks and nuns, influencing (as we have seen earlier) both longevity and the persistence of mental agility well into old age.[19]

Having a Good Cry: The Gift in Tears

While we typically associate tears with sorrow and pain, the supportive function of crying as a release from the physiological strains of suffering and even the transports of extreme happiness should not be overlooked in regard to the various dimensions of health. The importance of crying in western society is usually eclipsed by social embarrassment, which robs people of their cleansing and renewing effect.

Jesus wept over the death of his friend Lazarus, and he wept over Jerusalem (Jn 11:35 and Lk 19:41). Yet the resistance of adult western males to weeping, especially in public settings, is encapsulated in a terse reminder characteristically passed from fathers to sons: 'Real men don't cry.' So when men are moved to tears by overwhelming emotion, they become acutely embarrassed and socially dis-graced, as so memorably happened during the 1972 US presidential election campaign when Senator Edmund Muskie wept as he responded to a newspaper attack on the character of his wife. Perceived as weak and unstable, Muskie was defeated by Richard Nixon. (Later it was discovered that the attack on Muskie's wife was based on a false report contained in a letter planted by members of the Nixon campaign committee.)

Conversely, in many other parts of the world men are 'allowed' to weep and mourn openly and even vociferously, as I witnessed several times in Iraq. When assisting male clients to work through loss and suffering occasioned by divorce or death, however, I have also found that the turning point in the healing process arrived when resistance, anger and denial finally give way to acceptance – and tears. It was hardly a matter of wailing and streams of tears, but a silent flow that seemed to wash away the negativity that had held them in check. I am sure that had it been possible to run a chemical analysis of their tears, the hormone and enzyme content would have been revealing.

Tears are not only the messengers of sorrow and distress, however. Sometimes people laugh so hard that they cry. People burst into tears of joy. The gap between levity and gravity, between joy and sorrow, is not very wide emotionally. In the final analysis, if there can be such a thing, the 'gift' of tears sought by and sometimes granted to the mystic saints of old can truly be a grace to men and women today, a distinctively human response to moments of profound emotional elation as well as desolation. Over the whole range of expression, tears are both cleansing and healing – physically, psychologically and spiritually.

Physiologically, the chemistry of tears is revealing. Other higher animals may weep, but crying is a distinctively human trait, not least among the very young. As an expression of distress, tears are eloquent, but they are also cleansing. Their composition alters according to their function – we may cry when we stub our toe or slice onions, but those tears are different from both tears of laughter and tears of joy, which also differ from each other. Physically cleansing tears lack at least two chemicals found in healing tears associated with strong emotion: leucine-enkephalin and prolactin, which like other endorphins alleviate the effects of pain. Such tears wash away emotional distress. Conversely, stifling tears prevents their therapeutic action.[20]

Psychologically, tears not only express deeply felt emotions, releasing us from their power, but also affects the community of mourners (or, for that matter, revellers), creating a bond of sorrow or celebration. Apart from religious meaning, rites of mourning or even of public expiation of crimes are important expressions of social identity.

Tears also have a *sacramental* dimension, expressing and effecting states of soul and spirit that are directed not only at our fellow mortals, but to God. Weeping is often mentioned in Scripture as a sign of repentance and sorrow, a pledge of remorse and longing: 'By the waters of Babylon we sat down and wept, when we remembered Zion' (Ps 137:1). And the shortest verse in the New Testament is 'Jesus wept' (Jn 11:35).

But tears of joy also secure the bond between the individual or the people and their God, as when the Jews could not restrain themselves when the foundations of temple were re-laid after their return from Babylon: 'But many of the priests and Levites and heads of fathers' houses, old men who had seen the first house, wept with a loud voice when they saw the foundation of this house being laid, though many shouted aloud for joy; so that the people could not distinguish the sound of the joyful shout from the sound of the people's weeping, for the people shouted so loudly that the sound was heard far away' (Ezra 3:12-13).

One of the most touching traditions in western spirituality concerns what came to be known as 'the gift of tears', a mystical grace given to both women and men which spans the emotional range from longing to sublime happiness.[21] The following prayer is found in the lesser works of St Augustine:

> By your Holy Spirit who softens the hard hearts of sinners and moves them to tears, grant me the grace of tears, as you granted it to my ancestors, in whose steps I should follow: that I may bewail my whole life, as they bewailed themselves by day and night. By their prayers and merits who have pleased you and most faithfully served you, have mercy on me your most pitiful and unworthy servant and grant me the gift of tears. Water me from above, and water me from below, that day and night tears may be my bread. May I become in your sight, O my God, a sacrifice, rich and full of marrow, through

the fires of your compunction. May I be wholly consumed on the altar of my own heart, and may I as a most acceptable holocaust, be received by you as an odour of sweetness.[22]

But if crying is good for you, laughing can be positively miraculous.

Good Nick: Laughing Yourself Well

With mirth and laughter let old wrinkles come.
The Merchant of Venice, I, i. 86

As there is a time appointed to weep, there is also a time to laugh; a time to mourn, and a time to dance, as we recall from Ecclesiastes 3:4. Laughter is frequently mentioned in Hebrew scripture, even to the point of becoming a play on words. In the story of the birth of Isaac, the child of promise, there is a bright omen at the beginning of the story which suggests that despite great crises and terrifying struggles to come, comedy can also be divine. 'Then Abraham fell on his face and laughed, and said to himself, "Shall a child be born to a man who is a hundred years old? Shall Sarah, who is ninety years old, bear a child?"' (Gen 17:17. See also Gen 18:13-15, 21:6). For Isaac, the name the child is given, means in fact, 'he laughs' (Gen 17:19).

But is laughter really good for us? Apparently far more so than anyone suspected for a long, long time, especially physically. (Laughter is, however, primarily a psychological and even spiritual response to the perception of incongruity. About the only way to get a laugh out of someone purely physically is to tickle them.)

I remember poring over my parents' *Reader's Digests* when I was young. One of my favourite sections was called 'Laughter is the Best Medicine'. Much later I discovered that in many respects, it is. Or at least the most enjoyable. That was sharply brought home to me many years when I happened on a copy of Norman Cousins' justly famous book, *Anatomy of an Illness as Perceived by the Patient*. The long-time editor of the *Saturday Review*, and a formidable presence on the American literary scene, in midlife Cousins found himself not only mysteriously ill but received an electrifying diagnosis. Diagnosed (or possibly misdiagnosed) with a life-threatening and incurable condition, Ankylosing spondylitis, Cousins decided not to succumb to the gloomy prognosis of the medical team. As related in his book and the film based on it, after learning that a good bout of laughter reduced the pain considerably for as much as an hour or two, he determined to use laughter to help fight the progress of the disease. Relying primarily on old movies of the Marx Brothers, television shows featuring other comedians, funny books, as well as extensive bed rest and large doses of vitamin C, he did 'laugh himself well'.[23] Several years later, Cousins experienced a near-fatal heart attack. Again, he worked himself back to normal health by a positive attitude, a lot of laughter and excellent medical care. His book on the subject became another bestseller.[24] In 1978, Cousins was offered a faculty position at the University of California at Los Angeles Medical School, where he spent the remaining years of his life teaching ethics and promoting patient-centred health care centring on the close connection of emotional and mental attitudes and recovery.[25] Cousins died in 1990 at the age of 75.

Cousins left a great humanitarian legacy, not least being his elevation to public as well as professional visibility the role of the positive emotions, particularly the impact of laughter and fun, on serious illness. Thanks in large measure to his work, hope, love, faith and optimism were once again recognised as part of the healing pharmacopoeia.[26]

Clowning Around

The last book of my Dominican mentor and friend, Raymond J. Nogar, was called *The Emergence of Laughter: The Diary of a Clown*. I was able to read part of it, proofing a few chapters for him as the book progressed. He eventually finished it and sent it off to a friend for a final proofing, but died of a sudden heart attack before any of us knew where the manuscript had been mailed. It disappeared utterly. With it vanished what I thought was one of the most engaging autobiographical and theological studies of comedy I ever read.

Others have appeared. More will undoubtedly be written. What is important about all of them is that like medicine and prayer, laughter itself has beneficial physical, psychological and spiritual potency in regard to all dimensions of health. For some people, the art of telling jokes is difficult to master, but it's really not important to be a master joker. Someone else is usually around to fill that role. Or try to. The important thing is to laugh.[27]

St Thomas Aquinas was alert to the psychological and spiritual problem presented by someone entirely lacking a sense of humour, a condition he considered a severe personality defect if not downright sinful: 'Someone who is without mirth is not only lacking in playful speech but is also burdensome to others, since he is deaf to the moderate mirth of others. Consequently they are vicious, and are said to be boorish or rude.' Here he appeals to Aristotle (*Nichomachean Ethics*, Book IV, chapter 8) who gave us the charming word *eutrapelia* for 'playful wit' (*Summa Theologiae*, II-II, Q. 168, A. 4).

It is wise to be a bit cautious, however, because jokes can backfire. It was not by accident that a trained professional was hired to be a court jester. Amateurs have been known to stumble badly, some at the cost of their heads. A pastor recently told me that telling jokes in a sermon is particularly perilous, because many people may not 'get' them or find them inappropriate or offensive, or they could simply fall flat. Better, he said, to use a little humor to lighten the message, especially when the joke is directed at oneself.

And of course many great comedians also suffered from depression. Some likely candidates include Jonathan Swift, Ambrose Bierce, George Bernard Shaw, P.G. Wodehouse and James Thurber, and more contemporaneously, Peter Sellars, Spike Milligan, Stephen Fry and Paul Merton.

Nevertheless, they and their followers have managed to lighten the load that less gifted mortals find burdensome and not nearly so funny at the time – Laurel and Hardy, the Marx Brothers, Abbott and Costello, Bob Hope, Victor Borge, Ronnie Barket and Ronnie Corbett, Benny Hill, the Monty Python crew, Terry Thomas, Peter Cook and Dudley Moore, Dermot Morgan, George Carlin, and not a few women of past and present – Fanny Brice, Martha Raye, Imogene Coca, Lucille Ball, Carol Burnett, Lily Tomlin, Patricia Routledge, Dame Edna Everage (Barry Humphries), and one of the funniest comediennes of all, the late Canadian singer and satirist, Anna Russell.

Like Norman Cousins, true comedians seem to have learned that laughter can lighten the darkest moods. It gives us an alternative way of seeing things and often reveals the absurdity of annoying situations we find personally aggravating. Even 'gallows humour' or 'black humour' has an important contribution to make when people are immersed in terrible and often tragic situations. It has survival value, not least for the simple fact that laughter is the best medicine, physically, mentally and socially. Genuine humour, even in life's bleakest moments, steadies our nerves and in fact so relativises catastrophe as to provide enough hope to make the worst at least more endurable if not survivable. Who has not heard the story of St Lawrence, who tormented his tormentors with the jibe that he was sufficiently well roasted on one side to warrant turning him over! Or the jests with which St Thomas More met his executioner and in fact set the frightened man's mind at ease. (According to tradition, More, a consummate jester, is said to have informed his executioner, 'See me safe up: for my coming down, I can shift for myself.' And his final jest: 'Be careful of my beard, for it has committed no treason.'

Downside: Laughing Till it Hurts

Wit and humour can also be cruel, however. Sharpened to the point of hurtfulness, 'sarcasm' is justly named, for it tears the flesh. Mark Twain (Samuel L. Clemens) and H.L. Mencken were great humorists, but at heart both men were bitter and pessimistic. They did not so much laugh at themselves, but at others and caused millions of their readers to do the same, perhaps not realising that they were in fact often laughing at their own unrecognised foolishness.

Sigmund Freud was well aware that humour can have a knife-edge to it, masking deep underlying anger. Such humour is spiritually harmful, both to the joker and his target. Ridicule, sarcasm, even the sardonic down-putting or 'dissing' favoured by catty teenagers may well be expressions of illth, not health, the bitter fruit of envy and resentment. Practical jokes easily degenerate into meanness.

On the other hand, some corrosive humor is also corrective. Satire, the poet's scorn, was a feared weapon in the musical and poetic arsenal of the ancient Irish bards. An ungenerous host or a cruel master could be so socially wounded by such satire that some are said to have died of shame. And despite his own tendencies toward curmudgeonry, Clemens (1835–1910) was also wise and humane, and his remarks about comedy are characteristically sage: 'Humour is the great thing,' he wrote, 'the saving thing after all. The minute it crops up, all our hardnesses yield, all our irritations and resentments flit away, and a sunny spirit takes their place.'[28]

The Sacramental Dimension: Godly Laughter

Even God has a sense of humour. (As someone once said, any Creator who could put giraffes and hippopotamuses on the same planet had to have one.) But God's laughter, like the poet's, is often derisive, aimed at the selfish tyrants and sneaky crooks that work hardship on the poor and wretched:

> The kings of the earth set themselves, and the rulers take
>   counsel together,
> against the Lord and his anointed, saying,
> 'Let us burst their bonds asunder, and cast their cords from us.'
> He who sits in the heavens laughs;
>   the Lord holds them in derision. (Ps 2:2-4)

In Hebrew scripture God's laughter (*sachaq*, which is related to the name 'Isaac') is more often scorn than merriment, as in Psalms 37:13 and 59:8. The faithful will also enjoy some righteous laughter as they witness the fall of the haughty (Ps 52:6), and in the early Wisdom tradition Divine Wisdom mocks the foolish who refuse to wake up (Prov 1:26).

Laughter also figures in Christian scripture as ridicule, but mainly aimed at Jesus and his disciples as in the story of the raising of Jairus' daughter: 'And they laughed at him' (Mt 9:24, Mk 5:40, Lk 8:53). But one of the promises of the Kingdom is also a burst of honest joy: 'Blessed are you that weep now, for you shall laugh' (Lk 6:21).

In later Christian tradition, the virtue of mirth was highly recommended. *Hilaritas* was already one of the favourite 'Graces', muses who in Roman mythology lightened the dreary lot of mortals. These embodiments of social graciousness were happily baptised, not the least of them Hilaritas herself, the personification of Joy. (Some of the others were Faith, Abstinence, Patience, Simplicity, Innocence, Chastity, Concord, Truth and Charity – all eventually becoming favoured names for Christian girls and are occasionally still pressed into service.) Not surprisingly, hilarity became, in time, one of the virtues that were considered necessary companions of the desert monks, and later, monastic dwellers in the Benedictine and other traditions. A sad saint was truly a sorry saint, by this reading.[29]

Henri Nouwen enjoyed telling the story of St Philip Neri, who invented the musical form known as the Oratorio and amused the children of Rome by shaving off half his beard and dancing with pillows on his head, among other antics.[30] In today's world, robust humour can be both health-giving and life-enhancing. George Mulrain relates how laughter is a religious, even theological response of impoverished and often oppressed people who have little hope except in God:

> The folk from the Caribbean have this ability to laugh in the face of seemingly hopeless situations. This is not merely a mechanism of defence. In actual fact, it is the reflection of a theology that spells out hope in God. Even though people walk through the valley of the shadow of death, they will not fear. They will keep their minds fixed on God because they believe, just as the psalmists, that God is on their side. God will fight on their behalf in order that the enemies might be defeated. It is the hope, too, which amplifies the people's determination not to remain as victims, but to do whatever is humanly possible to ease out of difficult situations.[31]

In an insightful concluding essay to his edition of works on comedy by Henry Bergson and George Meredith, Wylie Sypher reminds us that 'The comic and the tragic heroes alike "learn through suffering," albeit suffering in comedy takes the form of humiliation, disappointment, or chagrin, instead of death'.[32] He adds, wisely, 'Tragedy needs a more single vision than comedy, for the comic perception comes only when we take a double view – that is, a human view – of ourselves, a perspective by incongruity. Then we take part in the ancient rite that is a Debate and a Carnival, a Sacrifice and a Feast'.[33]

Surely one of the elements of the tragic vision of life, memorialised in Miguel de Unomuno's classic work,[34] is death itself, ostensibly the great enemy of love, joy and laughter and perhaps the chief cause of tears. But can death, too, be addressed in ways that are personally and collectively health-giving rather than depressing and stressful? I am reminded here of a tradition that developed among the Dominican nuns of the southern Rhineland during some of the most difficult years of the fourteenth century. Strengthened by a healthy spirituality derived at least in part from the robust mysticism of Meister Eckhart and the Friends of God, many of the nuns were able, quite literally, to laugh in the face of death.

The prioress of Maria Medingen, Bl. Margaret Ebner, wrote in her journal around the year 1340:

> At this time one of our sisters lay dying. She had served God earnestly in suffering and poverty. And since she had already lain four days without eating I went to her and told her I noticed that she wanted to get to God before me. Then she clapped her hands together for joy and laughed so that it was heard everywhere in the room ... Then I replied, 'You act like someone who wants to go to a wedding'. Then she laughed so loudly that I noticed that God had granted her special grace. She assured me that this was true. And at that I laughed like her and was so happy that I could not sleep much that night because of the joy in my heart over the eternal joy for which she longed.[35]

NOTES

1. William Stringfellow, *The Politics of Spirituality* (Philadelphia: Westminster Press, 1984), p. 22.
2. Reginald Garrigou-Lagrange, OP, *The Three Ways of the Spiritual Life* (Rockford, IL: TAN Books and Pub., 1977 [orig.: London: Burns and Oates, 1938]), p. 1.
3. Freud's most explicit attack on religion was published in 1927 in what is essentially a philosophical essay, *The Future of an Illusion* (New York and London: W.W. Norton, 1976 ed.), although his disdain for religion was evident in many other works such as *Totem and Taboo* (1913), *Civilization and its Discontents* (1929) and *Moses and Monotheism* (1939), among others.
4. See, for instance, Steven A. Rogers, H. Newton Malony, Esther M. Coleman and Leslie Tepper, 'Changes in Attitudes toward Religion among Those with Mental Illness', *Journal of Religion and Health* 41 (June, 2002) 2:167–78. See also Steven A. Rogers, Evelyn L. Poey et al., 'Religious Coping among Those with Persistent Mental Illness', *International Journal for the Psychology of Religion* 12 (2002) 3:161–75.
5. One of the more important works in this area is H.G. Koenig, *Aging and God: Spiritual Pathways to Mental Health in Midlife and Later Years* (Binghamton, NY: The Haworth Pastoral Press, 1994).
6. See especially Robert M. Lawrence, 'Aspects of Spirituality in Dementia Care', *Dementia* 2 (2003) 3:393–402. Other important clinical literature includes K.I. Pargament, *The Psychology of Religion and Coping: Theory, Research and Practice* (New York: Guilford Press, 1997) and K.I. Pargament, H.G. Koenig, et al., 'Religious Struggle as a Predictor of Mortality among Medically Ill Elderly Patients: a Two-Tear Longitudinal Study', *Archives of Internal Medicine*, 161 (2001) 15:1881–85.
7. New York: Pantheon Books, Inc., 1955.
8. See her account of mental and spiritual suffering that so closely tallies with the descriptions in St John of the Cross' *Dark Night of the Soul: Come Be My Light*, ed. by Brian Kolodiejchuk, MC (New York and London: Doubleday, 2007). Not uncharacteristically, Christopher Hitchens followed up his 1995 attack on Mother Teresa's character with a virulent excoriation of her beatification. See Christopher Hitchens, *The Missionary Position: Mother Teresa in Theory and Practice* (London and New York: Verso Publishing, 1995) and Christopher Hitchens, 'Mommie Dearest: The Pope Beatifies Mother Teresa, a Fanatic, a Fundamentalist, and a Fraud,' *Slate*, www.slate.com/id/2090083/ posted Monday, Oct 20, 2003, at 4:04 PM ET.
9. London and New York: Sheed and Ward, 1952.
10. London: Burns and Oates, 1962.
11. Parts of this section are based on a lecture given on 4 June 1997 at Eckhart House, Dublin, 'Spirituality, Therapy, and the Miracle of Mental Health'.

12. In this regard, see the excellent article by Connie Fitzgerald, OCD, 'Impasse and Dark Night', in Tilden H. Edwards, ed., *Living with Apocalypse, Spiritual Resources for Social Compassion* (San Francisco: Harper and Row, 1984), pp. 93–116.

13. For a later exploration of this in specific detail, see Kenneth Wapnick, '*Mysticism and Schizophrenia*', in Richard Woods, *Understanding Mysticism* (Garden City, NY: Doubleday Image, 1981), pp. 321–37.

14. For an overview of much of this research, see Jeff Levin, op. cit., pp. 73–95.

15. See Mary K. Bade and Stephen W. Cook, 'Functions of Christian Prayer in the Coping Process', *Journal for the Scientific Study of Religion* 47 (Mar 2008) 1:123–33. Bade and Cook provide an extensive list of supportive studies reported in professional journals over several decades of investigation.

16. One of the earliest efforts to assess the psychophysiological effects of meditation in a comparative context was that published by William Johnston, SJ, *Silent Music: The Science of Meditation* (New York: Harper and Row, l974). Serious studies of the therapeutic effects of meditation include Jon Kabat-Zinn, *Coming to Our Senses: Healing Ourselves and the World through Mindfulness* (New York: Hyperion, 2005) and Deane H. Shapiro and Roger N. Walsh, eds, *Meditation: Classic and Contemporary Perspectives* (New York: Aldine Press, 1984). For practical guidance in learning the art of meditation, several recent books can be recommended, although a teacher is still the best resource: Thich Nhat Hanh, *The Miracle of Mindfulness: A Manual on Meditation* (Boston: Beacon Press, 1987); Lawrence LeShan, *How to Meditate: A Guide to Self-Discovery* (Boston: Little, Brown and Co., 1999 ed.) and Elaine MacInnes, OLM, *Teaching Zen to Christians* (Manila: Zen Centre for Oriental Spirituality, 1986). On centring prayer in the tradition of John Main (1926–1982), see Thomas Keating and Gustave Reininger, eds., *Centering Prayer in Daily Life and Ministry* (New York: Continuum Publishing Group, 1998).

17. Sara W. Lazar, Catherine E. Kerr et al., 'Meditation experience is associated with increased cortical thickness', *Neuroreport* 16 (28 Nov 2005) 17:1893–7 and Sharon Begley, 'Scans of Monks' Brains Show Meditation Alters Structure, Functioning', *Wall Street Journal*, 5 Nov 2004, p. B1.

18. In addition to the resources listed above for Shapiro and Walsh, see Bruce Bower, 'No Place Like Om: Meditation training puts oomph into attention', *Science News* 171 (12 May 2007) 19:291.

19. Benson discovered that the content of the mantras, beliefs and practices associated with Transcendental Meditation were irrelevant to the effect produced by silent 'chanting'. Meditative 'mantra-yoga' evoked calmness, contentment and, importantly, heart-healthy relaxation, a consequence that led to his development and advocacy of what he called 'the relaxation response'. See Herbert Benson and Miriam Z. Klipper, *The Relaxation Response* (New York: Harper Collins, 2001 ed.).

20. See William H. Frey II, with Muriel Langseth, *Crying: The Mystery of Tears* (Minneapolis: Winston Press, 1985); M. Badamchian, A. A. Damavandy, et al., 'Identification and quantification of thymosin beta4 in human saliva and tears', *Annals of the New York Academy of Sciences* 1112 (Sept 2007):458–65; Marjaneh M. Fooladi, 'The Healing Effects of Crying', *Holistic Nursing Practice* 19 (Nov–Dec 2005) 6:248–55; and Blain and Rita Justice, 'Shedding Tears, Healing Waters', *Health Leader*, University of Texas Health Science Centre at Houston.
www.healthleader.uthouston.edu/archive/Mind_Body_Soul/2004/shedding tears-0426.html.

21. A very interesting primer on the Gift in Tears can be found on line at www.helpforchristians.co.uk/articles/a28.asp. See also Frederic and Mary Ann Brussat, 'Tears Are for the Soul: Why many religious traditions consider the act of crying a gift from God', *BeliefNet*.
www.beliefnet.com/story/174/story_17455_1.html.

22. Slightly adapted from the *Book of Meditations I*, Ch. 36 (*Patrologia Latina* 40, col. 930.) www.lectionarycentral.com/trinity10/Augustine2.html.

23. See Norman Cousins, *Anatomy of an Illness as Perceived by the Patient* (New York: W.W. Norton Co, 2005 ed.).

24. Norman Cousins, *The Healing Heart: Antidotes to Panic and Helplessness* (New York: Avon Books, 1984).

25. Cousins' major work on medical ethics and the role of the positive emotions in healing, *Head First: The Biology of Hope and the Healing Power of the Human Spirit*, was published in New York and London by Penguin Books in 1990.

26. An important series of articles was published under the title 'Humour and Laughter may Influence Health' by Mary Payne Bennett and Cecile A. Lengacher in the journal *Evidence-Based Complementary and Alternative Medicine:* I. 'History and Background', 3 (Jan 2006)1:61–63; II. 'Complementary Therapies and Humor in a Clinical Population', 3 (1 June 2006)2:187–190; III. 'Laughter and Health Outcomes', 5 (1 March 2008)1:37–40; and IV. 'Humour and Immune Function' (5 Dec 2007), received July 25, 2007, accepted July 26, 2007, ecam.oxfordjournals.org/cgi/reprint/nem149v1. Other recent articles include 'University of Maryland School of Medicine Study Shows Laughter Helps Blood Vessels Function Better', *University of Maryland Medical Center*, 7 March 2005, www.umm.edu/news/releases/laughter2.htm; and Nigel Hawkes, 'Scientists laugh in the face of sickness', *Times On Line*, 8 March 2005, www.timesonline.co.uk/tol/news/uk/article421870.ece.

27. The origin of the English word 'joke', which dates only from the late seventeenth century, is the Italian *gioco* – jest, sport, or game. Before then, humorous wordplay was generally referred to as 'wit', which is related to the word 'wise'.

28. Mark Twain, 'What Paul Bourget Thinks of Us', *The Complete Essays of Mark Twain* (Cambridge, MA: DaCapo Press, 2000), p. 178.

29. In a recent sermon, Dean Robin Steinke noted the presence of 'hilaritas' in the spiritual world of Dietrich Bonhoeffer: 'On March 9, 1944, from his cell in Tegel prison he wrote to Eberhard Bethge, his dear friend and biographer, and described Mozart, Luther, Karl Barth among others as having a kind of hilaritas, "confidence in their own work, boldness and defiance of the world and of popular opinion, a steadfast certainty in their own work they are showing the world something good".' (*Letters and Papers from Prison*, p. 229) www.believersweb.org/view.cfm?id=1218&rc=1&list=multi. Posted on 16 May 2007. It was no less an attitude of mind shown by Bonhoeffer himself.

30. See *Clowning in Rome: Reflections on Solitude, Celibacy, Prayer, and Contemplation* (New York: Image Books, 2000).

31. George Mulrain, 'The Caribbean', in John Parratt, ed., *An Introduction to Third World Theologies* (Cambridge and New York: Cambridge University Press, 2004), p. 177. See also Peter Berger, *Redeeming Laughter: The Comic Dimension of Human Experience* (New York: du Gruyter, 1997).

32. Wylie Sypher, 'The Meanings of Comedy', in *Comedy*, ed. and intro. by Wylie Sypher (Garden City, NJ: Doubleday Anchor Books, 1956), p. 254.

33. Ibid., p. 255.

34. Miguel de Unamuno (1864–1936), *The Tragic Sense of Life (Del Sentimiento Trágico de la Vida)*, trans. by J. E. Crawford (Gloucester, MA: Peter Smith Pub. Inc, 1954 [orig. 1921]).

35. See *Margareta Ebner: Revelations and Pater Noster*, Leonard Hindsley, OP, and Margot Schmidt, eds and intro., preface by Richard Woods, OP (New York: Paulist Press, 1993), p. 197.

CHAPTER TEN
MAKING A GOOD END
THE SPIRITUALITY OF DEATH
AND DYING

> O death, where is thy victory?
> O death, where is thy sting?
> 1 Corinthians 15:55

'Dying is easy. Comedy is hard.' These, according to reports, were the last words of the great English stage and film actor Sir Donald Wolfit (*Room at the Top, Lawrence of Arabia, Svengali*, and other films). And perhaps only a stand-up comedian or a veteran actor would refer to a calamitous performance as 'dying on stage'. One way or another, dying and death – whether actual death or its metaphor – have figured prominently in human concern and discourse since mortal beings first realised that their days on earth were finite. Many scholars have argued that all religions were devised, especially in regard to beliefs about life beyond death, as a defense mechanism against the certain, sad, sometimes terrifying finality of simply being alive in the first place.

Coping with dying and death, whether our own or those of our loved ones, our fellow human beings, and even our animal kindred, is an index of spirituality as much or more than any other dimension of life – physically, psychologically and sacramentally. Volumes have been devoted to preparing for death, especially the *artes moriendi* of the past, and other visual, graphic and musical reminders assist us in recognising and even celebrating the final rite of passage. In this chapter, I cannot hope to cover the topic comprehensively or even adequately, but in terms of the spirituality of health and healing, several avenues for further exploration can at least be identified.

The need for a positive and holistic spirituality of dying and death arises largely because of what Ernest Becker aptly called 'the denial of death' in his famous book of that name.[1] Advances in medicine, pharmacology and surgical techniques over the last century and a half extended life expectancy considerably in the affluent, industrialised world and more slowly around the rest of the planet. Despite the horrific loss of life in the two world wars of the twentieth century, in the latter half of the twentieth century the prospect of outwitting or at least postponing 'natural' death – perhaps indefinitely – grew steadily alongside intellectual skepticism about the survival of bodily death that was developing in proportion to new achievements in science, medicine and even religious studies. Even theologians adapted increasingly to the predominant materialistic world view of the time. Existentialism aside, it was easier to ignore or even disguise death than to deal with it.

There was a 'downside' to the denial of death, however. Clinical therapists have argued from the time of Freud, perhaps none more eloquently than Becker, that the flight from death, basically a refusal to confront the inevitability and finality of dying, lies at the root of much if not most mental illth in western society. The claim may be extreme and as such undoubtedly faulty, especially in light of advances in understanding the physiological causes of mental illness, but it is not based on mere prejudice. In 1963, Jessica Mitford's *The American Way of Death* erupted on the literary scene as a sobering but sometimes comical examination of the lengths Americans in particular (but not exclusively) went to pretend that death is not 'the end'.[2] The same point had been made more comically, but hardly less grimly, in Evelyn Waugh's satirical 1947 masterpiece *The Loved One*.[3]

When Becker's book burst on the scene in 1971, it excited a great deal of interest, but in the end, seems not to have changed our behaviour all that much. We still prefer to pretend, thanks to the cosmetological arts of morticians, that our skillfully embalmed loved ones are only asleep, and that we ourselves are for all practical purposes immortal.

None of this is exactly new, of course. The denial of death goes all the way back. And it has been resolutely opposed by wise spiritual teachers. Most (not all) have pointed to the immortality of the human spirit as an alternative to utter extinction. But one way or another, faith in God or at least in the inextinguishable flame of life has been raised as a beacon in the darkness of fear and uncertainty. Romanticising and personifying death is not a solution, but it is an emblem of human hope and somehow survives despite materialism, science and religious skepticism:

> Death be not proud, though some have called thee
> Mighty and dreadfull, for, thou art not so,
> For, those, whom thou think'st, thou dost overthrow,
> Die not, poore death, nor yet canst thou kill me.
> From rest and sleepe, which but thy pictures bee,
> Much pleasure, then from thee, much more must flow,
> And soonest our best men with thee doe goe,
> Rest of their bones, and soules deliverie.
>   (John Donne, 1572–1631)

Death is without doubt the most personal of all experiences, at least inasmuch as we weren't paying much attention to what was transpiring as we were being born. If we're fortunate, we'll be able to depart with more awareness of what is happening. For death is not, nor should it be, an experience of fear and loneliness. Rather, it can be a moment of individual and communal transcendence, for Christians a journey into the mystery of eternal life with God in Christ.

Dying is one thing, but dealing with death – our own and that of other people – is an order of different magnitude, not least of which are preparation and celebration, the fond farewell of funerals. But before all that, there is the prospect of dying, which from midlife on provides the horizon of all earthly experience.

Body as Spirit: The Journey towards Death
It is a commonplace of ancient standing that we begin to die the day we are born. That isn't true, but our expiration date, although

indeterminate, is definite. Sooner or later, we will bow out, but normally, we have some time to prepare for the final curtain. As Eugene Bianchi put it:

> There is gradual slowing down and deterioration of the biological organism from early midlife to old age. In this context of decline toward death, the curve indicates negative, and even fearsome dimensions. Certain religious systems attempt to discount bodily deterioration by resorting to extreme forms of mind control or to descriptions of the afterlife that remove the negative and tragic sting from death. These mind-over-matter and easy-passage-to-the-next-life attitudes impoverish the growth potential of ageing. They fail to see that serious confrontation with the bodily limits of mortality, with all its emotional impact, can be part of the catalyst for human transformation in middle and later adulthood. Moreover, a facile interpretation of the first part of life as an ascendant period furthers an already exaggerated glorification of youth in a death-denying culture.[4]

Living Well to Die Well: the *Artes Moriendi*

Perhaps not surprisingly, from late Classical antiquity the Latin phrase *memento mori* was an important part of Christian spirituality – 'remember that you must die'. Especially after the social distress of the Black Death and the Wars of Religion two centuries later, portraits of saints often depicted them with a skull nearby, sometimes serving as a paperweight or simply an object of meditative contemplation. Less grim than the *danse macabre* or rotting corpses that began to figure in funerary monuments at this time, these reminders focused attention on how to live well in order to die gracefully, that is, in the state of grace. Eventually the attitude, one far more positive than might be at first expected, was embodied in a form of literature that came to be known as the *ars moriendi*, the art of dying.

At first practical manuals designed to assist both the dying person and caretakers to cope with the inevitability of death, they evolved into devotional manuals that appear among the first printed books and remained popular until the nineteenth century among both Catholics and Protestants. The first of these works seems to have been penned in Latin by a Dominican friar in early fifteenth-century Germany and was frequently copied (over 300 manuscript copies are known) and translated into German, English, Spanish, French and other languages well into the seventeenth century.[5]

The devotional aspect of the treatises aimed to help the dying person face death with optimism rather than dread, but (like the Tibetan *Book of the Dead* in some respects) goes on to describe the temptations that await as death approaches and how to resist them: doubt, despair, impatience, pride and avarice, among others. Attention turns next to Jesus and the power of divine love to overcome death and hell, especially by the imitation of Jesus' attitude toward his own impending death. Finally, the books typically conclude with prayers for the dying and practical advice on funeral ritual.

How We Die

Such ways and means of preparing ourselves for the last chapter of our life stories may seem a bit unreal if not morbid to contemporary Christians, who are more used to leaving such work in the hands of others. But until the modern era, especially the recent past, death was an inescapable reality in the life of the family and community, as it is, God knows, among the people of Iraq, the Sudan, Afghanistan, the Congo, and other violently troubled parts of the world today. In modern America, and increasingly in other parts of the affluent world, death has become an ever more remote experience, as professionals have increasingly removed the burden and the glory of accompanying our loved ones on their last great journey and preparing their bodies for burial. In our technological, specialised and mechanised society, people often die alone in hospital rooms surrounded by blinking machines amid a tangle of tubes and hoses. Bodies are removed and prepared for burial far out of sight of family and friends, and often, at least in major cities, the coffin is left in an 'interment chapel', awaiting actual burial when the 'ground crew' can get around to it, possibly on the next day. Gone are the days when burying our beloved dead meant seeing them into the ground and, as I have witnessed in devout Jewish funerals, the members of the immediate family adding a spadeful of earth to cover the casket.

In some respects, the tide of technologically distancing ourselves from our own mortality and that of our friends and loved ones is perceptibly if slowly changing. For several years, a movement has been growing toward a more direct and personal way of dealing with death and burial. The hospice movement has greatly returned human dignity to the prospect of dying, as we have seen earlier. The ritual of preparing and burying the dead has also seen a return to more natural and humane practice, including simplified (and far less costly) funeral arrangements and burial. But even the experience of dying has entered a new era of physical, psychological and perhaps especially spiritual significance.

Dying hasn't changed much since humans came on the world scene,[6] but how we interpret the experience certainly has. It is a final adventure that can hardly avoid fascinating as well as frightening us, as we face (as we certainly know in our honest moments of reflection that we must) the supremely unknown dimension of human existence, that 'undiscover'd country, from whose bourn / No traveller returns ...'[7] I recall how my father, as he approached the hour of his own death, was asked by the kind Franciscan chaplain at the hospital whether he was afraid of dying. My father, who over seven decades of life in the western United States had not been afraid of very many things, replied, 'Well, I've never done this before'.

He entered that country peacefully, however, and without any sign of fearfulness. As I kept vigil at his bedside over the next quarter of an hour I could not help but envy him a little as he embarked on the last great adventure of his life. But he didn't tell me what it was like. Some people do, however, especially if they are not sedated (as my father was, somewhat, because of advanced cancer) or unconscious.

Riders in the Chariot

A number of years ago, I came to know briefly one of the most interesting researchers I ever met, Dr Karlis Osis (1917–1997), whose specialty was for many years collecting the observations of doctors and nurses attending people who died in lucid consciousness. Osis collated their accounts in a fine monograph and went on to replicate his work in India, to determine to what extent cultural differences influenced the reports of the experience of dying.[8] His conclusions were not only consistent, but in many respects astonishing, given the tendency of physicians to view death as a clinical event rather than spiritual experience. Even more intriguing, many of Osis' findings matched those of other researchers, notably Dr Elizabeth Kübler-Ross, whose teaching and publications revolutionised the clinical-pastoral understanding and ministry of dying and death. (Not by accident, I am inclined to believe, I had attended a workshop administered by Dr Kübler-Ross a few years earlier, just as she was developing her revolutionary approach to the field.)

What Osis and Kübler-Ross discovered was that in a very large number of cases, one might say *typically*, the experience of dying passes through several stages. At first, the dying person is clearly aware of the people present in the room and converses with them. In the next phase, the dying person becomes aware of the presence of others in the room who are invisible and inaudible to the living people in the room, but converses with members of both groups. The dying man or woman's attention then shifts from the visible, audible persons present in the room to those their flesh and blood companions cannot see or hear, eventually ignoring the former altogether shortly before breathing their last. Sometimes the dying person is surprised and delighted to find family members and old friends among the presences unseen and unheard by the physicians, nurses and others in the room, and who seem, on later reflection, to have come in the role of escorts. (Occasionally unknown but friendly 'helpers', as Kübler-Ross called them, also come to assist; later she referred to them as 'angels'.)

People in the final stages of life sometimes see other beings – angels, saints, revered cultural figures and so forth. What Osis and his associates discovered is that we are prepared for these 'visits' by our belief systems. Both Catholics and Protestants may see Jesus, but Jews do not. Catholics sometimes see the Virgin Mary, but Protestants do not. All groups tend to see relatives and friends. In India, people see devas as well as ancestors, but do not see Jesus or Mary (unless they are Christians). In short, dying persons encounter those they might expect to encounter, even if they are sometimes surprised when they 'see' someone they did not know had died before them.

Does this mean that they are simply hallucinating, seeing what they 'want' to see? Not necessarily, although hallucinations cannot be ruled out, nor should they be. A hallucination is, after all, only a sensory experience that cannot be verified by independent observation. Dreams, visions and apparitions of the dead are also hallucinations in that sense, but the experience may be very real to those having it. Once we have settled our scores with what is and is not 'real', the subject might be treated more exactly. That I cannot see electromagnetic fields does not mean they are not 'there'. By the same line of reasoning, the clinically observed experiences of dying persons cannot be taken as 'proof' of life after death. But they certainly don't disprove it! In this regard, Osis' own conclusions are worth considering:

> Evidence for possible survival of bodily death comes mainly from research on the following phenomena: apparition experiences collectively perceived, some types of out-of-body experiences, certain aspects of near-death experiences, selected communications ostensibly coming from the dead ... Assessments of the evidence vary greatly among researchers, ranging from those who find no acceptable evidence for survival ... to those who find certainty ... The researcher's own philosophical outlook seems to have a strong influence on the conclusions that are reached. Most researchers take a position somewhere in the middle, and various theories of survival are presented by [Robert] Thouless (1984). Apparently, the

evidence is not yet strong enough to sway scholars whose philosophy has no place for disembodied existence.[9]

Final Passages

Christian concern with dying and death has characteristically reflected the enduring belief in the sacramentality of the body enshrined in late Jewish and early Christian traditions. Although connected with belief in the resurrection of the dead, there is also a compassionate dimension that has also influenced practice – the suitable disposition of human remains. In times past, refusing to allow the bodies of the dead to find proper internment was looked upon as the ultimate degradation. Bodies left hanging on gibbets as a deterrent to crime or rebellion were looked on with particular horror.

Well into the modern era, 'pious societies' existed in European cities that scoured the alleys and ditches where the dead bodies of the poor were often discarded so that they might at least have a decent Christian burial. Similarly, sodalities provided burial for those executed for crimes or political misprision. In those often more humane eras of the past, a portion of the local cemetery, sometimes called 'the Potter's Field', was reserved for the anonymous poor and outcast. (The English word 'cemetery' comes from the Greek *koimetarion*, 'sleeping place'.) Even those who died outside the favour of the Church were allowed proper burial, if only on the other side of the cemetery fence, as I remember well from my boyhood in New Mexico. As an altar boy occasionally (and happily) excused from school to serve a funeral mass, I was puzzled by the ragged-looking wooden crosses that clustered just across the wire fence near the poorest part of Mount Calvary Cemetery. Eventually I was told that that was where unbaptised babies, tramps and suicide victims were buried – customs now superseded or, more likely, abandoned. But even the lost sheep were cared for to that extent.

The life work and beatification in 2003 of Mother Teresa of Calcutta illuminated the importance of providing the poor a place to die in peace and possible comfort and to find rest, finally, for their haggard and wasted remains. Up to recent times, such concern was considered a chief act of Christian charity, one of the seven 'Corporal Works of Mercy'. In an epoch in which the cost of funerals has escalated into the tens of thousands of dollars, it is perhaps time to recover such a venerable and noble tradition on a much wider scale.

The final disposition of the deceased has acquired a different and distinctively contemporary spiritual significance in two related areas not so much denied as unimaginable to our ancestors – the donation of vital organs to those in need and the donation of our bodies to medical science. I remember keenly the first funeral of a good friend, Dr James Barry, whose funeral mass in 1990 was celebrated in the absence of a body, for he had willed his cadaver to a medical school. At the time, many of his friends were surprised, although such a gesture was hardly uncharacteristic of such a fine and thoughtful man. Since then, a number of friends and associates have offered this last and lasting gift of self for the sake of helping others to live. Similarly, the religious suspicion and sometime disfavour at signing organ donor cards has given way to acceptance and even enthusiasm. Resurrection can be realised in more ways than our ancestors ever dreamed.

Cremation, too, has gained acceptance in Catholic and other more traditional denominations after centuries of resistance. In times past, cremating bodies was sometimes a practical necessity during times of pestilence or particularly violent warfare, if only to prevent the spread of disease. But during more peaceful times cremation was sometimes interpreted as a sign of disrespect, and indeed for some unbelievers was deliberately chosen as a riposte against belief in life after death or the resurrection of the body. Land shortage and increasing costs have in some instances necessitated cremation, however. In Asian nations, where cremation is not looked on as a sign of disrespect, it has long been practiced by Christians there. On a visit to Japanese Catholic churches some years ago in Tokyo, Kyoto and Hiroshima, I was profoundly impressed by the burial chambers set aside in the churches where the ashes of parishioners were placed in small family vaults decorated with pictures and sometimes small keepsakes belonging to the recently departed. In a country where open land is very rare and the population large, cemeteries such as those in the United States and parts of Europe would be unthinkably expensive and, in fact, impossible.

The Eschatological Dimension: the Sacramentality of Death

Almost all Christians recite both the Apostles' Creed and the Nicene Creed, statements of faith refined by centuries of debate and controversy. Both creeds, and others from the dusty library of statements affirming Christian faith, specify belief in 'the resurrection of the dead' or 'the resurrection of the body', and 'life everlasting', as well as the judgement of 'the living and the dead'. Little authoritative detail was ever provided about the content of those beliefs, which have changed significantly over the centuries. But the traditional understanding and doctrine of 'eschatology' (from the Greek word *eschatos*, meaning 'the last in a series') came to focus on 'the four last things' – death, judgement, hell and heaven. Volumes have been written on all these items, much of it fanciful, some of it even lucid and helpful.

Vast tubs of ink and not a little blood were also devoted in past ages to quarrels about and expositions of the joys of heaven and the torments of hell, the problems of purgatory and limbo, the fate of unbaptised infants, and the lot of fallen angels, demons and the salvation of intelligent aliens. Some of the world's great literature arose from such preoccupations, not least among them the *Divine Comedy* of Dante Alighieri. In recent times, theological reflection has concentrated mainly on time and death, although bold ventures into investigations of the meaning of heaven, hell and life everlasting continue to appear on a fairly regular schedule. (Much of the contemporary publishing and popular frenzy about 'the End Times' – the Tribulation, the Rapture, the 'End of the World' and other Millenarian themes – has little to do with theology, spirituality, or indeed, solid biblical study.)[10]

In addition to theological studies of death, a number of recent works on near-death experiences, post-mortem experience and apparitions continue to stimulate discussion and the popular imagination. Beneath the fluctuating currents of popular and academic enthusiasm, it is clear enough that the sacramental or mystical dimensions of dying and death are never far from the medical and psychological accounts of the phenomenon of death. None of that is likely to diminish significantly in years to come.

Afterlife: Eschatology and Immortality

Some incoherence exists in the age-old attempts to make Christian sense out of the hopes and desires of people in regard to what happens after death. It is an incoherence not unlike that in *Hamlet*, in which the Prince of Denmark ponders death as 'The undiscover'd country, from whose bourn / No traveller returns ...' in the midst of an action initiated precisely by the return of one of those travellers, his own father (III, 2).

Theologians, poets, philosophers, novelists, film-makers and playwrights have attempted to portray the further adventures of 'souls' separated from their bodies in the 'afterlife', but despite good intentions and occasionally good literature, it remains an impossible task. Popular parabolic films such as *Ghost* (1990) or *What Dreams May Come* (1998) not to mention spooky entertainments such as *The Others* (2001), envision 'life after death' as some sort of continuation of life before death and owes as much to pre-Christian speculation by Greek dramatists and poets than (certainly) to Scripture, however moralistic they may appear.

The Medium and the Message

For those who believe one way or another in the survival of the human spirit or soul after death, making contact with those who have died (or their contacting us) has provided a perennial lure to peer behind the veil of mortality to glimpse something of that country from whose bourn no traveller at least ordinarily returns. In some cultures, spirit travel to the realm of the dead is almost taken for granted in the experience of shamans and witch doctors. For the ancient Hebrews, it was a crime worthy of death, as recounted famously in the story of King Saul and 'the Witch of Endor' (1 Sam 28:7-25). Spiritualism arose in the United States and England in the mid-nineteenth century, as ordinary people as well as writers, poets and scientists of the ilk of Charles Dickens, Samuel Taylor Coleridge, Alfred Russel Wallace, Sir Arthur Conan Doyle and Sir Oliver Lodge resorted to mesmerists and mediums to probe for apertures in the veil between this world and the next. Whether any of them succeeded in the slightest is at least open to quibble, but in the twentieth century, a new wrinkle was added in the form of electronic communication with the dead.

Voices of the Dead

Survival of bodily death is an item of belief in all Christian creeds, even if the meaning of the propositions vary from person to person and time to time. Visions of departed persons have been part of the circumstances of death and burial from earliest times. Such apparitions were studied intently at the end of the nineteenth century, and some of the research work has never been equalled. Interest has never waned, but today it is likely to be relegated to cable television channels where audiences follow the adventures of 'ghost hunter' teams as they explore haunted houses and other places of interest. The most lucid and interesting account of fairly recent attempts to fathom the afterlife is that by Mary Roach in her enjoyably kinky book *Spook*.[11] Unfortunately, she fails to do justice to the meticulous work of researches such as F.W.H. Myers at the turn of the century or more current research such as that done by Osis.[12] Roach does give fleeting mention, however, to one of the more fascinating researchers I have encountered, Dr Konstantin Raudive.[13]

I met Raudive and his wife in June 1972 when I visited them in their home in Tübingen, Germany, in the company of a Belgian electronics engineer I had invited along to verify the equipment the old Latvian had been using to record what he was convinced were 'voices of the dead'. I had read Raudive's difficult but absorbing book, *Breakthrough*, and some of his articles on electronic communication with the dead.[14] I was curious to say the least about his methods of recording as well as the communications he reported receiving from some of the departed. Dr Raudive confirmed that, among other events, he had been consulted by the Vatican about his reports, since they appeared to bear on the ordinary teaching of the Catholic Church about purgatory. To all accounts, there was nothing contrary to faith in his claims. Whether they were factual was a different matter.

What impressed me about Raudive, beyond his evident sincerity, even passion concerning his research, was the method he had finally selected to eliminate random broadcast signals as he recorded his 'voices' on his tape recorder. To block microphone interference, he inserted a short-stem diode into the microphone jack, which would (I was told by the engineer) permit reception of transmissions only in the immediate vicinity, specifically to the tape head itself.

Raudive claimed that some of the 'voices' he picked up belonged to well-known persons including Adolf Hitler (speaking German), Winston Churchill and John F. Kennedy. He also claimed to hear the voice of Pope John XXIII. The brief bursts of audible speech detectable when the tapes were played back at the highest volume did seem to manifest the timbre and pitch one might associate with such familiar voices. Uncannily so in the case of 'Churchill'. But what the voices said was garbled, at least to the untrained ear.

Although many attempts were made to replicate Raudive's research, as with cold fusion, none were very successful. Some of my own students attempted to record 'voices of the dead' by taking a tape recorder to a local and relatively quiet cemetery and recording both with a microphone and also without one. All they succeeded in producing (other than a good scare from being out on a dark autumn night in a chilly deserted cemetery) was a stream of static and occasional distant traffic noises.

A few commentators have suggested that Raudive's experiments were successful in some measure because he had, unknown to himself, mediumistic abilities which enabled him to channel voices of the departed to the tape head. That in itself would be a considerable feat, but Raudive always denied that he had any psychic powers.

It may be doubted whether anything at all was learned from the painstaking experiments of Raudive and others but it is highly probable that more electronically sophisticated attempts will be made in time to come. Ghost hunters equipped with infrared cameras and ultra-sensitive recording equipment will no doubt continue to populate satellite and cable television programmes as well, but like the media-savvy medium John Edwards, none have yet produced any evidence capable of surviving rigorous analysis. Clearly, however, at least the possibility of establishing some form of bridge between the living and the dead testifies to the enduring belief in post-mortem survival.

For those of more traditional persuasions, the testimony of sacred scripture remains sufficient and more than likely exclusive warrant. But even here, the content of belief is sometimes more surprising than common opinion suspects.

Immortality or Eternal Life?

One of the most probing analyses of (western) pagan and Christian eschatology – the doctrine of 'the last things' – was penned by Simon Tugwell in 1990.[15] Not even Tugwell's prodigious examination is able in the end to remove all the ambiguities and confusion from various, often conflicting accounts of possible post-mortem existence. It is nevertheless reassuring in the light of the April 2007 statement from the International Theological Commission, an adjunct of the Congregation for the Doctrine of the Faith, which relegated Limbo to the back shelves of mythology, that he just ignored it.[16] Tugwell's treatment of heaven, hell and purgatory is brief and bracingly sober, to say the least. To my mind, he properly focuses on the primary matters of death and judgement, which were traditionally the major themes of eschatological speculation, whether dogmatic or spiritual.

In particular, Tugwell avoids finding refuge in visions of immortality derived from Greek speculation on the immateriality of the soul, an opinion alien to the Hebrew conception of personality and early Christian attitudes which anchored hope not in metaphysics but God's power and mercy:

> Apart from its usefulness in interpreting and reinforcing belief in the resurrection, Christian tradition is remarkably uninterested

in claiming immortality for the soul by right, and the language of the Bible and the liturgy is, if anything, inimical to such a claim, treating immortality rather as something belonging only to God by right and then, by God's gift, to the risen Christ and those who are saved in him as a result of the resurrection. It is a hope proposed to the believer, not a property inherent in the human soul.[17]

While belief in life beyond death, if not immortality in the ancient pagan sense, remains part of the Christian tradition, it should be noted, if all too briefly, that in Christian practice, attention has shifted increasingly to the psychological and spiritual welfare of those 'left behind', the bereaved as they are euphemistically called. Over the last quarter century, bereavement ministry has taken its rightful place in the pastoral training of both lay and clerical students.[18] Partially as a result of reclaiming the care of the dying and grieving, new directions in funeral practice are developing, many of which reflect an emphasis on simplicity and social justice. One of the more interesting developments has been a movement toward simplified burial procedures.[19]

Not least in the concerns of the movement towards more natural forms of burial is the environmental aspect, as more and more urban land has been taken up (and certainly will in the future) for vast cemeteries and mausoleums. I was surprised twenty years ago to find that in congested areas of England, graves are only 'rented' for a limited time, after which the grave will be opened and another coffin placed on top of it. For people devoted to wandering through centuries-old cemeteries poring over weathered gravestones under sweeping yews and stately Cedars of Lebanon, modern funeral procedures must seem a bit heartless. Similarly, decorating graves, an annual event in many traditional communities, will become a very confusing outing if it is continued at all. Devising new procedures for burial or disposal of remains and new rituals of remembrance will undoubtedly figure in the mortuary practices of the near future.

In the meantime, people will of course continue to die, others will mourn their loss, and the bodies of loved ones will be committed to some kind of final resting place. And for us, the living, beacons of hope and remembrance will continue to burn if not as brightly as in simpler times, at least steadily in the thoughts of those who have gone ahead.

> Because I know the spark
> Of God has no eclipse,
> Now Death and I embark
> And sail into the dark
> With laughter on our lips.
> Joseph M. Plunkett, 'The Spark'

NOTES

1. See Ernest Becker, *The Denial of Death* (New York: Free Press, 1997 ed.). Becker's book, which may still be read with profit, won the Pulitzer Prize for non-fiction in 1974, just two months after his own death.
2. See Jessica Mitford, *The American Way of Death* (New York: Random House, 1983 ed.) and Jessica Mitford, *The American Way of Death Revisited* (New York: Knopf, 2000).
3. Evelyn Waugh, *The Loved One* (London: Chapman and Hall, 1948 and Boston: Little Brown and Co., 1977 ed.).
4. Bianchi, op. cit., pp. 6–7.
5. For an excellent online article on the *ars moriendi* manuscript tradition by Donald Duclow see www.deathreference.com/A-Bi/Ars-Moriendi.html.
6. The biological process of physical death, with its psychological and sociological aspects, was superbly treated in Dr Sherwin B. Nuland's book *How We Die: Reflections on Life's Final Chapter* (New York: Alfred Knopf, 1994).
7. *Hamlet, Prince of Denmark*, III. i. 79–80.
8. See Karlis Osis, *Deathbed Observations by Physicians and Nurses, Parapsychological Monographs* 3 (New York: Parapsychology Foundation, Inc., 1961) and Karlis Osis and Erlendur Haraldsson, *At the Hour of Death*, intro. by Elizabeth Kübler-Ross (New York: Hastings House, 1986 ed. [orig. New York: Avon Books, 1977]).
9. Karlis Osis, 'Life after Death?', *Encyclopedia of Death*, ed. by Robert and Beatrice Kastenbaum (Phoenix, AZ: Oryx Press, 1989), p. 174. Also see the *ASPR Newsletter* 16 (Summer 1990) 3:25–8. The reference is to an article by the distinguished English psychologist, Robert Thouless, 'Do we survive bodily death?' *Proceedings of the Society for Psychical Research* 57 (1984):1–52.

10. Among recent works see Joseph Rhymer, *The End of Time: Eschatology of the New Testament* (Slough and Maynooth: St. Paul Publications, 1992); Jeffrey Burton Russell, *A History of Heaven* (Princeton and Chichester: Princeton University Press, 1997); John Shea, *What a Modern Catholic Believes about Heaven and Hell* (Chicago: Thomas More Press, 1972); Reginald Stackhouse, *The End of the World? A New Look at an Old Belief* (New York: Paulist Press, 1997); and Alice K. Turner, *The History of Hell* (San Diego and New York: Harcourt, Brace and Co., 1993).

11. Mary Roach, *Spook: Science Tackles the Afterlife* (New York: W.W. Norton, 2005).

12. See especially Frederick W.H. Myers, *Human Personality and Its Survival of Bodily Death*, ed. and abridged by Leopold Myers (London: Longman, Green and Co., 1907. Orig: 2 volumes, 1902.)

13. See *Spook*, op. cit., pp. 183–5.

14. Konstantin Raudive, *Breakthrough: An Amazing Experiment in Electronic Communication with the Dead*, translated by Nadia Fowler, edited by Joyce Morton, with a preface by Peter Bander (Gerrards Cross, Buckinghamshire: Colin Smythe Ltd., 1971).

15. Simon Tugwell, OP, *Human Immortality and the Redemption of Death* (London: Darton, Longman and Todd, 1990).

16. See 'The Hope of Salvation for Infants Who Die Without Being Baptized,' *Origins*, Vol. 36, No. 45 (Washington, D.C., Catholic News Service, 2007). The text may also be accessed on the Vatican web site: www.vatican.va/roman_curia/congregations/cfaith/cti_documents/rc_con _cfaith_doc_20070419_un-baptised-infants_en.html.

17. Tugwell, op. cit., p. 163. He continues, 'All that christian orthodoxy is concerned to secure can surely be adequately safeguarded without appealing to any sort of "hybrid" view of human nature. The coincidence of mortality and immortality, of life and death, in the believer rests on the coincidence of divinity and humanity in Christ.' For a trenchant philosophical analysis of the belief in immortality, see William Ernest Hocking, *The Meaning of Immortality in Human Experience* (Westport, Connecticut: Greenwood Press, 1973). Other important works include John H. Hick, *Death and Eternal Life* (San Francisco: Harper and Row, 1976), Ignace Lepp, *Death and Its Mysteries*, trans. and intro. by Bernard Murchland (New York: Macmillan Co., 1968), and Karl Rahner, SJ, *On the Theology of Death* [*Quaestiones disputatae*] (New York: Herder and Herder, 1962).

18. Valuable pastoral resources include Jan C. Nelson and David Aaker, *Bereavement Ministry Program: A Comprehensive Guide for Churches* (Notre Dame: Ave Maria Press, 1998); Mauryeen O'Brien, OP, *Praying Through Grief: Healing Prayer Services for Those Who Mourn* (Notre Dame: Ave Maria Press, 1997); Harold Ivan Smith, *Death and Grief: Healing Through Group Support* (Minneapolis: Augsburg Fortress Press, 1997); *Harriet Young, Bereavement*

Ministry: A Leader's Resource Manual (Mystic, CT: Twenty-Third Publications, 1997); and, I would add, Lois Lindsey Hendricks, *Dreams That Help You Mourn* (San Jose, CA: Resource Publications, 1997).

19. See Jane E. Brody, 'Alternatives for the Final Disposition,' *New York Times*, 15 April 2008, p. D7, Lisa Carlson, *Caring for the Dead: Your Final Act of Love* (Hinesburg, VT: Upper Access Books, 1998), and Mark Harris, *Grave Matters: A Journey Through the Modern Funeral Industry to a Natural Way of Burial* (New York: Scribner, 2007).

CHAPTER ELEVEN
SOCIALITY
LOVE, SEX, MARRIAGE AND FRIENDSHIP

Love is not love
Which alters when it alteration finds,
Or bends with the remover to remove.
O no! it is an ever-fixed mark
That looks on tempests and is never shaken;
It is the star to every wand'ring bark,
Whose worth's unknown, although his height be taken.
William Shakespeare, *Sonnet 116*

By this point, it should be evident from decades of scientific research that spirituality and health are intimately connected with social bonds and, well, intimacy. As we have seen, married people tend to live longer than people who remain single (with the exception of community-bonded monks and nuns). Further, friendship has been regarded not only as a principal virtue and one of the greatest joys of life since Plato and Aristotle walked the streets of Athens, but also as health-protective. What is it that gives affectionate social connection the power to heal? We can begin to pursue an answer by looking at its opposite.

Loneliness has been described accurately in the subtitle of an early scientific study as 'the experience of social and emotional isolation'.[1] For the lonely person, the social network which supports, heals and enhances human life has been disrupted – not merely temporarily, but permanently and severely. In his classic little book, *On Caring*, Milton Meyerhoff described this state of affairs as a sense of being 'out of place' rather than 'in place'.[2]

Some years later, in a highly influential article, the Jesuit psychiatrist James Gill utilised the psychosocial network grid developed by Dr E. Mansell Pattison, a distinguished Christian psychiatrist, to describe the anxiety problems of celibates, among which loneliness is a preeminent problem:

> A normal network is one in which a person has ongoing relationships with 22 to 25 persons, with five or six persons in each of four subgroups (family, relatives, friends/neighbours, and social/work associates). An individual who has such a network around him, Pattison found, has frequent contacts with and a positive and strong emotional investment in most of these people. The relationships are valued and reciprocal, and those involved provide one another with concrete assistance when needed.

The neurotic network, by contrast,

> includes only about fifteen people, with fewer relatives, friends and co-workers, and a higher reliance on a person's own nuclear family. There are frequent negative and weak emotional interactions, and many of the fifteen persons are seen infrequently or not at all. The individual within this network interacts with only half as many persons in each subgroup ... as does a person in a normal network.[3]

Such a fragmentary style of life is characteristic of chronic loneliness and in many respects points to the negative dimension of enforced celibacy and the psychological adjustment problems that can arise from it both in the Church and in the wider society. It was therefore not surprising to learn that as Dr Lynch recognised, acute loneliness can break our hearts: 'The mortality statistics for heart disease among those adult Americans who are not married are striking – a death rate from heart disease that is as much as two to five times higher for non-married individuals, and those who are divorced, widowed or single, than for married Americans.'[4]

According to Pattison and others, the primary 'pool' from which healthier people draw their friends and associates tends to be the true kinship system – blood relatives. About half come from the extended family. The rest are evenly divided between workplace companions and friends made over a lifetime of contact from neighbourhood, school, church and other associations. Decades of research have identified the family, however, as the chief source of happiness and satisfaction in life. 'Family' ordinarily implies marriage, of course, and it is to marriage that we shall principally turn for a consideration of the health benefits of friendship. But family is not the only source. Close extra-familial friendships are also a potent source of mutual support, encouragement and health.

In beginning our quest for the health in love and companionship, we will start with the body, the foundation of all spirituality. Sexuality is the primary expression of family-based love and friendship (and sometimes the source of tension, conflict and suffering as well). The psychological and social aspects of marriage are vital in understanding both individual and community health, of course. And the sacramental dimension rises from human love to its incorporation in divine love, not only in the sacrament of marriage, but in the wedding feast of heaven, the favourite image used by Jesus to refer to the Kingdom of God.

Sexuality and Spirituality

To begin with, just as all spirituality begins with the body, so does sexuality: and the question naturally arises, why sex? What is it for? What does it do? (The answer, of course, is 'not quite everything, but a lot'.) *Functionally*, sexuality does much more than propagate one's own genes or even the genetic endowment of the tribe, clan, nation, or species. In humans particularly, sex becomes (ideally) an expression of love and affection. Physiologically, as a source of pleasure, it activates the entire endocrine system, relieving stress and rejuvenating the nervous system, cardio-vascular system and even the respiratory system.

Psychologically, consciously entering the world of sexuality in early adolescence constitutes a 'rite of passage' into adult life and responsibility – admittedly a raucous, scary and sometimes wounding experience. Sexual attraction coaxes people out of their introspective shells into the vibrant world of social competition, rivalry, bonding, and ultimately love and mating. Marriage is sanctioned as a social institution because it strengthens the network of relationships that unite a community, providing the protective environment for the next generation. Nuptial celebrations foster the unity and integrity of society and the world, forging social and political bonds among families, tribes, peoples and even nations.

Individuals can get lost in all of this, and it is not accidental that in both European and Asian literary traditions many of the great love stories, especially tragedies such as *Tristan and Iseult* or *Romeo and Juliet,* involve a conflict between individual desire and the social requirements regarding marriage and the impossible demands these place on young lovers. Social custom and pathology can turn sexuality into a weapon as well, as it finds use to demonstrate and enforce political supremacy, power and rank. Rape has long been the resort of those who wish to humiliate conquered peoples, and sexual mutilation has been imposed on both women and men as punishment and the ultimate mark of subordination and degradation.

In the West, the medieval institution of marriage was developed and surrounded by fences of ecclesiastical law for purposes of securing family hegemony, political, ethnic and economic alliances, and preservation of wealth.[5] The *sacramental* aspect, slow to be recognised in Christianity, was pressed into service of contractual obligation. Why it took a millennium for Christians to develop an authentic theology of marriage as a sacrament owes much to the social calamities following the collapse of classical antiquity. The fledgling egalitarianism of the late Roman Empire was not fully recovered until well after Charlemagne had instituted the new and 'Holy' Roman Empire in the ninth century.

However, the spiritual or sacramental dimension of marriage was present at a very early stage as a covenantal bond that not only symbolised our relationship with God as creator and lover but made it distinctively and solidly real. In pagan cultures marriage rites had for centuries displayed a cosmic dimension, as the lateral relationship of individual persons was taken to represent a vertical union with the gods, effecting and signifying the right order of the world. Ancient customs such as 'hierogamy', the ritual union of the king and high priestess at the beginning of the New Year, the dismal medieval privilege known as *le droit de seigneur* and the ritual copulation of peasants in the fields on the first of May insured the fertility of the land.[6]

As Christian society developed, the marital spirituality of Judaism and the reflections of Jesus and St Paul were brought together into a new and different synthesis. The mystical dimension of marriage as a sign of Christ's union with the Church in which we, too, are united with God began to vie with the contractual and cosmic interpretation:

> Husbands, love your wives, as Christ loved the church and gave himself up for her, that he might sanctify her, having cleansed her by the washing of water with the word, that he might present the church to himself in splendour, without spot or wrinkle or any such thing, that she might be holy and without blemish. Even so husbands should love their wives as their own bodies. He who loves his wife loves himself. For no man ever hates his own flesh, but nourishes and cherishes it, as Christ does the church, because we are members of his body.
>
> 'For this reason a man shall leave his father and mother and be joined to his wife, and the two shall become one flesh.' This mystery is a profound one, and I am saying that it refers to Christ and the church; however, let each one of you love his wife as himself, and let the wife see that she respects her husband. (Eph 5:25-33)

Adding the ecclesial, Christic dimension to marriage enriched its symbolic value immensely. But many troubling issues remain to be addressed even in a contemporary theology of marriage – physiological *dysfunction*, including infertility, anorgasmia and impotence; psychological *disintegration*, including rape, child abuse, incest; and (not to mince words) *sin*, the opposite of sacramentality, which amounts to 'sacrilege' – infidelity, religious misrepresentation and lovelessness.[7] Patriarchal domination, sexism of all stripes and the persecution of sexual minorities fall into this latter category, as increasingly recognised by the churches.

Sexuality is a complex and variable phenomenon, individually, socially, culturally and spiritually. People who do not share the predominant forms of sexual identity or adopt the sexual roles expected within their society often find themselves bearing the full weight of fear and dysfunction associated with sex in all its dimensions. Achieving sexual health in such circumstances is a truly Herculean task. But not an impossible one. Such healthiness means, fundamentally, being 'at home' with oneself and others, neither fearing discrimination nor oppressing others because of real or perceived differences. Maintaining such balance requires even greater reserves of psychological and spiritual stamina, but as a counsellor, therapist and confessor, I know it can be achieved because I have seen it in action.

Preserving the good will and promise of marriage is the most difficult of all such challenges in today's world, where so often infidelity is taken for granted if not actually expected, especially as reflected in popular entertainment media. And so it is to the promise and peril of marriage that we turn for an understanding of sexual health. For as Evelyn and James Whitehead said so well, 'As a religious covenant, marriage is a sign and source of God's love. The commitments of marriage – communion, fidelity, permanence – provide a framework that can protect and purify the promises of sexual love'.[8]

The Spirituality in Christian Marriage[9]
The Catholic Christian view of marriage is not what it used to be. At least not since it was redefined significantly during the Second Vatican Council, a revolution not much noticed at the time, but nevertheless both extensive in scope and profound in its implications.

Not least of these was the emphasis placed on the spirituality in marriage. In effect, the Council recognised Christian marriage as the primary source, the model and the sign of all Christian spirituality.

A number of books have been written on the subject since then, many of them excellent.[10] In this chapter, I intend to consider only two of the primary elements found in the spirituality of Christian marriage, the dual 'goods' of personal development and healing.

My perspective on marriage may seem a little biased. To begin with, as a Dominican friar, I am not now nor have I ever been a member of the married class. Yet over four decades of ministry, I have instructed a host of prospective brides and grooms, witnessed their marriages, baptised their children, and counselled them when difficulties arise. For over twenty-five years I worked as a marital therapist in the department of psychiatry at Loyola University's Medical Centre helping couples heal their relationships. Finally, I research, teach and write about Christian spirituality. The interplay of ministry, therapy and spirituality have proved to be a rich source of learning. For in the end, I am a student of marriage, not a marriage expert. Married people are the experts and many have been my teachers.

Among other things I have come to learn from my expert teachers is that spirituality and sexuality are not only intimately related but inextricably connected. I have also learned that the role of sexuality is only one of a number of components in marriage, several of which couples value even more highly – a fact some discover only late in life, but many come to appreciate early enough to preserve and enhance their relationship when sexual dysfunction occurs. And to one extent or another, it inevitably occurs. When it becomes serious and threatens the health of a relationship, some couples seek assistance at a clinic such as ours, and I can claim, thankfully, that about 85 per cent report improvement. But the real healing in a relationship does not occur on the sexual level alone, although it may take effect there. The most effective and deepest healing is emotional, cognitive and spiritual.

Plighting Our Troth

For those whose Middle English is a little rusty, *plight* is both a verb and a noun. The verb means to pledge, especially one's 'troth', to engage or commit oneself to someone. The noun means 'condition' and especially 'danger', which we may ascribe to an unhappy verbal coincidence. *Troth*, that which gets plighted, if even sometimes dangerously, simply means 'truth', and as a pledge, means giving one's word. 'Truth' signifies the quality of being true, and in Old and Middle English 'true' is a verb as well as an adjective. It means to bring something into the right or accurate position, alignment, or form and as an adjective denotes loyalty, sincerity and reality.

Today a bride and groom are more likely to 'promise to be true' than 'plight their troth', which means the same thing but with less of a flourish in the direction of Middle English. And what the couple promise is to be loyal, steadfast and faithful in bad times as well as good times, in sickness as well as health, to love and support each other until parted by death. Life doesn't always turn out that way, but that is the dream, the hope and the ideal. Like all such hopes, it is not something that simply happens, but a project that has to be made real. A good marriage is not made in heaven, by the way. It is made right here on earth. It is made, further, by days and years of hard work. We don't always succeed.

Nor is a good marriage made the way a car, a computer, or a television set is made, by assembling and reassembling pieces, but the way a garden is made, or a baby: for a marriage is a living thing, a real relationship that needs nourishment, care and sometimes healing in order to live, grow and thrive. It is that living heart of relationship that constitutes the spirituality in marriage.

Being a Christian ought to help, but that is not always the case. St Paul, for instance, had some sobering thoughts to offer the young Christians at Corinth:

> I want you to be free from anxieties. The unmarried man is anxious about the affairs of the Lord, how to please the Lord; but the married man is anxious about worldly affairs, how to please his wife, and his interests are divided. And the unmarried

woman or girl is anxious about the affairs of the Lord, how to be holy in body and spirit; but the married woman is anxious about worldly affairs, how to please her husband.

He goes on, although the selection read out in Sunday liturgies stops mercifully short of this passage:

I say this for your own benefit, not to lay any restraint upon you, but to promote good order and to secure your undivided devotion to the Lord. If any one thinks that he is not behaving properly toward his betrothed, if his passions are strong, and it has to be, let him do as he wishes: let them marry – it is no sin. But whoever is firmly established in his heart, being under no necessity but having his desire under control, and has determined this in his heart, to keep her as his betrothed, he will do well. So that he who marries his betrothed does well; and he who refrains from marriage will do better (1 Cor 7:32-40).

St Paul's advice for reducing religious anxiety seems clear enough: don't get married unless you must. As a marriage counsellor, I can agree with him at least this far: anyone who marries and tries to raise a family in today's world is going to worry. But if Paul thought that unmarried people didn't have cause to worry, he was very much mistaken. Besides worrying about getting married, they worry about many of the same things married people worry about.

In fact, what Paul was trying to get across is that often the real cause of worry, of mental suffering, is trying to have things both ways – trusting in God and also trying to please everyone else. Or at least not irritating them excessively. His ultimate message is still sound advice: start with God, and the rest should fall into place. And if it doesn't, our trust and reliance on God will steady us and provide the strength to get back into the struggle. But no one is really free from all anxiety. Paul himself spoke of the anxiety he felt for all the churches (2 Cor 11:28). Having peace of heart does not mean a life without suffering, anxiety and worry. It means having a sure way to cope with them.

This is true of marriage no less than any other aspect of life, and perhaps even more so. And if we were to conclude that St Paul's remarks about marriage in First Corinthians cast a gloomy shadow over marriage for later Christians, we would be mistaken, although Christians who had the effrontery to assert that celibacy was not a higher calling than marriage were periodically anathematised after the fourth century. (They are still frowned upon in certain clerical circles.)

Redefining the Spiritual 'Goods' of Marriage

Such attitudes have changed substantially and significantly in recent times, most notably in the statement found in *Gaudium et Spes*, the document known in English as 'The Church in the Modern World', of the Second Vatican Council.[11] The shift in emphasis is contained in paragraph 48. At first glance, it seems innocuous enough: 'Thus the man and woman, who "are no longer two but one" (Mt 19:6), help and serve each other by their marriage partnership; they become conscious of their unity and experience it more deeply from day to day.'[12]

Gaudium et Spes places a strong and, from a clinical perspective, a very appropriate emphasis on intimacy as a condition for and the consequence of a healthy marital relationship. In times past, such intimacy was interpreted, at least canonically, as physical accessibility, particularly what was referred to not entirely metaphorically as 'paying the marriage debt'. But today, emotional and spiritual closeness, openness and mutuality are seen as equally and in fact more important. Sex without emotional honesty and care may be technically sacramental, or canonically valid at any rate, but it is questionable as both a human and Christian value. And, as the Pastoral Constitution continues:

> The intimate union of marriage, as a mutual giving of two persons, and the good of the children demand total fidelity from the spouses and require an unbreakable unity between them. Christ the Lord has abundantly blessed this love, which is rich in its various features, coming as it does from the spring of divine love and modelled on Christ's own union with the Church.[13]

Besides intimacy and fidelity, *Gaudium et Spes* thus identifies the following characteristics of a truly Christian marriage: self-giving, the good of children and lasting unity – all of which are summed up as a encompassing love emanating from God and founded, as we read in the Epistle to the Ephesians, on God's presence to the Church in Christ. Compared with previous discussions of marriage, not least of them St Paul's disquisition in First Corinthians, this description is highly innovative, especially because of the emphasis placed on intimacy, mutuality and love.

Rethinking Christian Marriage as a Relationship of Love

One area in which contemporary thinking about marriage and clinical insights from marital therapy tend to converge is in regard to the affectionate bond between spouses as an essential element in a marriage. While we may take such an insight for granted, it is more revolutionary than it might seem from a theological perspective.[14]

Recent discussion about a marriage between Christians *not* based on mutual love and support has raised the question of whether such a relationship can in fact be sacramentally valid. Since the time of St Augustine, classical theology, supported by canon law, did not list reciprocal love as one of the goods of marriage or its goal or end, implying (and more than implying) that a loveless marriage could be both licit and valid. As a legal contract, that may well be the case. But it is increasingly being questioned whether a relationship devoid of love, or even one in which love has departed, can be Christian at all, much less a sacrament.

Strangely enough, St Augustine legitimated the act of Christian homicide in warfare by positing charity as the only possible motive, and the same argument can and has in fact been used to justify the execution of heretics and repentant criminals. How sad that he did not think of it in terms of marriage. It can certainly be said that any moral act performed by conscientious Christians will and must be informed by charity. That at least is a beginning, but it is hardly equivalent to recognising love as the essence of the sacramental union.

In the classical Augustinian theology of marriage that prevailed in the Catholic Church for the last millennium and a half, the 'goods' of marriage were considered to be offspring, fidelity and permanence, and, as seen in medieval perspective, the 'ends' of marriage, which gave it its 'finality' or ultimate meaning, were the procreation and nurture of children, mutual help and remedy for concupiscence.[15] As with intimacy, recent developments in marital theology and spirituality have, since the Second Vatican Council, pointed out how limited and limiting a vision of marriage, especially Christian marriage, such an understanding manifests.

In the world of classical antiquity, including the world of early Christianity from the time of St Paul to Augustine, loving friendship between spouses was not expected, partly at least because of the pervasive opinion going back to Aristotle and beyond, that authentic friendship required and fostered equality. And with certain exceptions, Augustine's theology and experience not being among them, equality was not a feature of male–female relationships such as marriage. Perhaps especially marriage.

Real partnership in marriage such as endorsed by *Gaudium et Spes* and which presupposes the equality of spouses is possible today in ways that even our great-grandparents would hardly have recognised, living as most did in societies in which voting, serving in public office and the military services, benefiting from higher education, and engaging in professional business or scientific or artistic careers were open only to males. Equality between the sexes is a thoroughly modern idea, and a thoroughly western one, although it has been developing gradually in other parts of the world as well.

Recognising the importance of mutuality and equality in marriage is not a capitulation of Christianity to secular values, but the consequence of the slow transformation of the western European tradition in particular by other Christian values. It is here, however, that the revolution of *Gaudium et Spes* departs from previous approaches. The constitution also redefines fidelity in a much more contemporary vein.

Faithful Friendship

As *Gaudium et Spes* reiterated, fidelity and constancy have always figured prominently among marital values, the 'goods' of marriage. Whether couples advert to it or not, such faithfulness constitutes a major portion of the spirituality in marriage. Marital fidelity does not mean simply refraining from sexual contact outside marriage. As one man told me recently (someone, I should add, who is a scientist and retired university professor, as well as something of a professed agnostic), 'Every day I have faith that this woman who married me still loves me. I *believe* that'.

Another wise man once said to me in view of his daughter's impending marriage, 'every person who marries undertakes the awful risk of burying their spouse'. What's more, they embrace that risk wholeheartedly. To be faithful and true until death *is* a risk – it's a pledge and promise to share a life together. All of it. And if spirituality means the very breath of life, marriage rests on a foundation of trust that only spirituality can provide. Money, security, youth, health – all fade. I have seen marriages founder on the rocks of illth. One woman I knew was abandoned by her husband of many years, the father of her children, a few years after she was diagnosed with multiple sclerosis. 'Who wants to be married to a sick woman?' he had complained.

Viagra, Cialis and Viramax (for all their real and supposed pharmaceutical benefits) will not save a failing marriage even if they delay its dissolution. Both wives and husbands sometimes leave their spouses and children to begin a new marriage with a much younger partner, attempting to hold on to or even recapture their vanished youth. And to be sure, disturbing trends revealed by statistical analysis indicate that fidelity is under siege in our times as never before and with disturbing consequences. In the United States, for instance, in 2002, 21 per cent of white families, about 6.5 million persons, were headed by women alone. Forty-three per cent of African-American households, 3.6 million families, were likewise headed by single women. Taken together with families of other racial and ethnic groups, that amounts to 28 per cent of all American children, about 20 million, living in households with only one parent, 16.5 million or 23 per cent with their single mother.[16] It has been estimated that by 2006, 32 per cent of all US children were living in single-parent families.[17]

In Ireland, over 80,000 single parents depend on social welfare as their main source of income, costing the state nearly €830 million a year. An additional €200 million is paid out to single-parent families in rent allowance and other supports. Moreover, children in single-parent families face a much higher risk of poverty than other members of the population. Similar situations exist in Great Britain and Australia.

As a clinician as well as a spiritual theologian, I am less impressed by statistical inferences than what is sometimes called the 'in-depth' information that comes from long-term experience with individual couples who can be taken to represent a cross-section of the married population, especially given the cumulative experience of the Loyola clinic in assisting over 3,000 couples over the thirty years of its existence. And the surprising fact has emerged that despite pressure from all sides promoting infidelity and marital breakup, faithfulness remains both a social and individual value as well as a feature of much married life.[18]

The Therapeutic Dimension: The Healing Gifts of Marriage

The role of healing in marital relationships has, I believe, two major dimensions. The first is the 'internal' spiritual, emotional and sometimes physical healing that the 'goods' of marriage (intimacy, fidelity and love) themselves produce for the couple. The second form of healing is that sometimes required from outside the relationship for it to regain and maintain its health.

One of the most impressive discoveries awaiting me in the practice and theory of marital therapy was that the intimacy and loving mutuality of a healthy adult relationship can compensate for and actually heal developmental wounds suffered in childhood and adolescence. Just as every family is to some degree dysfunctional, flawless psychological, social and spiritual development is an unattainable ideal. Fortunately, people have more than one chance to acquire the appropriate personal wholeness and interpersonal skillfulness we now recognise as psychological and social healthiness. The cognitive, emotional and spiritual demands of courtship and marriage not only require but tend to produce growth in maturity and responsibility which can overcome deficiencies acquired earlier in life. They do so by recapitulation – revisiting many of the same behavioural objectives that marked earlier transitions from infancy to childhood to youth and adulthood, only at a higher and in most respects faster turn of the spiral.

Over the course of a marriage, the healing capacity of intimacy and care continue, ideally, to provide renewed strength and vital energy to the partners with which they are enabled to meet the demands of life. I suspect that this has a great deal to do with the statistical finding that married people tend to live longer than persons who remain single. (Although one of my father's favourite quips comes to mind in this regard: 'Married people don't really live longer. They just seem to.')

Even in the golden years, grand-parenting presents a third developmental period in the life cycle in which intimacy and care can produce further healing and growth, both for the grandparent and also for the child. As one counsellor put it, 'Grandparents are God's special gift to children'. (Such grand-parenting does not have to be biologically based any more than parenting does. Elderly relatives, god-parents, teachers, even friends and neighbours can provide such mentoring, which is reciprocally beneficial.)

The healing potential of marriage and family life throughout the development cycle has received increasing attention in recent years, among both psychological and spiritual researchers. It is undoubtedly one of the most rewarding of the spiritual goods of marriage. As a therapist, however, my own work has concentrated on the reciprocal of that gift – the need for healing that occurs in a relationship when challenges begin to overwhelm the couple's joint resources. But here, too, the capacity for healing arises from within the relationship. Like physical medicine, marital therapy facilitates healing. It does not create it.

The Spiritual Dimension

The radical capacity for receiving and passing on the gift of life that constitutes what we mean by 'spirit' is expressed throughout a lifetime in any number of ways, becoming concrete and real through interactions with others in the midst of the world. But it is also shaped by our cultures and traditions, including religious affiliation and participation. But in general, a person's spirituality can be described as the particular way in which he or she (or they) organise and express their view of life in terms of both their ultimate aims and values and the ordinary details of everyday life. For the majority of people, that will include marriage and family life as a major, even predominant component of their spirituality.

The difference between a spiritual and psychological perspective on marriage and marital problems is noticeable but not vast. From a psychological perspective, the enemies of love that imperil a relationship include egotism or narcissism, insecurity, withdrawal, unexpressed anger and passive-aggressive behaviour. From a spiritual viewpoint they are selfishness, indifference, jealousy or possessiveness, and envy or resentment. St Paul's remarks on true love and its enemies in First Corinthians 13:4-7 is still very much to the point:

> Love is patient and kind; love is not jealous or boastful;
> it is not arrogant or rude.
> Love does not insist on its own way; it is not irritable or resentful;
> it does not rejoice at wrong, but rejoices in the right.
> Love bears all things, believes all things, hopes all things, endures all things.

Much of the healing that comes in marital therapy results from reversing or unlearning negative behaviour and developing positive responses by resensitisation in areas that have become numbed by familiarity or neglect. Clinically this is perhaps best achieved through a series of graded exercises in which couples develop or regain communication skills and expressions, including affectionate touch, that were once spontaneous and cheerfully honest. But married life itself can and very often does provide the same kind of opportunities, whether they are recognised as such or not.

Spiritual Exercises: Acceptance and Forgiveness

Perhaps the most sensitive zone in marital healing is that involving that most Christian of virtues, forgiveness. The capacity of couples to store up real and imagined hurts in order to produce a litany of wrongs at an opportune moment is both notorious and real. It is also very damaging.

Finger-pointing started just before the gate was slammed shut on Paradise. Adam blamed Eve and Eve blamed the serpent. In Genesis and according to St Paul, the penalty paid for sin was subjection. It has taken a long time to reverse that consequence, and the process is still unfinished. In regards to marriage and family life, the critical insight is not found in Paul's advice to husbands and wives, which was heavily burdened with the patriarchal baggage of Jewish culture, but what Jesus said in regard to human relations according to the mind of God:

> You know that the rulers of the Gentiles lord it over them, and their great men exercise authority over them. It shall not be so among you; but whoever would be great among you must be your servant, and whoever would be first among you must be your slave; even as the Son of man came not to be served but to serve, and to give his life as a ransom for many (Mt 20:25-28; Mk 10:42-45; Lk 22:25-27).

The ability to let go of old hurts and embarrassments plays a crucial role in all of life, and especially in marriage. Not least of its blessings is untying the knot of guilt that so easily prevents reconciliation and growth. Properly understood, Christian forgiveness is not self-administered. It is always a social transaction – we ask for forgiveness from others, just as they request it of us. Withholding forgiveness is a way of keeping others indebted to us, of exercising power over them in a word. But in the end, a relationship without forgiveness will be a relationship without love or reciprocity. Not surprisingly, assisting a couple to experience forgiveness becomes a major goal in therapy.

Thoughtfulness

One of the most effective devices that we encourage couples to practice outside the clinical setting in order to relearn sensitivity to their partners is the 'affectionate surprise', a small gesture calculated to amuse, delight, or impress their partner – small valentines that remind each other of the areas of like and dislike that are so easily taken for granted in a long-term relationship, an attitude effectively summed up in the title of a popular song of a number of years ago, 'You Don't Bring Me Flowers Anymore'.

A single rose or other favourite flower placed on a spouse's breakfast plate or on their pillow, a small gift of particular meaning, an anniversary surprise, a birthday treat – such seemingly minor gestures are the daily currency of attentiveness and positive regard. Conversely, forgetting special dates and occasions, being late for dinner, and other signs of routinisation show that we too easily take our 'other' for granted. The best birthday gift for a harried housewife is not necessarily a new steam iron.

It is not so much any one of the skills or experiences that renews the vitality in a relationship. Rather, it is the cumulative force of a progressive series of such exercises that has the power to awaken long-slumbering feelings of care, love, devotion and strong like (or dislike) that comprise a lot of the ordinary give-and-take of daily life. A clinical setting can provide a safe environment to practice them. Virtual reality is helpful. But the real work is done at home.

Married for Good

Marriage can be considered (and reconsidered) as a dynamic relationship in which the gift of life is received and transmitted in two especially important respects – the physical, emotional, mental and spiritual growth of marriage partners achieved through intimacy, commitment and love, and the healing gifts of marriage that enable spouses and their families to meet the failures, injuries and diminishment resulting from life experiences. In redefining both the goods and goals of marriage, it seems to me that they include preeminently the creation of a community of love, including but not limited to children, as the nuclear 'domestic church' alluded to in recent writings;[19] life-long commitment in love by marital partners; and the personal development and healing just mentioned. Such 'spiritual goods' are not opposed to the traditional values, but widen and deepen them. Among its revolutionary observations, *Gaudium et Spes* tells us that:

> True married love is caught up into God's love; it is guided and enriched by the redeeming power of Christ and the saving action of the Church, in order that the partners may be effectively led to God and receive help and strength in the sublime responsibility of parenthood.

After nearly forty years of service as a priest, therapist and teacher, I believe more strongly than ever that through marriage and family life, couples participate in a special way in the life of God as the effective sign of the inter-mutual love of the Trinity and Christ's redeeming presence in the Church *and* the world. Marriage and family are, precisely in this sense, the domestic church, the nucleus of Christian life. But while supreme today as always, family interests and values are not the only focus of Christian experience in the world. If our gaze does not turn outward, we miss the rest of the many-splendoured adventure of life, health and holiness.

Social Action: Being Well by Doing Good

Reaching out to others beyond the family pale has always figured in Christian thought as an emblem of discipleship, especially when the 'other' does not appear particularly lovable. Truly loving our enemies may seem impossible, but is still the task to which Jesus called us (Mt 5:43-44). Forgiveness and reconciliation are difficult, but if the world is to grow beyond the internecine conflicts of personal, ethnic and religious enmity that seem increasingly to darken our horizons, they are necessary. On a large scale, they occupy much of what we mean by social justice and social action.[20]

The health of the social enterprise we call civilization may well turn upon our success in turning our emotional swords into plowshares. Here religion and religious experience have a major contribution to make, one that is not strange or alien to its nature. It is important to acknowledge, however, that promoting the wellness of society can threaten the integrity of the hearth, a fact of discipleship that Jesus himself was fully aware of: 'Do not think that I have come to bring peace to the earth; I have not come to bring peace, but a sword. For I have come to set a man against his father, and a daughter against her mother, and a daughter-in-law against her mother-in-law; and one's foes will be members of one's own household' (Mt 10:34-36. See also Mt 10:21 and Mt 12:46-49).

Religion can certainly appear at times to weaken the fabric of society. Deeply felt spiritual experience often endows individuals with a measure of detachment from social norms and thereby at least some independence in thought and action, primarily by breaking down socially conditioned habits of behaviour.[21] The prophetic dimension of religion, allied to the mystical impulse, which relativises all social claims on ultimate allegiance, can drive a woman or man to extremes of lamentation, protest and action that shake the foundations of society. Such members of society are often considered mad or bad or both, and often meet a woeful end. Just as likely in later days they will be recognised as social heroes, assuming in their own life story the deepest and most noble aims of the society itself. In their perceived neuroticism and subversion, they call us back – and ahead – to our truest individual and social selves – Socrates, Jesus, Francis of Assisi, Catherine of Siena, Joan of Arc, Mohandas Gandhi, Martin Luther King, Jr. and Archbishop Oscar Romero among them.

By temporarily withdrawing a man or woman from society, whether physically or psychologically, the crises of lived religion, epitomised by the mystical impulse, actually catalyse the process of individuation. One departs into the real or metaphorical wilderness not stripped of the beliefs, values and mores of society, but dragging them along willy-nilly as so much baggage in desperate need of sorting. As with Jesus in his forty-day trial in the desert, such withdrawal (known as *anachoresis* in the ancient church) ideally leads to a dialectic of personal and social disintegration and reintegration, preparing the initiate to reenter the social world not only more creative and free, but as the living embodiment of the authentic ideals of the society. In this respect, profound religious experience can be considered society's way of rejuvenating its most profound inner resources by enhancing the identity of its most sensitive members, women and men who identify with their people on ever-expanding circles of inclusion, ultimately embracing the whole human race even, in Buddhist terms, every sentient creature.

These outstanding figures call us both back and also ahead to our truest selves, much as we might resist their challenge. The force of such resistance, strengthened by self-interest, ethnocentrism, or fear can, as it so often has, lead to persecution and even the death of such prophetic figures, as it so frequently has. But even in their death, perhaps because of it, their influence rises and increases and eventually moves both society and history onward. Let us look a bit more closely at this curious process of disengagement and renewal.

How to Renew the World

We may for convenience' sake designate this temporarily alienated member of society 'the mystic', someone intent on deciphering the 'secret orders' they feel will guide them past uncertainty, doubt and restlessness to the perception of the truth of their vocation and mission – and that of their society. As they break with former ways and even their families and friends to enter the wild laboratory of the Spirit, they experience confusion and possibly terror. They may in fact only dimly perceive the need for and nature of the disengagement from conventional attitudes and only reluctantly undertake surrendering them. But if they remain on the path they have chosen, the process of dis-integration and reintegration will occur despite initial resistance. Some risk is always involved.

In religious terms, the budding mystic is gradually 'mortified' in body, mind and spirit – reduced, that is, to the state of feeling utter dependence on God alone. This is accomplished by actively and passively stripping herself of all worldly attachments, not because they are evil, but simply because they are not God. But the 'path of negation' occupies only half of the mystic's method of purification and advancement.

All turning away is also a turning towards. The mystic, like the scientist and the artist, acquires by her negative discipline a new and powerful appreciation of the common world, finding there whole new realms of meaning and value. For the outcome of these activities is positive – detachment aims at re-attachment, disengagement aims at re-engagement, and withdrawal aims at return. Detachment from reliance on a single set of socially determined and sanctioned patterns of perception and behaviour enables the individual to acquire greater psychological independence from society. Her viewpoint is to some extent (if never totally) 'decentred', enabling her to recognise social norms more readily and to evaluate them as well as the institutions which embody and perpetuate them. The mystic thus enjoys greater freedom to see, judge and act. This freedom is reinforced by an assurance of self-worth and hope.

The dialectic of withdrawal, reintegration and return sensitises the mystic's conscience. Once returned to the world, she is better able to perceive both justice and injustice. Her capacity for friendship and love has expanded. But what stimulates the mystic's return to society is not love alone. Rather, the mystic is drawn to the world from which she had withdrawn in order to carry back the answers to the questions – her *society's* questions, which she had borne within her into her solitude, and which were raised to consciousness in the process of reflection, assessment and reintegration. Having recovered the integral vision of the society which produced her, the mystic must now communicate that vision in word and deed. A prophet has come into the world.

NOTES

1. Robert S. Weiss, *Loneliness: The Experience of Emotional and Social Isolation* (Cambridge: MIT Press), 1975 ed. See also Berna van Baarsen, 'Lonely but Not Alone: Emotional Isolation and Social Isolation as Two Distinct Dimensions of Loneliness in Older People', *Educational and Psychological Measurement* 61 (2001) 1:119–35.

2. Milton Meyerhoff, *On Caring* (New York and London: Harper and Row, 1971), pp. 54–6.

3. Dr James Gill, SJ, and Linda Amadeo, 'Celibate Anxiety,' *Human Development* 1 (Winter 1980) 4:6–17, p. 15. Pattison first presented his findings, 'Group Psychotherapy and Group Methods in Community Mental Health Programs', at the 25th and 26th annual meetings of the American Group Psychotherapy Association in 1969 and 1970.

4. Lynch, *The Broken Heart*, op. cit., p. 35.

5. See Georges Duby, *The Knight, the Lady and the Priest* (New York: Pantheon, 1983).

6. The beautiful if vaguely theistic love poetry of the Song of Songs reflects the cosmic dimension of royal marriage among the Israelites of the Middle Period.

7. See Evelyn Eaton Whitehead and James D. Whitehead, A *Sense of Sexuality: Christian Love and Intimacy* (Garden City, New York: Doubleday, 1989), pp. 30–1.

8. Ibid., p. 37.

9. Parts of this section have been adapted from a conference on Christian Marriage and Family Life given for the Diocese of Southwark, England, in Bromley, Kent, on 20 Feb 2000.

10. One of the more recent volumes was written by my colleague, Dr Kathy Heskin, *Marriage: A Spiritual Journey* (Mystic, CT: Twenty-Third Publications, 2002). Among other recent books, I would also recommend Leif Kehrwald, *Marriage and the Spirituality of Intimacy* (Cincinnati: Saint Anthony Messenger Press, 1997), and Julie McCarty, *The Pearl of Great Price: Gospel Wisdom for Christian Marriage* (Collegeville, MN: Liturgical Press, 2007).

11. Austin Flannery, OP, ed., *Vatican Council II: The Conciliar and Post Conciliar Documents* (Northport, NY: Costello Publishing Co., 1975), pp. 903–1014.

12. The Pastoral Constitution on the Church in the Modern World (*Gaudium et Spes*), n. 48, op. cit., p. 950.

13. Ibid.

14. 'It was only at Vatican II that conjugal love was given a central role in marriage, when marriage was described as "a community of love" and an "intimate partnership of married life and love". The Council recognised that conjugal love is a unique kind of love that is warm, intimate, self-giving and both expressed in and nurtured by sexual acts. It was stressed that out of this unique love come offspring, and that this love also enables the couple to experience the

divine in their lives.' Brennan R. Hill, 'Reformulating the Sacramental Theology of Marriage', in Michael G. Lawler and William P. Roberts, eds, *Christian Marriage and Family* (Collegeville, MN: Liturgical Press, 1996), p. 11.

15. For a concise statement of classical marital theology, see Brennan R. Hill, art. cit., p. 4.

16. Figures compiled from the US Census Bureau Report for 2003.

17. The Annie E. Casey Foundation, www.aecf.org/AboutUs.aspx, accessed 31 March 2008.

18. Although it is often claimed that over half of marriages today end in divorce, that is a statistical error. In the United States, according to 2004 data from the US Census Bureau, 58 per cent of all women and 54 per cent of all men had been married only once. Of men and women *currently* married, 79 per cent have been married only once. Divorce has unquestionably increased over the last century throughout the western world. But it is also true that couples who divorce are more likely to divorce again. Thus, tallying the numbers of marriages and divorces performed is not the same as estimating the stability of marriage: repetition skews the statistics. See www.census.gov/Press Release/www/releases/archives/marital_status_living_arrangements/010624 .html. Similar figures exist for the United Kingdom. See www.statistics.gov.uk/

19. Cf. *Gaudium et Spes*, n. 48: 'The Christian family springs from marriage, which is an image and a sharing in the partnership of love between Christ and the Church; it will show forth to all Christ's living presence in the world and the authentic nature of the church by the love and generous fruitfulness of the spouses, by their unity and fidelity, and by the loving way in which all members of the family cooperate with each other.' (op. cit., pp. 951–2.)

20. Both revisioning our attitude toward 'otherness' and the possibility of turning towards others with sincere and unconditional love have preoccupied several contemporary schools of thought and service. See especially Stephen G. Post, *Unlimited Love: Altruism, Compassion, and Service* (Philadelphia and London: Templeton Foundation Press, 2003) and Edith Wyschogrod, *Saints and Postmodernism: Revisioning Moral Philosophy*, (Chicago: University of Chicago Press, 1990).

21. See in this regard, Arthur J. Deikman, MD, 'Deautomatization and the Mystic Experience', *Psychiatry* 29 (1966): 324–38. Reprinted in Woods, op. cit., pp. 240–60. For a more recent, if less analytical, description, see Marsha Sinetar, *Ordinary People and Monks and Mystics* (New York: Paulist Press, 1986).

CHAPTER TWELVE
INEXPLICABLE HEALING
THE BEYOND OF HEALTH

Great floods have flown
From simple sources: and great seas have dried
When miracles have by the greatest been denied.
All's Well that Ends Well, II. i. 144–6

As urban civilization advanced along great rivers from the sea coasts and cities were built around fortresses, palaces and temples, houses of healing were almost invariably erected for petitioners afflicted with disease and injuries. Medical arts developed among the priests at shrines dedicated to the gods of health and healing, some of them specialists in particular situations such as childbirth, blindness, or diseases of the skin. Even small towns might have a shrine nearby where pilgrims would come with their burdens of illth and hope.

Some shrines were located at natural sites felt to possess a mysterious aura that at least hinted of a divine presence – caves, springs, grottoes, mountain tops and groves of holy trees. Human construction added to the sites, sometimes enlarging them to immense proportions. In all of this the belief was operative that healing powers from the earth, sea, air, or fiery depths would channel health to those suitably disposed.

It is perhaps too easy to dismiss all this as primitive superstition, but the survival for thousands of years of such shrines and the expectation that healing was a divine gift that might be graced to petitioners argues that the gift was sometimes granted.

Spontaneous healing occurs even today – mysterious recoveries from sometime fatal illnesses, the mending of muscle and bone, the recovery of sight and hearing. When such events occur at a site renowned for facilitating inexplicable cures, the world takes notice.

We will return to the topic of healing shrines and inexplicable healing. But first it will be helpful to consider the primary miracle of health in some of its more unusual forms.

Superhealth

Occasionally news accounts feature stories of extremely elderly people in various parts of the world who have enjoyed robust health throughout their many years, sometimes despite a lifetime of hard manual work and even some habits that might seem otherwise hazardous to health. (As my neighbours say with a wink, 'Drink may have been taken'.) Genetic endowment may well account for such marvels, or it could be wisdom in making life choices, or just plain luck. But such instances are often as inexplicable as they are unpredictable. For most people, life expectancy is ruled more or less rigorously by actuarial tables, which is to say we tend to live about as long as other people in our society barring accident or misfortune. Those figures vary considerably, however, depending on the part of the world and the social class one inhabits.

It is nevertheless evident, as I have argued throughout these pages, that a healthy diet, sufficient exercise, a benevolent physical environment and a society not given to poverty, violence and excessive stress can offer each of us a long and hopefully happy life – between seventy-five and ninety years if all goes well, perhaps longer. Religious affiliation and an active spiritual life clearly contribute to longevity and, when illness occurs, to recovery. It has been estimated that if the world situation does not deteriorate significantly over the next few decades, the present generation (at least those lucky enough to be born in more affluent societies) may live to be as old as 150 years or more.[1] (No human being has been known to have lived more than 122 years.)

There is another kind of 'super health' that warrants exploration, however. Spontaneous inexplicable healing has mystified physicians for centuries, but that it happens is not in question. *How* it happens is subject to debate.

Healing Signs

Unexpected and sometimes astonishing healing events are found in very early portions of the Bible, including the touching and even homely accounts of the prophet Elijah's compassionate acts for the widow of Zarephath (1 Kings 17:8-24) and that of Elisha on behalf of the Syrian warlord, Naaman the leper (2 King 5:1-19). One of the more primitive stories centres on an emblem that became the lasting sign of extraordinary healing – the Nechushtan.

Chapter 36 of the second book of Chronicles describes how the Babylonians conquered Jerusalem in the sixth century before Christ, carrying off 'all the vessels of the house of God, great and small' to Babylon, where they were destroyed. Not among them, however, was a wooden pole with a brass serpent attached to it called *Nechushtan* ('a thing of brass'). Scholars tell us that it was probably a religious emblem the Hebrews had looted from one of the pagan temples they destroyed during the conquest of Canaan. In any case, at the end of the eighth century, King Hezekiah had it removed from the Temple and destroyed, even though its origins has been attributed to Moses himself, because people were worshipping it with incense (2 Kings 18:4).

According to Numbers 21:9, during their wanderings in the wilderness God had sent serpents among the Hebrews to punish them for their loss of faith. When the people turned to Moses for help, he was instructed by God to make an image of a serpent and place it on a pole. 'And if a serpent bit anyone, if he looked at the bronze serpent he would live.' It is probably worth noting that serpents were sacred in the Middle East to the mother goddess of fertility and vegetation, and were also associated with healing, as in the story of Asklepios, the Greek god of medicine. That is why the symbol of healing is still two snakes entwined on the physician's staff. But in John's gospel, Jesus looks back to this strange figure as a portent of his own crucifixion. 'As Moses lifted up the serpent in the wilderness, so must the son be lifted up, that whoever believes in him may have eternal life' (Jn 3:14). Not merely healing, but life itself, eternal life.

The Latinate word 'miracle' appears nowhere in the New Testament. When Jesus and his disciples heal the sick, restore sight to the blind, hearing to the deaf, use of their limbs to cripples and even life to those recently dead, these acts are called 'signs' and sometimes 'powers' or 'energies', or even 'wonders'. When nature bends to Jesus' command people are, naturally, astonished and marvel. They did as much for Honi the Rainmaker or Rabbi Hanina, noted Jewish wonderworks of the time. But several points are worth noting here. No one attributes divinity to Jesus because of these events. They wonder, however, 'Who then is this, that even wind and sea obey him?' (Mk 4:41; see also Mt 8:21 and Lk 8:25).[2] Second, Jesus and his disciples violate no laws of nature. As with contemporary instances of spontaneous, inexplicable, or, if you prefer, miraculous healings, bone is joined to bone, eye functions return to normal, auditory function resumes or begins. People do not grow new arms or legs, develop third eyes in the middle of their foreheads, or sprout ears on their chins. That *would* violate natural process or what is sometimes referred to as 'the law of nature'. Rather, such events restore and in that sense fulfill nature. It must also be granted, however, that when contemporary neurosurgeons temporarily graft body parts to areas of the body where they do not normally appear in order to preserve the living tissue, no natural laws are in fact being violated – just stretched a bit.

The difference lies either in the speed with which bone knits and vision is cleared, or in the activity of the 'triggering' event that initiates a rapid healing process, or perhaps both. But it is Lazarus who appears at the opening of the tomb, not King Arthur or Tom Cruise. When Jesus calms the storm, the wind stops blowing and the waves subside, just as they do regularly, but not instantly. It did not suddenly begin to rain daisies nor did the Sea of Galilee suddenly turn to glass. (One recent debunker did suggest that when Jesus walked on the sea he was actually standing on a slab of ice that had suddenly but quite naturally formed – presumably without anyone's noticing! To keep his balance on a chunk of ice in choppy water during a storm would, I suspect, have been just as great a marvel as calming the storm. Regrettably, no accounts exist that Jesus invented surf-boarding or skipped from one piece of ice to another like Eliza in *Uncle Tom's Cabin*.)

The 'miracles' of the New Testament are not Hollywooden, computer-enhanced special effects of the kind illusionists such as David Copperfield perform today to stupefy and amaze an audience. Some of the witnesses even fail to believe they happened at all. Miracles, as C.S. Lewis wisely remarked half a century ago, are simply events without a history. They do not proceed against nature, but enhance nature. Thomas Aquinas said as much in his long treatise *De Potentia Dei*, 'On the Power of God'. For Thomas, though God at times does something apart from the natural order of things, God does nothing *contrary* to nature. 'Such an event is not against nature simply speaking because it is consonant with nature by and large, which includes the order of all creatures related to God.'[3]

Things happen that simply weren't in the cards. But what happens is not outrageous or bizarre. In fact, such events restore the right order of things and, to Jesus' way of thinking, disclose the presence of the Kingdom already in our midst. Walt Whitman had it right: 'To me every hour of the light and dark is a miracle, / Every cubic inch of space is a miracle' ('Miracles', *Leaves of Grass*).

While miracles of healing occupy a position in Christianity that is historically more central than they do in other major world religions, the possibility and actuality of inexplicable cures mediated by healers and shrines in other religions is by no means absent. In 2007, *Eye on Religion*, a special issue of the *Southern Medical Journal,* considered traditions of miraculous healing in Christianity, Judaism, Hinduism and Buddhism – all of which share if not a common heritage, a remarkably similar approach – cautious, but not skeptical.[4]

One of my spiritual teachers, a swami, described an Indian healer's method of curing pox. On entering a village where someone was suffering from smallpox or another form, he would sit and meditate until the pox was transferred from the victim to himself. Then, covered with the pox sores, the healer would walk into the forest where he would select a tree and sit beneath it and meditate until he had transferred the pox to the tree.

'What happened to the tree?' I wondered.

'The tree was wise. It knew what to do.'

The Power of Faith

There seems to have been little doubt in Jesus' mind about what made his healing 'work'. In the synoptic tradition, Jesus' remark to those he heals is almost invariably the same – 'Your faith has made you well.'[5] Often the crowds pressed on Jesus hoping simply to touch the fringe of his garment, so trusting was their faith in his power to heal: 'And when the men of that place recognised him, they sent round to all that region and brought to him all that were sick, and besought him that they might only touch the fringe of his garment; and as many as touched it were made well' (Mt 14:35-36; Mk 6:56; Lk 6:19).

Faith healing has been a continuous tradition in Christianity ever since. It did not, however, displace the ministrations of the medical profession until very late, most probably not before the nineteenth century. But when physicians were in short supply, or the task was beyond them, spiritual healers were known to appear. Again, Christian scripture is generous in early examples, especially in the Acts of the Apostles, which according to tradition was written by a physician: the cure of a lame man by John and Peter (Acts 3:1-11), Peter's astonishing revival of Tabitha (Acts 9:40), Paul's resuscitation of a young man named Eutychus who had fallen out of a window (Acts 20:9-10). Even the impact of Peter's shadow was sufficient to excite healing faith:

> And more than ever believers were added to the Lord, multitudes both of men and women, so that they even carried out the sick into the streets, and laid them on beds and pallets, that as Peter came by at least his shadow might fall on some of them. The people also gathered from the towns around Jerusalem, bringing the sick and those afflicted with unclean spirits, and they were all healed (Acts 5:14-16).

Paul's handkerchiefs were similarly endowed with sufficient authority as to effect cures: 'And God did powerful deeds [*dunameis*] by the hands of Paul, so that handkerchiefs [*soudaria*] or aprons [*simikinthia*] were carried away from his body to the sick, and diseases left them and the evil spirits came out of them' (Acts 19:11).

The choice to accept such accounts as fact or to regard them as mythical symbolism is itself a matter of faith. What is not in question is the origin and continuity of the belief that faith did heal and continued to. Occasionally someone asks, 'But how?'

Placebo Effects

An ardent Christian's recent dismissive snort to someone who relied strongly on the power of faith to heal, 'You have faith in faith', meaning not faith in God, presumably, misses that point – or refuses to concede it. It is faith that makes us well – faith in Jesus, faith in God, faith in Our Lady of Lourdes, faith in our doctor, faith in medicine, and yes, even faith in faith.

It is faith to all appearances that gives the 'powerful placebo' the power to heal. Skeptics such as R. Barker Bausell see that as an invalidating power, endowing sham treatments with bogus efficacy. But the fact remains that even when deliberately deceived by researchers, people's faith is still what makes them well. Wolfgang Goethe perhaps put it better than anyone in *Faust*: 'The dearest child of Faith is Miracle' (*Das Wunder ist des Glaubens liebstes Kind, Faust* I, 1, 413).

Placebos, which were known in the ancient world, if not by that name, were described medically in 1811 as 'any medicine adapted more to please than benefit the patient'. Inert substances (or innocuous procedures) which a patient accepts as medicine or therapy but actually lack specific therapeutic capability, placebos have been drawn into the controversy over unexpected and often inexplicable healing on both sides of the debate. The Latin term *plac?bo* ('I will please') has its origin in the Christian liturgy as a title given to the Evening Prayer for the Dead, which began with Psalm 114:9: 'I will please the Lord in the land of the living.'[6] By the fourteenth century, it had come to mean 'flatter'. 'Placebo effects', which include patient improvement from substances lacking therapeutic potency, began to be described in the 1920s and were well known by 1950. Today, the power of placebos must be taken into consideration in controlled laboratory tests as part of standard protocol. How placebos activate the capacity of real healing remains controversial but also undeniable.

But for Bausell and other skeptics, such effects simply invalidate virtually all claims of healing achieved by non-conventional means.[7] A more balanced view, such as that of Anne Harrington, situates placebos in the context of the healing potential of the human body and mind operating together to mobilise the capacity to fight disease and debility.[8] Harrington's approach is close to the even more positive appraisal by Norman Cousins.[9] Skeptics aside for the moment, both extensive medical research and religious inquiry agree that with faith come hope, expectation, optimism, perhaps even cheerfulness and at least sometimes, undeniable healing. For those who benefit, the scorn of skeptics tends to rings hollow. 'The one thing I know is that I was blind, and now I see' (Jn 9:25). 'Placebo' may be just a different name for 'faith'.

Moving Violations

Eighteenth-century rationalists such as David Hume and Immanuel Kant rejected all 'miracles' which were (rather arbitrarily) defined as 'violations' of the laws of nature, meaning, presumably, the Creator's laws, since few of the philosophers at the time were out-and-out atheists. 'A miracle,' Hume noted, 'may be accurately defined [as] a transgression of a law of nature by a particular volition of the Deity, or by the interposition of some invisible agent.'[10] Since, however, the Deity would not suffer contradiction, miracles are impossible. The same line of reasoning is used today to disqualify belief in anything pretending to 'supernatural' status, as the Bishop of Durham quipped: 'What sort of God are we portraying and believing in if we insist on what I will nickname "the divine laser beam" type of miracle as the heart and basis of the Incarnation and the Resurrection?'

It doesn't require a great deal of thought, however, to figure out that no physical 'laws' of the universe are 'violated' by so-called miraculous healing except in the sense that an automobile driver might exceed the posted speed limit on a city street. Healing occurs the way it always tends to, only much faster and at least in some reported cases, more completely. The question not easily answered is not 'how' inexplicable healing occurs but 'why'. What is it that often suddenly initiates and accelerates the healing process, sometimes to what appears to be instantaneity? The clear answer on one hand is faith – the faith of the 'patient' or of his or her loved ones. But the *source* of that faith must be considered also, for the act of faith is not only 'internal'. What corresponds from outside the inner world of belief remains mysterious, perhaps indeterminate, but it must be real. It can be a sense of a presence, actual visitation to a shrine, or the imposition of hands in a healing service, or just the object of prayer.

It is important to bear in mind in regard to improbable and inexplicable healing that it is focused and localised. The ill person is not cured in every possible respect, nor does the recipient of healing become invulnerable to infection, accident, or, eventually, death. The woman with a healed hip joint is not also given perfect eyesight or permanently cured of that nagging ringing in her ears, seasonal allergies, or dental caries. A cancer patient may find that a life-threatening tumour is gone, but still has heart disease or arthritis. (Or possibly not. Sudden healings have been known to be more rather than less comprehensive, but total, much less absolute healing is just not the issue.)

'Spontaneous Healing': A Miracle by Any Other Name
'There is only one kind of healing,' an elderly doctor once told me in the midst of a difficult case, 'the kind that works.'

He had asked my assistance for a woman who was near death not because of a specific illness but because she had been ritually cursed by a rival for her husband's affections. This was no 'ordinary' case of jealousy and ill will. The woman had been targeted by a series of deadly black-magic spells. Although a well-educated woman of some means, married to a doctor, she was an Italian immigrant who knew from her childhood what these dreadful signs meant in her homeland. Subconsciously they began to undermine her physical, mental and spiritual health until she had lost not only the will to live but was in actual danger of dying.

Her doctors, including a psychiatrist, were unable to block or remove the effects of the curses. Not even hypnotherapy was of avail. Her priest had prayed with her and had even performed a private exorcism. Not even that arrested the course of her decline. Finally, her elderly physician contacted me in Chicago and asked me to put him in contact with a group of spiritual healers, a band of women and men who believed in the curative powers of Nature. The group operated under the leadership of a psychiatric social worker I had met some time earlier, a remarkable woman who in addition to her professional skills was also recognised as a *curandera*, a healer. Some might call her a witch doctor or Wiccan or Pagan, but she was not particularly concerned about labels. Although she had no Latino ancestry, she worked in a largely Spanish-speaking part of Chicago and had found that her healing abilities were instantly recognised and sought out by people suffering from a variety of afflictions that were unresponsive to conventional intervention.

I agreed to make the contact but disclaimed any responsibility for the results. That was no problem for the good doctor who by then was convinced that the only procedure that could save his patient was to fight fire with fire, or at least with holy water, whatever the spring from whence it flowed.

It worked. On a pre-arranged date and time, the healing circle placed a photograph of the ailing woman in their midst and began a long chanted ritual to lift the death spell and return the victim to full health. As I was informed the next day, the 'client' began to recover almost immediately. Soon she was in full recovery. Receipt of yet another death threat sent her into a brief relapse, but a second healing session arranged directly by her doctor with the healers reversed it and the woman recovered completely. I never learned whether she got her husband back, however.

The Power of Prayer
For several years I taught a special undergraduate philosophy course subtitled 'The Farther Reaches of Human Nature' that was partially based on the book by that name by psychologist Abraham Maslow.[11]

A number of my students were in the School of Nursing. Among other topics we studied was atypical or extraordinary healing which included, among other areas, the role of prayer, the use of visual imagery and the effects on healing of hope and optimism. Some years before, under the guidance of one of my theology professors, I had studied a number of cases reported in the Medical Bulletin of Lourdes – the famous healing shrine. More recently, I had analysed a number of cases of unusual, often sudden healing in the files of the Religious Experience Research Unit at Oxford University (now the Alister Hardy Research Centre, located at the University of Wales in Lampeter). I was by then less skeptical of claims of unconventional healing than were many of my colleagues, to say the least. That I was even permitted to offer such an elective course was a tribute, I believe, to the openness of the departmental chair of what was a highly trained and critical department.

One of my students, a highly talented music major, discovered in the middle of the term that she had a growth on her larynx that the doctors feared was malignant. As she and her mother tearfully told me, they were afraid that even a biopsy might ruin any chance she might have for a singing career. They asked for my prayers and said that through prayer and meditation, they believed that the growth could be reduced. The next tests were scheduled for a week later. About two weeks later, she and her mother returned to my office beaming with the news that not only had the tests been negative, there was no sign of the growth. It had disappeared.

Spontaneous healing does occur, just as there are faulty diagnoses. A single case cannot prove that prayer and meditation can heal cancer or any other illness. Nor is it possible to predict that a given case will end in healing. But that is of little concern to those who find their health inexplicably restored. A number of such cases in my own experience have taught me to be open to unusual and sometimes sudden healing.

A few years later, I was teaching a graduate course in the Institute of Pastoral Studies on 'Spirituality and the Body', in which a section was devoted to non-conventional healing – the body's sometimes uncanny ability to heal despite what appears to be overwhelming disease. One of the students was a surgical nurse from a well-known Catholic hospital who was also a religious sister. After the course had ended she confided in me that she had recently been diagnosed with a serious form of cancer. I was shocked, not just by the diagnosis but by her response.

'I have decided not to undergo chemotherapy or radiotherapy,' she said, 'partly because of what I learned in your course. I have thought and prayed about this all summer and I am sure that I can beat the cancer by hope, prayer and meditation. On the other hand, I'm pretty sure that the chemotherapy would probably kill me.'

As she was a health care professional, I respected her knowledge as much as I admired her courage and faith. Feeling apprehensive, even though she had absolved me of any moral or spiritual liability for her decision, I told her I would pray for her and begged her to stay in touch. She did – through the rest of that summer, the year afterwards, and for many years to come. Not only did she beat the cancer, she went on to leave active nursing to undertake a second career in spiritual direction and counselling, particularly with people suffering from serious illness.

One of the most dramatic cases involved a request from the local Archdiocese to investigate a reported and inexplicable healing following a prayer service. A more than middle-aged woman I'll call 'Dorothy' who lived in northern suburb had been suffering from advanced hip socket erosion and was scheduled for hip replacement surgery. A few days before the date set for the operation, a number of friends and neighbours, members of a charismatic prayer group, came to her house and held a healing service. Dorothy had to be carried upstairs to her bedroom, as by then she was barely able to walk. During the prayer service, she felt 'different', as she explained to me a few days later. But shortly afterwards, she was able to rise by her own power, walk down the stairs, and even dance a little.

Her doctors were dumbfounded. I was able to view X-ray film taken before and after the prayer service and could clearly see the extensive damage to the hip joint in one set, and the apparently normal bone in the second set. The possibility that Dorothy had simply anaesthetised herself to the excruciating pain under the influence of suggestion (or some other 'placebo effect') was ruled out: bone had regenerated in a matter of minutes. I issued an informal report, but the case was quietly closed as the family did not want any publicity. Nor did they need it.

Such 'anecdotal' evidence for the efficacy of prayer to facilitate healing is abundant. While to those who find themselves inexplicably well after suffering for years from a variety of major and minor diseases, or who have regained the use of paralysed limbs, or their sight or hearing, or some other bodily function, no explanation is needed. 'I was blind, and now I see' (John 9:25). On the other hand, for those prepared to deny in advance the possibility of extraordinary healing, no explanation is possible. As one debunker whispered to me on national television one day, 'They're all fakes'. At the end of the day, as the saying goes, while experimental evidence has been unable to demonstrate unequivocally positive effects of prayer on physical health, some reports are significant enough to warrant further study.[12]

Healers

Over the years, I have come to know a number of 'faith healers' – people who seem to have the gift (or grace) of healing, which they can impart to others, often simply by touching them or praying for them. Usually, some kind of physical contact or at least presence is characteristic of their ministry. Others simply pray. I'm sure that my friends Ambrose and Olga Worrall would not mind standing in for the rest.

I met English-born Ambrose (1899–1972) and his wonderful American wife Olga in the 1970s at several healing events sponsored by the Spiritual Frontiers Fellowship and other groups in the midwestern United States and California. Both were very active in the healing ministry. Ambrose died in 1972, and Olga in 1985. As she survived Ambrose by several years, I came to know her better if unfortunately we saw each other only occasionally. In addition to her remarkable healing abilities, I recall her truly prodigious hats. Both were very down-to-earth, commonsense people, largely of a Methodist disposition. Engaged in a purely spiritual ministry, neither ever charged for their time or services. And by all accounts, Olga's abilities were astonishing. For almost a decade, she was one of the most famous spiritual healers in the United States, overshadowed only by the showmanship of Kathryn Kuhlman and other media stars.[13]

The Worralls and other healers have sometimes belonged to formal associations who provide support and share information, not at all a bad idea for a profession or ministry which is often the target of heated attack in the public media. But many healers do not have a notable public ministry, but carry on their work quietly, sometimes anonymously, in small churches or in homes. Few if any of their 'cures' receive publicity of any kind and in all honesty they prefer it that way.

For millions of people throughout the world, healing is sought and sometimes obtained not from human ministry as such, but from the proximity of sacred sites known for their aura of superhuman, even divine power. Such shrines are as old as humankind itself; some have become world famous. The 'ministry' involved is often carried out by volunteers who, like the thousands of guides who bring pilgrims to Lourdes each year, are strictly speaking, amateurs – 'people who love to love'.

Healing Shrines

Healing shrines survived the emancipation of medicine from religion, even without temple custodians to listen to the dreams of clients, read their symptoms, diagnose their ills by means of augury, prophetic utterance and scrolls, and supervise treatments and even surgery. After the appearance of Christianity and Islam, ancient healing shrines continued to attract devotees until they were destroyed or fell into ruin. Even then, a few survived as places of clandestine pilgrimage.

For Christians of late antiquity, the source of divine healing emanated from the power of faith literally embodied in the mortal remains of those who had been healing channels of grace during their lives, as Peter Brown relates: 'The shrines of martyrs were visited with increasing fervour in the fifth and sixth centuries, as places where new life and healing bubbled up for the faithful from the cold graves of the dead. For the martyrs' shrines contained the bones of men and women on whom the Holy Spirit had come to rest.'[14]

While any number of reported healings at shrines can be dismissed as exaggeration, propaganda, misdiagnosis, or the result of the power of suggestion or the almighty 'placebo effect', all of which are part of the debunkers' arsenal, it is very difficult to dismiss highly critical analysis of claims made, for instance, at Lourdes. There a medical bureau was established at an early date which meticulously examined each case presented as an instance of miraculous healing. Physicians and scientists, some of them atheists, pored over every aspect of the case and applied the most stringent norms. Among them, the condition had to be medically certified, the patient could not be receiving specific medical treatment for the condition at the time, the healing had to be immediate (that is, not prolonged over a period of weeks or months), the cure had to be clinically verified, it had to be inexplicable by medical standards of treatment, and there could be no relapse for at least five years or longer.[15]

Needless to say, not many cures of some of the millions of people who have thronged to Lourdes over the past century could be expected to pass all these requirements. But the sixty-seven that have are all the more impressive, particularly when the nature of the illnesses are taken into consideration, including ulcerative limbs with extensive gangrene, cardiac hypertrophy, pulmonary tuberculosis, amyotrophic lateral sclerosis of the spinal cord, tubercular peritonitis, bilateral optic atrophy, cancer of the uterus, rheumatic spondylosis, multiple sclerosis and so on. One may simply deny that such illnesses were 'real', or that the cures were 'real'. That, however, is far more prejudicial than the considered investigations that led to the conclusion that medical science simply could not explain the thoroughness or rapidity of these sixty-seven healings.

Statistically, the immediate spontaneous recovery of patients with acute, debilitating and often lethal illnesses is theoretically possible, especially given the vast numbers of sick people who come to Lourdes and other healing shrines. If their faith in statistics is strong enough, it may provide the answer for skeptics, but statistical analysis does not and so far as I am aware cannot explain why so many supposedly 'random' cures happen at healing shrines rather than, say, shopping malls or, for that matter, hospitals.

Science and medicine are not competent to declare an event of any kind a miracle, for that is a theological category and bears primarily on faith. It is, as Goethe claimed, 'Faith's dearest child'. If it takes faith to perform or receive a miracle of healing, it also takes faith to believe in it. Scientifically, the event remains, as it must, 'inexplicable'. For the pilgrims who come to Lourdes, Knock, Einsiedeln, Compostella, Guadalupe, St Anne de Beaupré, or the scattered holy wells of Ireland and Wales, it needs no explication.

NOTES

1. See Theo Richel, 'Will Human Life Expectancy Quadruple in the Next Hundred Years? Sixty Gerontologists Say Public Debate on Life Extension Is Necessary', *Journal of Anti-Aging Medicine* 6 (2003) 4:309–14.

2. For an excellent and exhaustive study of the 'miracles' of Jesus, see John P. Meier, *A Marginal Jew: Rethinking the Historical Jesus*, Vol. 2 (New York: Doubleday, 1994) and also Joseph Rhymer, *The Miracles of Jesus* (Slough: St Paul Publications, 1991). See also Mark Corner, *Signs Of God: Miracles and Their Interpretation* (Hampshire UK and Burlington, VT: Ashgate Publishing Co., 2005) and Bruce Epperly, 'Miracles without Supernaturalism: A Process-Relational Perspective', *Encounter* 67 (Winter 2006) 1:47–61.

3. Disputed Question VI, *De Potentia Dei*, 1 ad 1. Slightly more wide-eyed, St Augustine considered a miracle 'something difficult, which seldom occurs, surpassing the faculty of nature, and going so far beyond our hopes as to compel our astonishment'. *De utilitate credendi*, xvi.

4. See Charles Pinches, 'Miracles: A Christian Theological Overview', *Southern Medical Journal* 100 (Dec 2007) 12:1236–42; Chün-fang Yü, 'Miracles in the Chinese Buddhist Tradition,' *Southern Medical Journal* 100 (Dec. 2007) 12:1243–5; Faiz Khan, MD, 'Miraculous Medical Recoveries and the Islamic Tradition', *Southern Medical Journal* 100 (Dec 2007) 12:1246–51; Aaron L. Mackler, 'A Jewish View on Miracles of Healing', *Southern Medical Journal* 100 (Dec 2007) 12:1252–4.

5. The catalogue is worth noting: Mark 5:34 (the woman with issue of blood); Matthew 9:22; Luke 8:48; Mark 10:52 (a blind beggar); Luke 18:42; Matthew 15:28 (the Syro-Phoenician woman); Luke 7:9 (the centurion's boy); Luke 8:50 (the daughter of Jairus); Matthew 9:18-25; and Mark 5:41 (one of the rare instances where Aramaic was preserved: 'Talitha kum'); Luke 17:19 (the ten lepers).

6. As numbered and translated in the Septuagint and Vulgate; Psalm 116:9 in the King James Version and later translations as 'I will walk before the Lord in the land of the living'.

7. Bausell, op. cit., pp. 137–8, 206–8 et passim.

8. Harrington, op. cit., pp. 65–6, 125–38 et passim.

9. See Head First: The Biology of Hope and the Healing Power of the Human Spirit (New York and London: Penguin Books, 1990), pp. 229–42.

10. David Hume, On Miracles, pt. I, note.

11. Abraham Maslow, The Farther Reaches of Human Nature (New York: Viking, 1971 / Harmondworth, UK: Penguin Books, 1973).

12. See Paul N. Duckro and Phillip R. Magaletta, 'The Effect of Prayer on Physical Health: Experimental Evidence', Journal of Religion and Health 33 (1994) 3:211–9 and Martha G. Meraviglia, 'Prayer in People With Cancer', Cancer Nursing 25 (Aug 2002) 4:326–31.

13. For an account of their ministry, see Ambrose A. Worrall with Olga N. Worrall, The Gift of Healing: A Personal Story of Spiritual Therapy (New York: Harper and Row, 1965 (repr. Ariel Press, 1989)).

14. Peter Brown, The Body and Society: Men, Women, and Sexual Renunciation in Early Christianity (New York: Columbia University Press, 1988), p. 445.

15. The Medical Bureau at Lourdes publishes an official bulletin three times a year in French, Italian, English, Spanish and German. Articles include discussions on reported cures from a medical and pastoral perspective as well as on questions regarding theology, faith and science. A searchable database of articles published since 1998 is available on subscription. See www.amil-lourdes.com. A number of books and articles on Lourdes are published every year, among the more recent: James Martin, SJ, Lourdes Diary: Seven Days at the Grotto of Massabieille (Chicago: Loyola Press, 2006), and Jason Szabo, 'Seeing is Believing? The Form and Substance of French Medical Debates over Lourdes', Bulletin of the History of Medicine 76 (Summer 2002) 2:199–230.

CHAPTER THIRTEEN
HIGH FETTLE
HEALING THE WORLD

Be that thou know'st thou art, and then thou art
As great as that thou fearest.
Twelfth Night, V. I. 136–7

I have always liked the word 'fettle', which I think I first heard from the lips of my Irish grandmother. In any case, one still hears it used now and then among the people who live beyond the Pale of increasingly urbanised Dublin. Actually, *fettle* stems from Middle English verb *fetlen*, 'to set in order', originally 'to gird up', itself coming from an Old English word '*fetel*', a belt or girdle. Basically it came to mean 'condition' or 'state', and people in the English-speaking world still speak of being in 'good fettle' or even 'high fettle', and sometimes in 'poor fettle'.

The fact of the matter is that the world seems to be in pretty poor fettle at the moment when we consider the condition we have put it in – war has devastated the Middle East for sixty years now and bids fair to continue doing so for some time. Financial mismanagement, corporate greed and reckless spending have ruined national and local economies. Hunger and poverty stalk billions of children, women and men in Africa, Asia and Latin America. Global climate change has wrought ecological catastrophe around the world, destroying lives and displacing millions of people from their homes. Plant and animal species are disappearing at an alarming rate because of habitat degradation, poaching and global warming.

On a fine spring day, sitting in a park in San Francisco, Dublin, or Kyoto, we might not notice any of this, for biological and geological processes proceed slowly and by degree. But they proceed inexorably, sometimes moving with what can eventually be seen in hindsight as terrible speed toward some dreadful and perhaps irreversible tipping point. Whether in political matters, as witnessed by the events of 11 September 2001, or natural disasters such as the wreckage resulting from the Great Tsunami of 2004 or Hurricane Katrina, slow decades of carelessness, heedlessness and recklessness can culminate very suddenly in cataclysm.

The challenge facing the present and certainly future generations is how to put the world in better fettle. Eden Garden, once a Paradise, has fallen into serious disrepair. It wants healing. Politicians and corporate leaders may deride the prophets of doom that have sounded the tocsin on global climate change, but ignoring the symptoms will only aggravate the eventual disaster. The old cliché is still true: an ounce (or perhaps I should say twenty-eight grams) of prevention is worth a pound (or half a kilogram) of cure. It is always more costly to repair damage than to prevent it. We might as well face the fact that saving the world is going to be expensive. It will also be difficult. But it will only become more expensive and more difficult, if not beyond remedy, if we dither. As recently proposed by the eminent biologist E.O. Wilson, only by joining the resources of religion and science will the inhabitants of Spaceship Earth, especially those who occupy the control deck, be able to address the pressing environmental challenges that threaten the planet with ecological disaster.[1]

Whether experienced as the 'global village' created by instantaneous electronic communication on a worldwide scale, or met in the struggle to engineer a world with minimal economic frontiers by means of so-called Free Trade Agreements, or even by fighting global pandemics such as AIDS, SARS, and the avian flu, clearly the geological, climatological, biological and sociological systems of the world are now *felt* to constitute an interconnected whole. As a consequence, the differentiating characteristic of our era has been identified accurately to be globalisation. Any spirituality for a possible future must necessarily take that into consideration.

Living in a Globalised World

Early in June, 2006, my vintage Nissan died abruptly near the intersection of State Street and Jackson Avenue in the heart of Chicago's Loop. The electrical system seemed to be working properly, but nothing would persuade the engine to turn over. In desperation, I called my Motor Club on my cell phone, that icon of post-modern interconnectedness. A fellow answered politely and requested some unusual bits of information – my area code and postal code, among other things. I repeated my location, somewhat startled that someone wouldn't have a clue as to the dilemma of someone stuck in traffic at 7 p.m. in downtown Chicago.

'Where are you?' I asked.

'In India,' came the response.

'What are you doing in India?' I asked.

'I live here,' he said.

'Imagine,' I said, 'that I am stopped dead and blocking traffic in the heart of Mumbai and desperately need to get my car moving again.'

'Would you like me to put a "rush" on that?' he asked cheerfully.

'That would be a good idea,' I said.

As it turned out, relief was dispatched and within forty minutes, the old Nissan had received a jump and I was on my way. It was eighteen years old and still managed to squeeze out twenty-nine miles to the gallon, by the way.

Something similar had happened two weeks earlier, when I was involved in making and remaking a plane reservation for a trip to the Pacific Northwest for two talks and a family wedding. I first spoke to a ticket agent in India, then the Philippines, then Canada. But in the end, the reservations were charged to me twice, and it took over a month to unravel the snarl.

In 2007, when I took some university souvenirs with me on a trip to China to serve as small gifts for our hosts and guides, I was amused to learn on closer examination that all the pens, penlights and calculators had been made in China to begin with. (As my students are fond of saying, 'What goes around, comes around'.)

Globalisation is a phenomenon we are going to be getting used to for a while. As we observe the stories about illegal immigration and global warming on television and even in our movie theaters (Al Gore's superb *An Inconvenient Truth* comes to mind as an example), to claim that there is an important connection with spirituality might seem stretched. But I am persuaded that globalisation presents a particular, inescapable and vital challenge for Christian spirituality as well as health now and especially in the years ahead.

Certainly one of the greatest tasks facing this and the next generation is to find ways to live harmoniously and well in a world that is both shrinking and expanding at the same time, as population continues to increase disproportionately and at the same time, boundaries between nations and states become more fluid. Immigration and the movement of refugees are blurring ethnic and linguistic distinctions. Traditional cultures are disappearing or combining in new and sometimes startling ways. Moreover, our era is one in which the global village is being taken over by Wal-Mart and Tesco. The classical role of national governments is being superseded by the rule of multi-national corporations. It might be taken as a sign of the times that in 2007 the Halliburton Corporation moved its corporate headquarters from Houston, Texas, to Dubai.

First of all, what is globalisation? In his timely book, *Globalization and Its Discontents*, which has become something of a classic in recent years, Nobel laureate Joseph Stiglitz described it as:

> the closer integration of the countries and peoples of the world which has been brought about by the enormous reduction of costs of transportation and communication, and the breaking down of artificial barriers to the flows of goods, services, capital, knowledge, and (to a lesser extent) people across borders. ... Globali[z]ation is powerfully driven by international corporations, which move not only capital and goods across borders but also technology.[2]

As a conjoined political, economic, social and cultural phenomenon, globalisation actually presents not one but a *host* of challenges to any spirituality for a possible future, four of which I think are now of cardinal importance for humanity as a whole and the health of the world.

First, on the most personal scale I would begin with insurgent individualism and the privatisation of experience as an unanticipated consequence of instantaneous electronic communication, particularly the internet and the ubiquity of mobile phones, both of which are changing personal and corporate experience in profound ways. Second, globalisation is producing continuous and perhaps increased political instability on a national and international scale, especially in the developing world. Related to this is the likelihood that asymmetrical warfare, terrorism, will dominate the boundary zones between East and West, the north and south, and the rich and poor – that is between those aspiring to share in the world's bounty and those determined to hoard it. If not an outright clash of civilizations, the coming struggle will be a violent contest of bitterly opposite ideologies and religious sectarians.

The third challenge concerns the increasing militarisation of national economies and political agendas, not least in the United States but also in many poor nations, a trend which will continue to contribute to the deterioration of support for education, health services, scientific research and the arts. Fourth, globalisation has already accelerated ecological devastation on an unprecedented scale, producing severe and destructive climate change, particularly what we have begun to call global warming, with consequent population displacement, epidemics and famine.

It is especially the last of these that has absorbed much of my own concentration over the last twenty years and to which I would like to focus attention briefly.

Health and the Environment: World Illth

As the people of the world become more aware and sometimes frightened of the consequences of global climate change, the impact on health can hardly be underestimated. Health has always been affected by climate. Particular diseases tend to proliferate in areas characterised by geography and climate – respiratory infections and diseases of the skin in hot, moist areas; eye infections in desert conditions; malaria, dengue fever and a host of viral and bacterial infections in the tropics. Urban civilization produced its own range of illnesses, many of them stress-related, other exacerbated by poverty and congestion.

None of that is exactly 'news'. The difference in years to come – and sooner, I think, than later – will lie in the extent to which these diseases will spread and at an ever-faster rate of acceleration because of global climate change. The present health disasters of sub-Saharan Africa may be only a harbinger of catastrophes to come unless immediate and effective action is taken on a massive scale. Some threats to global health are already beyond control.

According to a recent report issued by the World Health Organisation, an increase of only 1 degree Fahrenheit over the last quarter century resulted in an annual loss of approximately 150,000 lives and 5.5 million years of healthy life. In 2003, Europe's hottest summer since the sixteenth century, some 30,000 people, mostly the elderly and infants, died from heat-related causes. In France alone over 14,000 died in just three scorching August weeks. Within the next twenty years, the global toll is expected to double as average global temperatures continue to rise. In addition, four million children under the age of five die each year, we are told, from environmental hazards such as polluted water and air and exposure to toxic chemicals.[3]

The dilemma facing us is deadly serious: can we reverse the direction of planetary violation and strive for a sustainable harmony among all creatures of the earth before the escalation of disasters brought about by greed and carelessness ends in global catastrophe? We might well begin by recalling Genesis 1:31, 'And God saw everything that he had made, and behold, it was very good'. The religious view of life affirms that the planet and its resources are not merely useful commodities to be exploited and discarded, but as works of divine benevolence are simply good *in themselves* and therefore worth cherishing and protecting. From a scriptural perspective, the divine order of the world, *ho kosmos tou theou*, intends harmony among human beings, among the human and animal realms, and even among animals and plant life.[4] To the extent that we disturb that primordial harmony, we do so at our peril. To the extent that we strive to heal the world and its systems, we become co-creators with God. Our task now is to save the world.

At Home in the World

The iridescent Emerald Ash Borer arrived in the United States from its native Asia sometime in 2002 or 2003. Following in the wake of the Longhorned Asian Beetle that had decimated the maple trees, elms, horse chestnuts and willows of New England and the Chicago area a few years earlier, the newcomer killed well over 30 million ash trees in Michigan, Ohio and Indiana in a period of just four years. Most of the devastation was in southeastern Michigan. In the meantime, some long-time residents, pinebark beetles, managed to destroy over 70 million lodgepole pine and spruce trees in the Rocky Mountains, the Pacific Northwest and Western Canada. Something there is that doesn't love a tree.

Although human beings also migrated from place to place over our first few million years on this planet, we are not an invasive species by nature nor necessarily as voracious as bark beetles. We tend to stay put, enhance our surroundings and largely feel that we belong to one another. We tend to regard strangers as, well, strange. And possibly dangerous. Especially if they don't look like us, speak like us, dress like us, eat like us, or worship the way we do. Still, we have managed to remain a single species, every single member just as human as any other, like it or not.

In his engaging excursion into everything, Bill Bryson notes that 'if all your DNA were woven into a single fine strand, there would be enough of it to stretch from the Earth to the Moon and back, not once or twice but again and again'.[5] Yet our genome is constructed of only four elements, the nucleotide bases adenine, thymine, guanine and cytosine. What's more, each of our genomes is 99.99 per cent exactly the same as everyone else's, and only about 2 per cent different from some of our near-relatives among the primates (the great apes, not the bishops). Our individuality, if you will, is determined by only .1 per cent of our total heredity.[6] We are, to say the least, more alike than different. And yet that difference is, in a way, everything. William James put it well when he said, long before scientists really knew much about heredity at all:

> An unlearned carpenter of my acquaintance once said in my hearing: 'There is very little difference between one man and another; but what little there is, is very important.' This distinction seems to me to go to the root of the matter.[7]

The Spiritual Connection

James, and following him Alfred North Whitehead, also famously described religion and, in our sense, spirituality, as 'the feelings, acts and experiences of individual men in their solitude, so far as they apprehend themselves to stand in relation to whatever they may consider the divine'.[8] Granting that he would surely intend to include women in the generic term, even those of us who admire James are more inclined today to define spirituality as what people do with their life as a whole and in society. James himself was closer to the mark when he wrote, 'Religion ... is a man's total reaction upon life'.[9] I'd certainly agree, but would still call it spirituality, which I regard as more, not less encompassing than religion. In this respect, I still find myself instinctively falling back on William Stringfellow's marvellous description from *The Politics of Spirituality*, one of the guiding stars of these reflections:

> spiritual maturity or spiritual fulfillment necessarily involves the *whole* person – body, mind, soul, place, relationships – in connection with the whole of creation throughout the era of time. Biblical spirituality encompasses the whole person in the totality of existence in the world, not some fragment or scrap or incident of a person.[10]

Seen in this light, any spirituality worthy of the name Christian involves the total life of the whole person. It will, consequently, address the context of life holistically, including the natural as well as social environment.

Such observations specify not only the integral aspect of spirituality, its holistic character, but also its dynamic and relational character. In this respect, I would say today that spirituality refers to our total and unfolding involvement with the universe as a whole precisely as we are consciously aware of it and endeavour to enhance that mutual encounter in action. The unitary experience implicit in these descriptions of spirituality point to its mystical and ethical character in terms relevant to the present ecological crisis and Christian responsibility in general.

Today however, and perhaps more than ever, the urbanised, consumer public seems to be aware of a sense of separation from a rightful place in the order of things: a social, economic and political estrangement from goods and services once freely available. In the wake of terrorism and counter-terrorism, we also feel increasingly powerless to decide our own destinies. A generation ago, Bishop Robinson expressed this malaise and a possible response to it in prophetic terms (if couched in the less than inclusive language of the time):

> The redemption of man today means his release to become, not an individual – for in independence he is powerless in the face of the giant State – but a person, who may find rather than lose himself in the interdependence of the community. The content of social salvation for the modern man is to discover himself as a person, as one who freely chooses interdependence because his nature is to be made for others, rather than as one who is engulfed in it because the pressures of his age demand it. The alternative to the 'They' is not the 'I' but the 'We'.[11]

As with most prophetic utterances, Robinson's was little heeded in his day but surely deserves a new hearing in ours. For he was right: the independence of the coming era must be a consciously cultivated interdependence embracing all peoples and the planet as our collective home.

Losing Our Nerve

A few years ago, the film version of Dan Brown's exuberant but ultimately shallow novel *The Da Vinci Code* became a religious cause célèbre. At this remove, it is difficult to understand exactly why the novel and its film version created such a fuss, but after being invited to give three lectures and to participate in several panels on the phenomenon in various parts of the United States, it seemed undeniably clear that the story touched a nerve – although even more clearly it neither shook the foundations of western civilization nor drove thousands of believers out of the church as had been promised. If anything, it made people more attentive to the origins of Christian belief, the place of Mary Magdalene and other women leaders in the earliest stratum of Christianity, and the formation of the canon of scripture.

But a deeper, and in some respects, darker face of recent events in the church fed the suspicion that doubt and betrayal do in fact lurk at the heart of institutional religion, specifically in regard to the sexual abuse scandals and episcopal efforts to deny, then cover up the evidence. Whether by art or chance, by aiming his barbs not at the ordinary faithful, but at the hierarchy and easy targets such as Opus Dei, Dan Brown scored a hit.

One way or another, many Catholics in North America and other parts of the world are experiencing a sense of spiritual uneasiness, a crisis of confidence in church leadership as they attempt to find their way between blind trust and critical faith. Not surprisingly, people are questioning authority more openly and in some cases looking for alternatives to the rigid control over religious experience traditionally exercised by the hierarchy. It has become easier to say 'I am spiritual, but not religious'.

Here, however, we may simply be meeting once again the old polarity between intimate, personal experience of God and the social regulation of conduct, worship and religious life by church authorities. This tension, which can be creative and constructive, no doubt lies at the bottom of the distrust that has often existed between religious authorities and mystics. These latter women and men of all traditions and periods tend to follow a way that by-passes organisational cooptation by accentuating the direct and immediate relationship to God that every human person is granted at the core of their experience of self, the world and others. That is why there are Protestant mystics and Catholic and Orthodox mystics as well as Jewish mystics, Buddhist mystics and Hindu mystics of all stripes and persuasions. Why, also, virtually every founder of a great religious or spiritual tradition was a mystic, not least of all Jesus himself, whose Spirit can never be confined nor diminished by institutional boundaries or bounders.

The implications of this powerful polarity between institution and charism for a spirituality adequate to meet the requirements of a post-modern world and contribute to the health and ultimately the salvation of the world, are, I think, immense.

Contemplative Action

Another recurrent and troubling problem in spirituality concerns the disjunction between contemplative development and prophetic reform. The turn to social action in the dual form of friendship and justice is the natural expression of any spirituality that fosters physical and psychological wholeness and well-being. For no one can be truly healthy or holy in isolation. Individual welfare depends upon, as well as enhances, community welfare. So much we have seen already. But if the spiritual life of both individuals and groups tends to social action as an expression of completeness, it does not begin there. In fact, premature involvement in social reform can not only injure society, it will also interfere with the appropriate spiritual development of individual persons.

I have proposed that an essential moment in the spiritual development of the greatest saints, prophets and social reformers was their withdrawal from society in order to gain adequate self-awareness and social insight for the prophetic task ahead of them. From a holistic perspective, it would thus be a mistake to oppose mystical contemplation to prophetic action. They are reciprocal phases of the same process, components in a real dialectic of spiritual growth. But the mystical aspect, the progressive realisation of oneness with God, the experience of the presence of God, precedes as well as follows prophetic involvement in the world. Meditative contemplation is the ground and wellspring of social action. Social action is the flowering and fruit of contemplation. But social action also contains new seeds of contemplation. The growth process, both interior and public, moves ahead reciprocally.

Holistic spirituality naturally tends to focus social activity on issues that affect the whole of life. Among the important areas of such concern are world hunger, peace and disarmament, economic and political injustice and oppression and environmental deterioration. Importantly, holistic social action is not wedded to any partisan ideology, whether right or left. It is not Catholic, Protestant, or Jewish. It is human. Its concern is for the welfare of all peoples in specific concrete matters – adequate food, clothing and shelter; educational and occupational opportunity; political liberty; freedom from economic coercion; the right to enjoy and use natural resources responsibly. In a word, to live freely, fully and happily, at peace with oneself, other people and God.

If holistic spirituality means anything, it is that health and well-being, food and dance, song and art, meditation and social action are integral elements of everyone's experience. It means, further, that our participation in these forms of human involvement is in itself spiritual, whether we know it or not. Developing our spirituality means raising that fact to full awareness.

Healing: The Cosmic Dimension

As inclusive concepts, healing and health refer not only to physical illness and recovery, but to mental and spiritual integration as well. But dimensions of healing extend beyond the individual to communities, to the global environment itself, and ultimately to the cosmos as a whole. That may seem like an impossibly large order, but it is based on the simple perception that we are connected to the whole of the universe in every aspect of our existence.

In his insightful book on the meaning of the 'Little Stories' that built up around the figure of St Martín de Porres in seventeenth-century Peru, Alex García-Rivera focuses on the significance of the Dominican saint's healing, especially of domestic animals: 'Healing is a metaphor with profound meanings. The anthropology of healing provides some general guidelines toward determining those meanings: "rituals of healing redress the fragmented social, personal, temporal, physical and metaphysical tissues constituting the whole of the universe".'[12] 'This comes about,' he continues, 'by a connection made between physiologies and the universe.' Thus in specifically human terms, following Geneviève Calaume-Griaule:

> Cosmologies and physiologies are cultural constructs that offer systematic appraisals of the order in which disease insinuates itself to inspire disorder ... The body serves as a microcosm where the powers of disease can be located, contested, pacified, eliminated, or accommodated ... The cultural rendering of the dynamics of the body fan outward to relate patients and doctors to the organised processes of the world.[13]

All healing is a contribution to the development of universal harmony, much as the ancient Chinese, Egyptians, Indians, Greeks and Hebrews had thought. In regard to our present concerns, the approach of Pope John Paul II is pertinent. In his 1987 encyclical *Sollicitudo Rei Socialis*, the pope cited three moral considerations which relate social development in particular to the cosmic mystery of creation: 1) the very nature of the beings which make up the cosmos demand human respect and reverence because of the natural connection, the appropriate place, that each shares in the order of creation, an order which in Christian perspective is divinely willed and blessed; 2) because natural resources are limited and many are non-renewable, no one has the right to deprive future generations, much less others now living, of their availability as if these were inexhaustible; and 3) the harmful effects of industrialisation, especially pollution of the environment, pose a serious threat to health and life on a global scale.[14]

Laurie Garret and other researchers have indeed drawn back the veil of time and shown us, like the ghost of Christmases yet to come, the spectral countenance of future plagues, potential epidemics and pandemics far more virulent and devastating than AIDS that can threaten the entire world. How can we be ready for such disasters? More urgently, how can we prevent them? By learning now what we will need to know then. And what will we need to know? To begin with, as Bernie Siegel puts it succinctly:

> It is important that we realise that we can never cure everything. We will never find homes for all the homeless, or food for all the hungry, or cures for all diseases. But we can, as doctors, as family and as friends, care for everyone. And in that caring, true healing will occur – the healing of the spirit and of lives.[15]

That is therapy. It is also spirituality, the healing of the injuries, disease and disability that afflict our sisters and brothers throughout the world, beginning at our doorstep. It also points to the healing of the wound of sin that infects the planet and even the cosmos itself, this great body of God groaning in travail, awaiting the revelation of the full glory of all God's children.

'The end is where we start from ...'

In the preceding pages we have explored together a number of areas in which a spirituality of wellness offers promise to enable people to live longer, healthier lives, contribute to society and alleviate or even avoid many of the 'discontents' of our hectic technology-driven, commercialised, artificial and often lethal way of life in today's world. We traced the path of wellness from its origins in classical antiquity and a biblically based, wisdom-oriented approach to life, through the benedictions of medieval monastery gardens, and the recovery of holistic medicine in the last century, delving into the findings of recent studies of longevity, alternative health care, fitness and exercise, diet and nutritional studies, botanic medicine, even the role of laughter and tears in promoting human welfare.

From a holistic perspective, I have sought to show that wellness is a unified and unifying phenomenon – the total response of human persons, individually and socially, to the gift of life. Physical, emotional, mental and social health are all dimensions of 'wellness', and all are important. Spirituality is the link that raises the unity of these only apparently diverse components of our corporal, mental and spiritual experience to full visibility. In Christian spirituality, the sometimes intricate interaction of Function, Symbol and Sacrament provides a way of understanding how ageing gracefully, the place of food, drink, exercise and grooming, sexuality, family life and friendship, death itself – all have necessary and complementary roles to play in keeping each of us and all of us together in good nick and fine fettle.

The interface of individuals and the planetary population as a whole has never been more evident or more significant than it is today. In terms of wellness, it is more urgent than ever to realise the truth in Donne's great insight – no one is an island. We are *all* part of the main, responsible to and for one another, perhaps more now than ever before. I remain convinced that as the planet as a whole becomes more and more interlaced in terms of health, illth and survival itself, only a spirituality that embraces the wholeness of life thankfully and responsively will enable the human, animal and plant populations to survive and thrive. The challenge of choosing life in its fullness is now not if, but when.

Nevertheless, as the integrating pattern of life's journey toward completeness, spirituality becomes concrete, visible and therefore real only in the actual experience of individual persons. In itself, spirit – the radical capacity in each human being to receive and pass on the life of God – remains a hidden and elusive dimension. It takes on concrete character and meaning only when actualised in concrete, specific encounters in the world of nature and other persons. Spirituality defines spirit.

Developing spiritually is, of course, a temporal process – for each of us and for all of us. We are participants in a continual dialogue between the past and the future, our forms of spirituality being the ways in which we respond to the self-communication of God in the historical moment we are given. Our word or song or image may be remembered for generations, echoing through the centuries like those of Francis, Teresa and Ignatius. Or it may seemingly vanish from the human scene on utterance. In either case it remains our contribution, our story, one which only God can and will truly assess. But it also has its place as the way the gift of life became manifest in our moment, adding its unique weight and value to the worth of the whole.

NOTES

1. See E.O. Wilson, *The Creation: An Appeal to Save Life on Earth* (New York: W.W. Norton, 2006).
2. Joseph Stiglitz, *Globalization and Its Discontents* (New York and London: Penguin, 2002), p. 10.
3. 'Climate Change and Human Health', *Bulletin of the World Health Organization*, Volume 85, Number 11, November 2007, pp. 830–2.
4. See Robert Murray, SJ, *The Cosmic Covenant: Biblical Themes of Justice, Peace and the Integrity of Creation* (London: Sheed and Ward, 1992).
5. Bill Bryson, *A Short History of Nearly Everything* (New York: Doubleday, 2003), p. 483.
6. Ibid., 481.
7. William James, 'The Importance of Individuals' in *The Will to Believe and Other Essays in Popular Philosophy* (New York: Longman, Green and Co., 1897), p. 256.
8. James, op. cit., lecture 2, p. 42. Whitehead's characterisation, 'Religion is what the individual does with his own solitariness', is found in *Religion in the Making* (New York: The Macmillan Co., 1926), p. 16.
9. Ibid., p. 45.
10. Stringfellow, *The Politics of Spirituality* (Philadelphia: Westmister Press, 1984), p. 22. See also, Chapter One, p. 25, n. 13 and Chapter Nine, p. 160.
11. Robinson, op. cit., p. 8.
12. Alex García-Rivera, *St Martín de Porres: The 'Little Stories' and the Semiotics of Culture*, foreword by Virgil Elizondo, intro. by Robert Schreiter (Maryknoll, NY: Orbis Press, 1996), pp. 66–7 citing Lawrence Sullivan, 'Healing', in *The Encyclopedia of Religion*, ed. by Mircea Eliade, Vol. 6 (New York: Macmillan, 1986), p. 233.
13. Ibid., citing Geneviève Calaume-Griaule, 'Diseases and Cures', trans. by Brunhilde Biebuyck, in *The Encyclopedia of Religion*, ed. cit., p. 368.
14. *Sollicitudo Rei Socialis (The Social Concern of the Church)*, No. 34. www.vatican.va/holy_father/john_paul_ii/encyclicals/documents/hf_jp-ii_enc_30121987_sollicitudo-rei-socialis_en.html.
15. Bernie Siegel, MD, *Peace, Love, and Healing* (New York: Harper and Row, 1989), p. 227.

BIBLIOGRAPHY

BOOKS

James F. Balch, MD, Phyllis A. Balch, CNC, *Prescription for Nutritional Healing*, Garden City Park, NY: Avery Publishing, 1990.

R. Barker Bausell, Snake Oil Science: *The Truth about Complementary and Alternative Medicine*, Oxford and New York: Oxford University Press, 2007.

Eugene C. Bianchi, *Aging as a Spiritual Journey*, New York: Crossroad, 1993.

Jane Brody, *Jane Brody's Nutrition Book: A Lifetime Guide to Good Eating for Better Health and Weight Control*, New York: Bantam, 1982.

Theodore Burang, *The Art of Tibetan Healing*, trans. by Susan MacIntosh, London: Watkins, 1974.

Jean Carper, *The Food Pharmacy*, New York: Bantam, 1988.

Mary Carse, *Herbs of the Earth: A Self-Teaching Guide to Healing Remedies*, Hinesburg, VT: Upper Access Publishers, 1998. (NA herbs)

Deepak Chopra, MD, *Ageless Body, Timeless Mind: The Quantum Alterative to Growing Old*, New York: Harmony Books, 1993.

Norman Cousins, *The Anatomy of An Illness as Perceived by the Patient*, New York: W.W. Norton & Company, 2005 ed.

Norman Cousins, *The Celebration of Life: A Dialogue on Hope, Spirit, and the Immortality of the Soul*, New York: Bantam Books, 1991.

Norman Cousins, *Head First: The Biology of Hope and the Healing Power of the Human Spirit*, New York and London: Penguin Books, 1990.

Andrew T. Crislip, *From Monastery to Hospital: Christian Monasticism and the Transformation of Health Care in Late Antiquity*. Ann Arbor, MI: University of Michigan Press, 2005.

Norman Cousins, *The Healing Heart: Antidotes to Panic and Helplessness*, New York: W.W. Norton & Company, 1988.

Charles Davis, *Body as Spirit: The Nature of Religious Feeling*, New York: Seabury, 1976.

Richard Dawkins, *The God Delusion*, New York: Houghton Mifflin, 2006. London: Black Swan, 2007.

BIBLIOGRAPHY

Daniel Dennett, *Breaking the Spell: Religion as a Natural Phenomenon*, London and New York: Penguin, 2007.

Michele Dillon and Paul Wink, *In the Course of a Lifetime: Tracing Religious Belief, Practice, and Change*, University of California Press, 2007.

James A. Duke, *The Green Pharmacy*, Emmaus, PA: Rodale Press, 1997.

Meyer Friedman and Ray. H. Rosenman, *Type A Behavior and Your Heart*, New York: Fawcett Columbine, 1981 (1974).

Laurie Garrett, *Betrayal of Trust: The Collapse of Global Public Health*, New York: Hyperion, 2000.

Laurie Garrett, *The Coming Plague: Newly Emerging Diseases in a World Out of Balance*, New York: Farrar, Straus and Giroux, 1994.

Anne Harrington, *The Cure Within: A History of Mind-Body Medicine*, New York: W. W. Norton, 2008.

Sam Harris, *The End of Faith: Religion, Terror, and the Future of Reason*, London and New York: Free Press (Simon and Schuster), 2006.

Lois L. Hendricks, *Dreams that Help You Mourn*, San Jose, CA: Resource Publications, Inc., 1997.

Christopher Hitchens, *God is Not Great: How Religion Poisons Everything*, New York: Twelve Books (Hachette) 2007. London: Atlantic Books, 2007.

Ivan Illich, *Medical Nemesis: The Expropriation of Health*, London: Calder and Boyars, 1975.

Michael Kearney, *A Place of Healing: Working with Suffering in Living and Dying*, Oxford and New York: Oxford University Press, 2000.

Michael Kearney, *Mortally Wounded: Stories of Soul Pain, Death and Healing*, Dublin: Marino, 1996 / New York: Simon and Schuster, 1997.

Barbara Kingsolver, *Animal, Vegetable, Miracle: A Year of Food Life*, New York: HarperCollins, 2007.

Harold G. Koenig, *The Healing Power of Faith: How Belief and Prayer Can Help You Triumph Over Disease*, New York: Simon & Schuster, 2001.

Ernest Kurtz and Katherine Ketcham, *The Spirituality of Imperfection*, New York: Bantam, 1992.

Jeff Levin, *God, Faith, and Health: Exploring the Spirituality-Healing Connection*, New York and Chichester: John Wiley & Sons, 2001.

Andrew Lockie and Nicola Geddes, *Homeopathy: The Principles and Practice of Treatment*, London and New York: DK Publishing, 1995.

Patrick Logan, *Irish Country Cures*, Belfast: Appletree Press, 1981.

Helen M. Luke, *Old Age*, New York: Parabola, 1987.

James J. Lynch, *The Broken Heart: The Medical Consequences of Loneliness*, New York: Basic Books, Inc., 1979 ed. [1977].

Martin E. Marty and Kenneth L. Vaux, eds, *Health/Medicine and the Faith Traditions: An Inquiry into Religion and Medicine*, Philadelphia, Fortress Press, 1982.

Martin E. Marty, *Health and Medicine in the Lutheran Tradition*, New York: Crossroad, 1983.

Richard A. McCormick, *Health and Medicine in the Catholic Tradition*, New York: Crossroad, 1984.

Chris D. Meletis, ND, *Complete Guide to Safe Herbs*, London and New York: DK Publishing, 2002.

Caroline Myss and C. Norman Shealy, The Creation of Health: The Emotional, Psychological, and Spiritual Responses that Promote Health and Healing, New York: Three Rivers Press, 1993 ed.

Henri Nouwen, *Gracias!* New York: Orbis Books, 1993.

Mary Elizabeth O'Brien, *Spirituality in Nursing: Standing on Holy Ground*, Sudbury, MA: Jones and Bartlett, Publishing, 2003.

Karlis Osis, *Deathbed Observations by Physicians and Nurses*, Parapsychological Monographs 3, New York: Parapsychology Foundation, Inc., 1961.

Mehmet C. Oz, MD, *Healing from the Heart*, with Ron Arias and Liza Oz, New York: Penguin Putnam, 1998.

John Allen Paulos, *Irreligion: A Mathematician Explains Why the Arguments for God Just Don't Add Up*, New York: Hill and Wang, 2007.

Stephen G. Post, *Unlimited Love: Altruism, Compassion, and Service*, Philadelphia and London: Templeton Foundation Press, 2003.

Stephen G. Post and Jill Neimark, *Why Good Things Happen to Good People*, New York: Broadway Books, 2007.

J. A. T. Robinson, *The Body: A Study in Pauline Theology*, London: SCM Press / Philadelphia: Westminster Press, 1952.

Louis Rose, *Faith Healing*, Harmondsworth, UK: Penguin Books, 1971.

Bernie Siegel, MD, *Love, Medicine, and Miracles*, New York: Harper and Row, 1986.

Bernie Siegel, MD, *Peace, Love, and Healing*, New York: Harper and Row, 1989.

David Snowdon, *Aging with Grace: What the Nun Study Teaches Us about Leading Longer, Healthier, and More Meaningful Lives*, New York and London: Bantam Books, 2001.

Rodney Stark, *The Rise of Christianity: How the Obscure, Marginal, Jesus Movement Became the Dominant Religious Force*, Harper SanFrancisco, 1997.

Paul Tillich, *The Meaning of Health: Essays in Existentialism, Psychoanalysis, and Religion*, Chicago: Exploration Press, 1984.

Paul Tillich, *The Meaning of Health: The Relation of Religion and Health*, Richmond, CA: North Atlantic Books, 1981.

Simon Tugwell, OP, *Human Immortality and the Redemption of Death*, London: Darton, Longman and Todd, 1990.

Kenneth L. Vaux, *Health and Medicine in the Reformed Tradition*, New York: Crossroad, 1984.

Heinrich Wallnofer and Anna von Rottauscher, *Chinese Folk Medicine*, trans. by Marion Palmedo, New York: New American Library, 1972.

Andrew Weil, M.D., *Healthy Aging: A Lifelong Guide to Your Physical and Spiritual Well-being*, New York: Alfred A. Knopf, 2005.

Andrew Weil, MD, *Natural Health, Natural Medicine: The Complete Guide to Wellness and Self-Care for Optimum Health*, New York: Houghton Mifflin Co., 2004.

Andrew Weil, MD, *Spontaneous Healing: How to Discover and Enhance Your Body's Natural Ability to Maintain and Heal Itself*, New York: Alfred A. Knopf, 1995.

David Winston and Steven Maimes, *Adaptogens: Herbs for Strength, Stamina, and Stress Relief*, Rochester, VT: Healing Arts Press, 2007.

Ambrose A. Worrall and Olga N. Worrall, *The Gift of Healing: A Personal Story of Spiritual Healing*, New York: Harper and Row, 1965.

Matthew Wood, *The Practice of Traditional Western Herbalism: Basic Doctrine, Energetics, and Classification*, Berkeley, CA: North Atlantic Books, 2004.

ARTICLES

S.M. Bauer-Wu and C.J. Farran, 'Meaning in life and Psycho-spiritual functioning. A comparison of breast cancer survivors and healthy women', *Journal of Holistic Nursing* 23 (2005) 2:172–90.

Maureen Benjamins, 'Predictors of Preventive Health Care Use among Middle-aged and Older Adults in Mexico: the Role of Religion', *Journal of Cross-Cultural Gerontology* 22 (June 2007) 2:221–34.

Robert Roy Britt, 'Churchgoers Live Longer', *Livescience.com*, <http://www.livescience.com/health/060403_church_good.html> posted 03 April 2006.

Stuart M. Butler, Harold Koenig, et al., 'Is Prayer Good for Your Health? A Critique of the Scientific Research', *Heritage Letters* 816, Washington, DC: The Heritage Foundation, 2003: 1–24.

Eamon Duffy, 'The Art of Dying', *Priests and People* 8 (Nov. 1994) 11:409–13.

C.J. Farran, O. Paun, and M.H. Elliott, 'Spirituality in multicultural caregivers of persons with dementia', *Dementia* 2 (2003) 3:353–77.
Laurie Garrett, 'The Challenge of Global Health', *Foreign Affairs* 86 (Jan.–Feb. 2007) 1:14–38.

Edda Hedlund, Jaakko Kaprio, et al., 'Migration and Coronary Heart Disease: A Study of Finnish Twins Living in Sweden and their Co-twins Residing in Finland', *Scandinavian Journal of Public Health* 35 (Oct. 2007) 5:468–74.

Karen H. Kim, 'Religion, Body Satisfaction and Dieting', *Appetite* 46 (May 2006) 3:285–96.

H. G. Koenig, 'Religion, Spirituality and Aging', *Aging and Mental Health* 10 (Jan. 2006) 1:1–3.

Loren Marks, 'Religion and Bio-Psycho-Social Health: A Review and Conceptual Model', *Journal of Religion and Health* 44 (Summer 2005) 2:173–86.

Kenneth Pargament, 'The Bitter and the Sweet: An Evaluation of the Costs and Benefits of Religiousness', *Psychological Inquiry* 13 (2002) 3:168–81.

Murali S. Rao, MD, DFAPA, 'Spirituality in Psychiatry?' *Psychiatry* 2005 2 (Sept. 2005) 9:20.

Glorian Sorensen, Phyllis Pirie, Aaron Folsom, Russell Luepker, David Jacobs, Richard Gillum, 'Sex Differences in the Relationship between Work and Health: The Minnesota Heart Survey', *Journal of Health and Social Behavior* 26 (Dec. 1985) 4:379–94.

BIBLIOGRAPHY

Paul D. Tyson, 'Buddhist and Western Perspectives on Suffering, Stress, and Coping', *Journal of Religion and Health* 46, 3:351–7.

Sandra Millon Underwood and Rhonda L. Powell, 'Religion and Spirituality: Influence on Health/Risk Behavior and Cancer Screening Behavior of African Americans', *Association of Black Nursing Faculty Journal*, Jan.–Feb. 2006:20–31.

John M. Wallace, 'Is Religion Good for Adolescent Health? A National Study of American High School Seniors', Waco, TX: Baylor University, Center for Religious Inquiry across the Disciplines, 2006.

Kenneth Wapnick, 'Mysticism and Schizophrenia', *The Journal of Transpersonal Psychology* 1 (Fall 1969) 2:49-66. Reprinted in Richard Woods, ed., *Understanding Mysticism*, New York: Image Books, 1980, 321–37.

A. Weaver, S.D. Kilpatrick, M.E. McCullough, C. Puchalski, D.B. Larson, J.C. Hays and C.J. Farran, 'A review of spiritual and religious measures in nursing journals: 1995–1999', *Journal of Religion and Health* 44 (2005) 1:55–66.

INDEX

WELLNESS: LIFE, HEALTH AND SPIRITUALITY

INDEX

INDEX

definitions, 13–14, 18
and health, 13–26
holistic spirituality, 19–20, 254
and mental health, 159–182
sexuality and, 204–207
'spontaneous healing', 234–235
Spook (Roach), 195
St John Ambulance, 63–64
St John's Wort (*Hypericum perforatum*), 111
Stark, Rodney, 40
starvation, 130
Stiglitz, Joseph, 246
stinging nettle (*Urtica diotica*), 112
stress, 131–134
Stringfellow, William, 20, 135, 160, 250
suffering. *see* pain and suffering
superhealth, 227
Synesius of Cyrene, 150
Sypher, Wylie, 178

T

tarragon (*Artemisia dracunculus*), 111
tears, 169–172
Tennyson, Alfred Lord, 85
Therapeutae, 27, 36–38
Thomas Aquinas, St, 23, 144, 151, 174, 230
Thomas More, St, 175
thoughtfulness, 218
Tibetan medicine, 29–31
traditional care, and the treatment of pain, 106–109
traditional Chinese medicine (TCM), 29–31
traditional healers, 108
traditional medicine, 22
Tugwell, Simon, 197
turmeric, 113

V

Vata, 29
vegetables, 122–123
Vincent de Paul, St, 64–65

W

water, 123–125
Waugh, Evelyn, 184
We Neurotics: A Handbook for the Half-mad (Bassett), 163
well-being, 74
white meats, 121
Whitehead, Alfred North, 250–251
Willow bark, 112
Wilson, E.O., 244
wine, 39, 125–127
Wolfit, Donald, 183
world illth, 247–249
Wormwood (*Artemisia absinthium*), 111
Worrall, Ambrose and Olga, 238–239